Card Sketches
FOR PAPER CRAFTERS

OVER **500** PROJECTS USING OVER *145* SKETCHES

LEISURE ARTS
the art of everyday living
www.leisurearts.com

PaperCrafts
MAGAZINE

Find us on
Facebook

Follow us on
twitter

www.PaperCraftsMag.com
www.PaperCraftsConnection.com

Card Sketches
FOR PAPER CRAFTERS

Editorial

Editor-in-Chief Jennifer Schaerer

Managing Editor Kerri Miller

Creative Editor Susan R. Opel

Trends Editor Cath Edvalson

Senior Editor Courtney Smith

Editor P. Kelly Smith

Editorial Assistant Ahtanya Johnson

Design

Art Director Matt Anderson

Graphic Designer Holly Mills

Photography bpd Studios

Offices

Editorial
Paper Crafts magazine
14850 Pony Express Rd., Suite 200
Bluffdale, UT 84065-4801

Phone 801-816-8300

Fax 801-816-8302

E-mail *editor@PaperCraftsMag.com*

Web site *www.PaperCraftsMag.com*

Published by Leisure Arts, Inc., 5701 Ranch Drive, Little Rock, Arkansas 72223-9633. 501-868-8800. *www.leisurearts.com*

Library of Congress Control Number: 2011943055
ISBN-13: 978-1-60900-385-2

Leisure Arts Staff

Vice President and Editor-in-Chief Susan White Sullivan

Director of Designer Relations Cheryl Johnson

Special Projects Director Susan Frantz Wiles

Senior Prepress Director Mark Hawkins

Imaging Technician Stephanie Johnson

Prepress Technician Janie Marie Wright

Publishing Systems Administrator Becky Riddle

Mac Information Technology Specialist Robert Young

President and Chief Executive Officer Rick Barton

Vice President of Sales Mike Behar

Director of Finance and Administration Laticia Mull Dittrich

National Sales Director Martha Adams

Creative Services Chaska Lucas

Information Technology Director Hermine Linz

Controller Francis Caple

Vice President, Operations Jim Dittrich

Retail Customer Service Manager Stan Raynor

Print Production Manager Fred F. Pruss

Creative Crafts Group, LLC

President and CEO: Stephen J. Kent

VP/Group Publisher: Tina Battock

Chief Financial Officer: Mark F. Arnett

Controller: Jordan Bohrer

VP/Publishing Director: Joel P. Toner

VP/Production & Technology: Barbara Schmitzr

VP/Consumer Marketing: Nicole McGuire

Visit our web sites:

www.PaperCraftsMag.com
www.PaperCraftsConnection.com
www.MoxieFabWorld.com

PUBLICATION—*Paper Crafts*™ (ISSN 1548-5706) (USPS 506250), is published 6 times per year in Jan/Feb, Mar/Apr, May/June, Jul/Aug, Sept/Oct and Nov/Dec, by Creative Crafts Group, LLC, 741 Corporate Circle, Suite A, Golden CO 80401. Periodicals postage paid at Salt Lake City, UT and additional mailing offices.

REPRINT PERMISSION—For information on obtaining reprints and excerpts, please contact Wright's Reprints at 877/652-5295. (Customers outside the U.S. and Canada should call 281/419-5725.)

Made in China

Posted under Canadian Publication Agreement Number 0551724

Card Sketches
FOR PAPER CRAFTERS

contents

Sketches take the guesswork out of designing cards. In this inspiration-packed book, you'll find over 145 sketches with a variety of takes on each one to jump-start your creativity. You'll be amazed by the different looks that can be achieved by flipping or stretching the sketch. No matter your style or skill level, you'll go to this sketch resource again and again!

Shaped Sketches:

The playful nature of a shaped card is sure to delight the recipient, and you'll have fun creating them, too!

Square Sketches:

Some designs call for the symmetrical nature of a square. No matter the size, a square card can be a fun break from the norm.

NOTE: Because these projects are from past issues, some products may no longer be available. Luckily, the Internet provides a wonderful way to search for similar items so you can still create a beautiful project using these inspiring designs. So, if you can't find a product, use your creativity to adapt the project and find a replacement.

Horizontal Sketches:

Breathe new life into your designs with a variety of great ways to create lovely horizontal cards.

Vertical Sketches:

Who says the traditional vertical card has to be boring? You'll find lots of ideas in this section to inspire you!

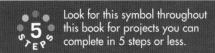

Look for this symbol throughout this book for projects you can complete in 5 steps or less.

editor's note

Revealed: Design Secrets!

Card sketches can be your secret weapon – not only are they time-saving and handy for making the most out of your scrap pile, they are also perfect for breaking up a creative roadblock when you don't know where to begin. Whether you're new to sketches or just looking for a new batch from which to create, this book is full of inspiration just for you.

You'll see how versatile sketches are, too, because each sketch in this book is used in at least three different designs. Sometimes the sketch is used as it appears and other times it's rotated, flipped, inverted or cropped (see adjacent page for more on how to stretch a sketch). The possibilities are endless, especially when you let your imagination lead the way. You'll definitely want to study the many ways a single sketch has been used to inspire a card or project and give your paper crafting a creative boost.

I know you'll keep this book within close reach and use it again and again, so go ahead and get sketchy!

Birthday Pocket & Tag

Designer: Betsy Veldman

See more designs using this sketch, on facing page.

POCKET

1 Make card from cardstock.

2 Cut strip of cardstock; punch border and adhere.

3 Stamp sentiment on cardstock; trim and adhere.

4 Cut canvas pocket to fit card front; stitch border and adhere.

5 Cut strip of patterned paper; ink edges, stitch border, and adhere.

6 Die-cut flowers and stems from patterned paper; layer together and adhere.

7 Thread buttons with twine; adhere. Wrap ribbon around card front; tie bow.

Finished size: 4¼" x 5¾"

SUPPLIES: *Cardstock:* (Aqua Mist, Pure Poppy) Papertrey Ink *Patterned paper:* (Farm House from Farm Fresh collection) October Afternoon; (Apron Strings from Early Bird collection) Cosmo Cricket; (Bonded from My Friend collection) My Mind's Eye *Clear stamp:* (happy birthday from Birthday Basics set) Papertrey Ink *Chalk ink:* (Creamy Brown) Clearsnap *Specialty ink:* (Pure Poppy hybrid) Papertrey Ink *Accents:* (brown, red buttons) Papertrey Ink *Fibers:* (jute twine) The Beadery; (yellow ribbon) Papertrey Ink *Dies:* (flowers) Provo Craft *Tools:* (border punch) Fiskars; (corner rounder punch) EK Success *Other:* (tan canvas fabric)

Tips for getting the most from sketches

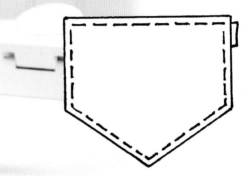

1. Dawn McVey used the sketch as inspiration for making the pocket into a gift card holder

2. Heidi Van Laar made a pocket shaped tag.

3. Julie Campbell put the pocket shape on a card base and made a play on words with her sentiment.

Rotate

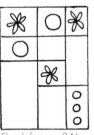

Sketch from p. 246

Flip

Sketch from p. 178

Crop

Sketch from p. 184

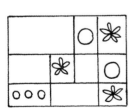

Special Mom Card p. 247

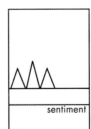

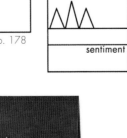

Christmas Greetings Card p. 179

Every Day is a Gift p. 185

SHAPED SKETCHES

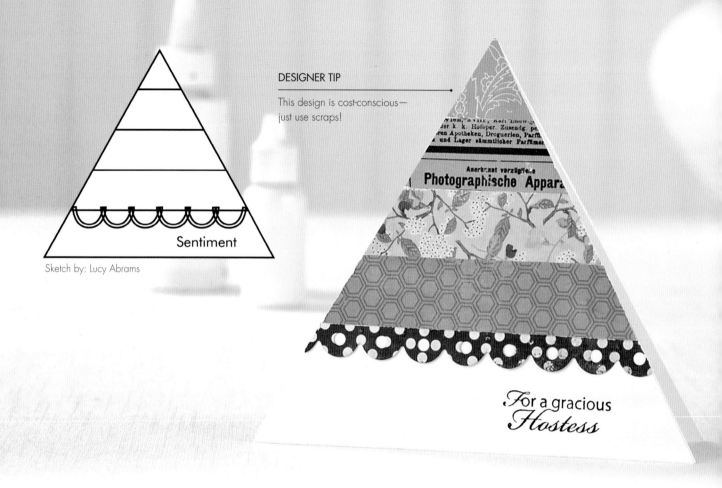

DESIGNER TIP

This design is cost-conscious— just use scraps!

Sentiment

Sketch by: Lucy Abrams

For a gracious Hostess

5 STEPS For a Gracious Hostess

Designer: AJ Otto

❶ Make card from cardstock.

❷ Adhere patterned paper strips and trim.

❸ Die-cut border from patterned paper; adhere.

❹ Stamp sentiment.

Finished size: 5¼" x 4½"

SUPPLIES: *Cardstock:* (white) Neenah Papers *Patterned paper:* (Vintage Linen from For the Record collection) Echo Park Paper *Rubber stamp:* (sentiment from Fine Furnishings Additions set) Gina K Designs *Dye ink:* (Tuxedo Black) Tsukineko *Die:* (scalloped border) Spellbinders

DESIGNER TIP

With shaped cards, it's easiest to adhere patterned paper first and then trim off the excess.

FIND IT

Pattern on p. 283

Simply Amazing

Designer: Ashley Cannon Newell

❶ Trim cardstock into two triangles; adhere together to form card. ❷ Stamp simply amazing. ❸ Wrap twine around card and form bow; thread button with twine and adhere.

Finished size: 5¼" x 4½"

Wassup Gnomey?

Designer: Heidi Van Laar

❶ Make card from cardstock, following pattern on p. 283. ❷ Trim cardstock triangle and adhere; ink cheeks. ❸ Adhere patterned paper pieces. ❹ Punch border strips from cardstock; adhere. ❺ Print "Wassup Gnomey?" on patterned paper; adhere to patterned paper sign post. Adhere sign. ❻ Punch circle from patterned paper for nose; adhere. Adhere pearls.

Finished size: 5"x 5"

Triangle Baby

Designer: Becky Olsen

❶ Make card from cardstock. ❷ Adhere patterned paper triangle; trim patterned paper strips, ink edges, and adhere. ❸ Adhere trim. ❹ Loop and adhere twine. ❺ Die-cut label from patterned paper and ink edges. Punch holes and tie on ribbon; adhere. ❻ Affix stickers to spell "Baby".

Finished size: 6" x 6"

SUPPLIES: *Cardstock:* (Aqua Mist) Papertrey Ink *Clear stamp:* (simply amazing from Handwritten Notes set) Papertrey Ink *Dye ink:* (Tuxedo Black) Tsukineko *Accent:* (pink button) Papertrey Ink *Fibers:* (natural twine) May Arts; (natural trim) Hero Arts, May Arts, Prima

SUPPLIES: *Cardstock:* (white) Georgia-Pacific; (Vanilla) Bazzill Basics Paper *Patterned paper:* (Picnic Table, Bandana, Adventurer, S'mores from The Great Outdoors collection) GCD Studios *Chalk ink:* (pink) Hampton Art *Accents:* (brown pearls) Kaisercraft *Font:* (Sunshine Poppy) www.dafont.com *Tool:* (embossing border punch) EK Success

SUPPLIES: *Cardstock:* (white) Bazzill Basics Paper *Patterned paper:* (Portobello Road You & Me; Party from Lost & Found collection) My Mind's Eye *Dye ink:* (Frayed Burlap) Ranger Industries *Stickers:* (Rockabye alphabet) American Crafts *Fibers:* (white ribbon) May Arts; (cream trim) Prima; (cream twine) Prima *Die:* (label) Spellbinders

Sketch by: AJ Otto

DESIGNER TIP

Adding a bit of glitter to part of a sentiment gives it a unique, gradient look and makes it really pop!

Hold on to the Magic

Designer: Kalyn Kepner

❶ Cut circles from cardstock. Adhere left side of circles to form card; ink edges.

❷ Trim and adhere patterned paper. Stitch edges.

❸ Wrap twine around card front; adhere.

❹ Thread buttons with floss and adhere.

❺ Trim label from patterned paper; adhere with foam tape.

❻ Apply glitter glue.

Finished size: 5¼" diameter

SUPPLIES: *Cardstock:* (Cream Puff) Bazzill Basics Paper *Patterned paper:* (Deck the Hollies, Elements, green plaid from Mitten Weather pad) Cosmo Cricket *Chalk ink:* (Creamy Brown) Clearsnap *Accents:* (red, green buttons) Papertrey Ink; (red glitter glue) Ranger Industries *Fibers:* (natural twine) Westrim; (white floss) DMC

INSIDE

DID YOU NOTICE?

Giovana left a small section of the card outside the die when she cut it to keep the front and back of the card attached.

Love You to the Moon

Designer: Aly Dosdall

❶ Die-cut circle from cardstock. ❷ Die-cut circle from patterned paper; adhere. ❸ Affix label and stars. Affix alphabet stickers to spell "And back". ❹ Die-cut circles from patterned paper; trim one and adhere. ❺ Affix border, label, and star. Affix alphabet stickers to spell sentiment. ❻ Punch heart from cardstock; adhere with foam tape. ❼ Attach brad.

Finished size: 6" diameter

SUPPLIES: *Cardstock:* (red) Bazzill Basics Paper *Patterned paper:* (All Systems Go, Captain's Log, Deep Space Probe, Space Station from Rocket Age pad) October Afternoon *Accent:* (red brad) The Paper Studio *Stickers:* (labels, red stars, yellow border) Jillibean Soup; (Tiny alphabet) Making Memories *Die:* (circles) EK Success *Tool:* (heart punch) EK Success

Welcome, Little One

Designer: Giovana E. Smith

❶ Die-cut card from cardstock. ❷ Die-cut circles from patterned paper; trim, mat with die cut cardstock circle, and adhere. Stitch edges and seam. ❸ Stamp sentiment on cardstock. Die-cut into label. Adhere with foam tape. ❹ Adhere flower and rhinestones.

Finished size: 3¾" diameter

SUPPLIES: *Cardstock:* (Grass Green, Sweet Corn, white) Gina K Designs *Patterned paper:* (Measuring Up from Material Girl collection) Cosmo Cricket *Rubber stamp:* (sentiment from Basket Blessings set) Gina K Designs *Dye ink:* (Certainly Celery) Stampin' Up! *Accents:* (yellow flower) Little Yellow Bicycle; (green rhinestones) Kaisercraft *Dies:* (circles, label) Spellbinders

Chemistry Friends

Designer: Laurel Seabrook

❶ Die-cut circles from cardstock; adhere at side. ❷ Die-cut circle from patterned paper; adhere. ❸ Die-cut smaller circles from patterned paper; trim and adhere. Stitch edge. ❹ Wrap twine around card front and adhere. ❺ Adhere die-cut with foam tape. ❻ Stamp beaker on cardstock. Paper-piece liquid; adhere.

Finished size: 4" diameter

SUPPLIES: *Cardstock:* (Honey) Close To My Heart; (white) *Patterned paper:* (Bunch of Matter, Cup of Equations, Quart of Quarks from Atomic Soup collection) Jillibean Soup *Rubber stamp:* (beaker from Love Potion #9 set) Unity Stamp Co. *Dye ink:* (Cocoa) Close To My Heart *Accent:* (green friends die cut) Jillibean Soup *Fibers:* (teal/white twine) The Twinery *Dies:* (circles) Provo Craft

Sentiment

Sketch by: Lucy Abrams

DESIGNER TIP

Not enough ribbon for a bow?
Twist twine around the end and
add a button for a cute effect.

Spooky Pumpkins

Designer: Sherri Thompson

1 Cut circles from cardstock; adhere at top to form card.

2 Trim and adhere patterned paper.

3 Apply rub-on.

4 Adhere ribbon; thread button with twine and adhere.

5 Affix pumpkins.

6 Affix alphabet stickers to spell "Spooky". Adhere rhinestones.

Finished size: 4½"diameter

SUPPLIES: *Cardstock:* (kraft) The Paper Company *Patterned paper:* (Wicked Whimsy from Hallowhimsy collection) Imaginisce *Chalk ink:* (Creamy Brown) Clearsnap *Accents:* (orange rhinestones) Queen & Co.; (brown button) *Rub-on:* (black stitching) Die Cuts With a View *Stickers:* (pumpkins) Imaginisce; (Tiny Type alphabet) Cosmo Cricket *Fibers:* (green dot ribbon) American Crafts; (cream twine) *Tool:* (circle cutter) Creative Memories

DESIGNER TIP

To eliminate air pockets and ensure precise dots, gently tap the tip of the pearlescent glue a few times on scrap paper between applications.

DESIGNER TIP

Create your own handmade flowers by wrapping trim in a circle. Color with shimmer spray for an antique look.

DESIGNER TIP

Cut a small amount off the back of a circle card to create a flat bottom. This will allow the recipient to display the card without it rolling.

Rose in Life's Garden

Designer: Ashley Cannon Newell

❶ Die-cut circles from cardstock; adhere at top to form card. ❷ Die-cut circles from patterned paper; ink one with shimmer spray. Trim and adhere. ❸ Tie on ribbon; stitch to card. ❹ Stamp sentiment. ❺ Ink trim with shimmer spray; form and adhere into flowers. ❻ Die-cut leaves from patterned paper; adhere. Adhere pearls.

Finished size: 4¾" diameter

The Love Sub

Designer: Regina Mangum

❶ Die-cut large ovals from cardstock; adhere at top to form card. ❷ Cut submarine top from cardstock; ink edges and adhere. ❸ Punch small ovals from cardstock; adhere. Cut out periscope and adhere. ❹ Die-cut oval from cardstock; punch circles. Ink edges and adhere with foam tape. ❺ Trim, ink, and adhere cardstock strip. Adhere pearlescent glue dots. ❻ Punch hearts from cardstock and adhere with foam tape. ❼ Affix stickers to spell sentiment.

Finished size: 5½" x 4½"

Li'l Monster

Designer: Sarah Jane Moerman

❶ Die-cut circles from cardstock; adhere at top to form card. ❷ Trim and adhere patterned paper. ❸ Stamp mouth on cardstock; cut out and adhere. ❹ Adhere eyes. ❺ Stamp sentiment on cardstock; die-cut into tag. ❻ Wrap twine around card and thread through tag. Tie and adhere.

Finished size: 4¼" diameter

SUPPLIES: *Cardstock:* (kraft) WorldWin *Patterned paper:* (Love Letters from Sweetness collection; Beautiful Butterfly from Parisian Anthology collection) Pink Paislee; (Little Boy Blue Rough & Tough from Quite Contrary collection) My Mind's Eye *Clear stamp:* (sentiment from Roses in Bloom set) Waltzingmouse Stamps *Dye ink:* (Chocolate Chip) Stampin' Up! *Specialty ink:* (Sand shimmer spray) Tattered Angels *Accents:* (white pearls) Kaisercraft *Fibers:* (natural twill) Frost It Pink; (cream trim) May Arts *Dies:* (circle, leaf) Spellbinders

SUPPLIES: *Cardstock:* (Delightful Daffodil, Basic Gray, Real Red) Stampin' Up! *Patterned paper:* (Sweater Weather from Jolly by Golly collection) Cosmo Cricket *Accents:* (pearlescent glue) Ranger Industries *Stickers:* (Mini Market alphabet) October Afternoon *Die:* (oval) Spellbinders *Tools:* (circle punch, oval punch, heart punch) EK Success

SUPPLIES: *Cardstock:* (Summer Sunrise, Spring Rain) Papertrey Ink *Patterned paper:* (Hub from Wander collection) BasicGrey *Rubber stamp:* (mouth from Mr. Smiles set) Claudia & Company *Clear stamp:* (sentiment from Monster Fun set) Hero Arts *Dye ink:* (Barn Door) Ranger Industries; (black) Stewart Superior Corp. *Accents:* (wiggle eyes) *Fibers:* (red/white twine) The Twinery *Dies:* (circle) Silhouette America; (tag) Sizzix

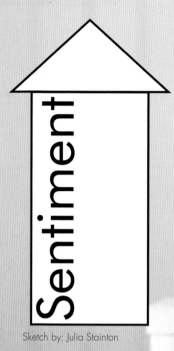

Sentiment

Sketch by: Julia Stainton

DESIGNER TIP

Use a double-sided patterned paper for your card base—it's a fun surprise when opened!

New Home

Designer: Linda Beeson

① Make card from patterned paper.

② Trim cardstock into triangle for roof; adhere.

③ Punch border sections from patterned paper; sand edges and adhere. Turn up edges with your fingers.

④ Punch circle from patterned paper; adhere. Adhere button and pearl.

⑤ Affix stickers to spell "New home".

Finished size: 4½" x 8½"

SUPPLIES: *Cardstock:* (white) Core'dinations *Patterned paper:* (Cedar River Trail from Campy Trails collection) American Crafts; (Workbook from Schoolhouse collection) October Afternoon *Accents:* (red button) Papertrey Ink; (red pearl) Queen & Co. *Stickers:* (Lush alphabet) Making Memories *Tools:* (circle punch) EK Success; (decorative-edge scissors) Plaid

INSIDE

Welcome

Designer: Vera Wirianta Yates

Ink all edges. ❶ Die-cut house from cardstock; adhere vellum for windows. Fold and adhere to form envelope. ❷ Die-cut house insert from cardstock. Trace roof section on cardstock; cut out and adhere. ❸ Stamp welcome repeatedly on roof. ❹ Die-cut welcome; adhere. ❺ Slip insert inside house envelope. Adhere pearl.

Finished size: 4¼" x 6½"

Shoot for the Stars

Designer: Leigh Ann Baird

❶ Make card from cardstock. ❷ Trim and adhere patterned paper. ❸ Trim patterned paper block and triangle to form rocket; ink edges and adhere twine tails. Adhere rocket with foam tape. ❹ Stamp sentiment. ❺ Punch stars from patterned paper; adhere. ❻ Print sentiment on cardstock. Cut out, ink edges, and adhere with foam tape.

Finished size: 4¼" x 5½"

Family Tree

Designer: Laurel Seabrook

❶ Make card from cardstock. ❷ Trim patterned paper panel; adhere. ❸ Die-cut grass from patterned paper; adhere. Stitch card edges. ❹ Punch border strips from cardstock; adhere in layers. Stitch roof edge. ❺ Adhere rhinestones and twine bow.

Finished size: 4" x 7½"

SUPPLIES: *Cardstock:* (pink, yellow) The Paper Studio; (tan) Bazzill Basics Paper; (kraft) Michaels *Vellum:* The Paper Studio *Clear stamp:* (welcome from Round and Round set) Papertrey Ink *Dye ink:* (Worn Lipstick, Antique Linen) Ranger Industries *Accent:* (pink pearl) Michaels *Dies:* (house, welcome) Silhouette America

SUPPLIES: *Cardstock:* (white) Papertrey Ink *Patterned paper:* (Sunny Days Border, Blue Sky, Citrus Circle, Whimsy Stripe from Sweet Summertime collection) Echo Park Paper *Pigment ink:* (Wheat) Tsukineko *Fibers:* (orange/white twine) The Twinery *Fonts:* (AR Berkley, AR Cena) Adobe *Tool:* (star punch) Fiskars

SUPPLIES: *Cardstock:* (Cocoa) Close To My Heart; (white) *Patterned paper:* (Borders N' Blocks, Tight Knit from Family Dynamix collection) Bella Blvd *Accents:* (green rhinestones) Kaisercraft *Fibers:* (natural twine) May Arts *Die:* (grass) Provo Craft *Tool:* (border punch) Stampin' Up!

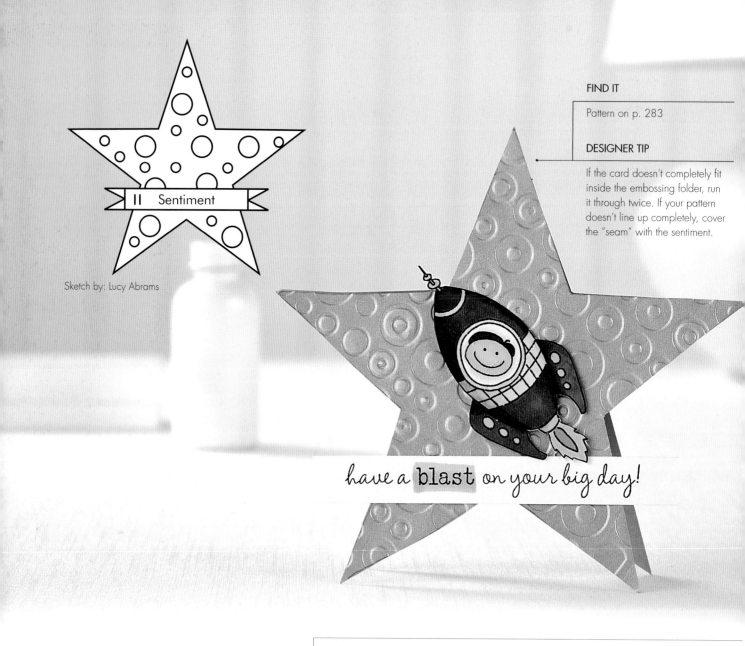

Sketch by: Lucy Abrams

have a **blast** on your big day!

FIND IT

Pattern on p. 283

DESIGNER TIP

If the card doesn't completely fit inside the embossing folder, run it through twice. If your pattern doesn't line up completely, cover the "seam" with the sentiment.

Have a Blast

Designer: Belinda Chang Langner

❶ Cut two stars from cardstock, following pattern on p. 283. Emboss one with template; adhere to second star.

❷ Stamp rocket and face on cardstock. Color with markers; cut out and adhere with foam tape.

❸ Stamp sentiment on cardstock; color blast with marker. Trim into banner and adhere.

Finished size: 5¾"x 5½"

SUPPLIES: *Cardstock:* (white, silver) Papertrey Ink *Clear stamps:* (rocket, face, sentiment from Half Pint Heroes set) Waltzingmouse Stamps *Dye ink:* (Tuxedo Black) Tsukineko *Color medium:* (assorted pens) Copic *Finish:* (dimensional glaze) *Template:* (embossing dots) Provo Craft

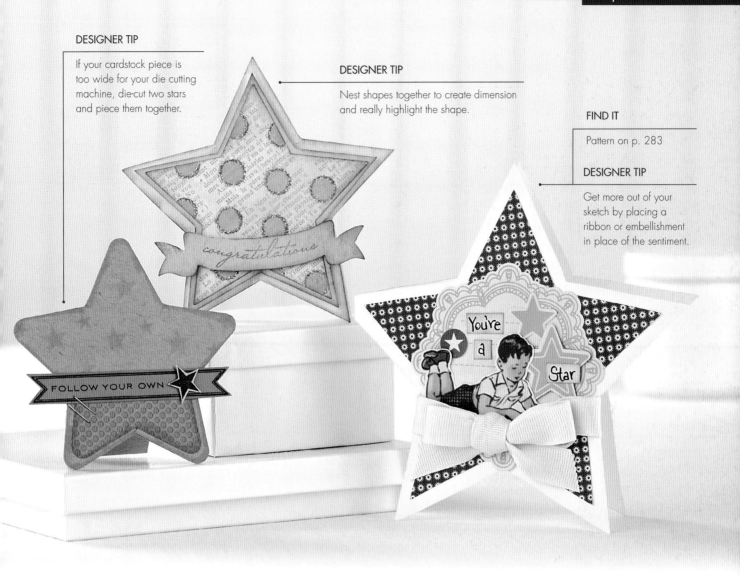

DESIGNER TIP

If your cardstock piece is too wide for your die cutting machine, die-cut two stars and piece them together.

DESIGNER TIP

Nest shapes together to create dimension and really highlight the shape.

FIND IT

Pattern on p. 283

DESIGNER TIP

Get more out of your sketch by placing a ribbon or embellishment in place of the sentiment.

⁵ Follow Your Own Star

Designer: Marcie Sharp

❶ Die-cut star from cardstock; ink edges. Cut cardstock strip and adhere to back of star. ❷ Stamp stars. ❸ Die-cut star from patterned paper; trim and adhere. ❹ Stamp sentiment and banner on cardstock; cut out, ink edges, and adhere. ❺ Stamp star on cardstock; cut out and adhere with foam tape. Attach staples.

Finished size: 4"x 4"

⁵ Congratulations

Designer: Ashley Cannon Newell

Ink all edges. ❶ Die-cut two stars from cardstock; adhere together to form card. ❷ Die-cut stars from patterned paper; adhere together and adhere with foam tape. ❸ Die-cut banner from patterned paper; stamp congratulations. Adhere with foam tape.

Finished size: 5"x 4¾"

⁵ You're a Star

Designer: Kristii Lockart

❶ Cut card from cardstock, following pattern on p. 283. ❷ Cut patterned paper star, following pattern; adhere. ❸ Affix stickers. ❹ Write sentiment with pen on cardstock strips; ink edges and adhere. ❺ Tie on ribbon.

Finished size: 6" x 6"

SUPPLIES: All supplies from Papertrey Ink unless otherwise noted. *Cardstock:* (Orange Zest, Hawaiian Shores, kraft) *Patterned paper:* (orange dot from Dotty Biscotti collection) *Clear stamps:* (banner, stars from Banner Builder set; sentiment from Star Prints set) *Dye ink:* (Tuxedo Black) Tsukineko; (Chamomile) *Pigment ink:* (Hawaiian Shores) *Accents:* (aqua staples) Making Memories *Dies:* (stars) Making Memories

SUPPLIES: *Cardstock:* (Rustic Cream) Papertrey Ink *Patterned paper:* (Portobello Road You & Me from Lost & Found collection) My Mind's Eye *Clear stamps:* (congratulations from Masculine Motifs set) Papertrey Ink *Dye ink:* (Twilight) Close To My Heart; (Vintage Photo) Ranger Industries *Dies:* (banner, stars) Spellbinders

SUPPLIES: *Cardstock:* (French Vanilla) Bazzill Basics Paper; (Rustic Cream) Papertrey Ink *Patterned paper:* (Workbook from Schoolhouse collection) October Afternoon *Color medium:* (black pen) American Crafts *Stickers:* (stars, schoolboy, doily journaling card) October Afternoon *Fibers:* (cream ribbon) Papertrey Ink

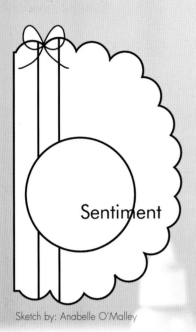

Sentiment

Sketch by: Anabelle O'Malley

DESIGNER TIP

Adding a touch of black really gives your other colors the star treatment!

PRAYING FOR YOU

Praying for You

Designer: AJ Otto

❶ Die-cut and emboss scalloped card from cardstock.

❷ Die-cut scalloped circle from patterned paper; trim and adhere.

❸ Tie on ribbon.

❹ Die-cut scalloped circle from cardstock; adhere.

❺ Die-cut and emboss circle from cardstock; stamp flower, stem, leaf, and sentiment. Adhere with foam tape.

❻ Adhere rhinestones.

Finished size: 4¼" x 5¼"

SUPPLIES: *Cardstock:* (white) Neenah Paper; (Basic Black) Stampin' Up! *Patterned paper:* (Mabel Joy from Stella & Rose collection) My Mind's Eye *Rubber stamps:* (flower, stem, leaf, sentiment from Lean on Me set) Gina K Designs *Dye ink:* (Tuxedo Black) Tsukineko; (Peach Parfait, Pear Pizzazz) Stampin' Up! *Accents:* (orange, clear rhinestones) Kaisercraft *Fibers:* (black/white ribbon) May Arts *Dies:* (circles, scalloped circles) Spellbinders

Love Every Day

Designer: Kandis Smith

❶ Make card from cardstock. ❷ Adhere patterned paper; trim card around scalloped edge. ❸ Stamp Large Solid Flower, sentiment, and hearts. ❹ Tie on ribbon. Tie key to ribbon with twine.

Finished size: 4" x 6"

Sweet Baby

Designer: Chan Vuong

❶ Die-cut two circles from cardstock; trim and adhere at left edge. ❷ Stamp flourish. ❸ Tie on twine. ❹ Stamp frame and sweet baby on cardstock. Punch into circle and attach brad. Adhere with foam tape.

Finished size: 2¾" x 3¾"

Happy I Do Day

Designer: Alicia Thelin

❶ Make card from two scalloped note cards. ❷ Stamp and emboss sentiment on cardstock. Punch into circle; adhere. Zigzag-stitch edge. ❸ Stamp sentiment on cardstock. Punch circle; adhere with foam tape. ❹ Apply dimensional glaze; adhere glitter. ❺ Trim card edges; tie on ribbon.

Finished size: 3¾" x 5½"

SUPPLIES: *Cardstock:* (Coconut Cream) Core'dinations *Patterned paper:* (red scallop from Love Notes collection notebook) Making Memories *Rubber stamps:* (sentiment, heart from Love Every Day set; Large Solid Flower) Hero Arts *Dye ink:* (Soft Sand) Stewart Superior Corp.; (red) Inkadinkado *Chalk ink:* (Night) Hero Arts *Accent:* (key) K&Company *Fibers:* (black/white ribbon) Making Memories; (natural jute twine) Darice

SUPPLIES: *Cardstock:* (Aqua Mist, white) Papertrey Ink *Clear stamps:* (round frame from Daily Designs set; sweet baby from Daily Designs Sentiments set) Papertrey Ink; (flourish from Wild Flowers set) BasicGrey *Pigment ink:* (Turquoise Gem, Onyx Black) Tsukineko *Watermark ink:* Tsukineko *Accent:* (giraffe brad) Michaels *Fibers:* (aqua/white twine) *Die:* (scalloped circle) Spellbinders *Tool:* (circle punch) EK Success

SUPPLIES: All supplies from Stampin' Up! unless otherwise noted. *Cardstock:* (white); (aqua) Roberts Crafts *Rubber stamp:* (sentiment from Word Play set) *Dye ink:* (Kiwi Kiss) *Pigment ink:* (Whisper White) *Embossing powder:* (white) *Finish:* (dimensional glaze) *Accent:* (iridescent glitter) *Fibers:* (green polka dot ribbon) Hobby Lobby *Tools:* (circle punches) *Other:* (scalloped note cards)

Sketch by: Nina Brackett

BONUS IDEA

With a different sentiment, this design would make a terrific teacher card!

To My Core

Designer: Kalyn Kepner

1. Cut circle card from cardstock, following template.

2. Die-cut scalloped circle from patterned paper; adhere.

3. Cut circle from patterned paper, following template; adhere.

4. Trim patterned paper and adhere in quadrants; stitch edge. Zigzag-stitch seams.

5. Die-cut scalloped circle from cardstock; stitch edge and adhere with foam tape.

6. Stamp apple on cardstock and patterned paper; paper-piece and adhere with foam tape.

7. Stamp sentiment on cardstock; color hearts with marker. Trim and adhere with foam tape.

Finished size: 5¼" diameter

SUPPLIES: *Cardstock:* (orange, yellow, green, brown, white) Bazzill Basics Paper *Patterned paper:* (Strawberry Jam, Dandelions from Fly a Kite collection) October Afternoon; (Girl Lovely, Zoo Cuties from Alphabet Soup collection; Little Miss Muffet Celebrate Happy Houndstooth, Little Boy Blue Little Man Zig Zag from Quite Contrary collection) My Mind's Eye *Clear stamps:* (apple, sentiment from Falling for You set) Paper Smooches *Dye ink:* Chestnut) Clearsnap *Color medium:* (pink marker) Copic *Template:* (circle) Provo Craft *Dies:* (scalloped circles) Spellbinders

DESIGNER TIP

Distress the scalloped circle by wrinkling and creasing it with your hands.

Happy Thoughts

Designer: Tosha Leyendekker

❶ Die-cut circle card from cardstock. ❷ Die-cut scalloped circle from cardstock; distress, ink edges, and adhere. ❸ Die-cut circle from felt. Insert batting and stitch to card. ❹ Die-cut flowers and leaves from felt. Adhere and attach brad. ❺ Stamp happy thoughts on canvas; adhere. ❻ Adhere pearls.

Finished size: 4¼" diameter

Circle of Thanks

Designer: Rita Cortum

❶ Die-cut scalloped circle card from cardstock. ❷ Die-cut circle from cardstock; adhere. ❸ Cut small squares from various cardstock and adhere together in a large square. Die-cut and emboss into circle; adhere. ❹ Punch circles from patterned paper; adhere. ❺ Punch tree from cardstock; adhere. ❻ Stamp sentiment on cardstock; punch into tag and adhere.

Finished size: 4½" diameter

🔵5 Happy Holidays

Designer: Rae Barthel

❶ Die-cut card from cardstock. ❷ Adhere die cut. ❸ Die-cut circle from cardstock; score. Tie on twine and adhere. ❹ Apply rub-on. ❺ Affix frame sticker. Affix Santa and holly stickers with foam tape.

Finished size: 5½" diameter

SUPPLIES: *Cardstock:* (Vintage Cream) Papertrey Ink *Clear stamp:* (happy thoughts from Amazing Wishes set) Verve Stamps *Dye ink:* (Antique Linen) Ranger Industries *Solvent ink:* (Jet Black) Tsukineko *Accents:* (white pearls) Michaels; (white pearl brad) Eyelet Outlet *Dies:* (circles, scalloped circle, flowers, leaves) Spellbinders *Other:* (brown, green, pink felt; natural canvas; cotton batting)

SUPPLIES: *Cardstock:* (Wild Wasabi, Bashful Blue, Tangerine Tango, Daffodil Delight, Soft Suede) Stampin' Up!; (white) Georgia-Pacific *Patterned paper:* (Sweet and Sassy Green Floral) The Paper Studio *Rubber stamp:* (sentiment from Pocket Silhouettes set) Stampin' Up! *Dye ink:* (Chocolate Chip) Stampin' Up! *Dies:* (scalloped circle) Stampin' Up!; (circles) Spellbinders *Tools:* (tree punch) Fiskars; (circle) EK Success; (tag) Stampin' Up!

SUPPLIES: *Cardstock:* (Vintage Cream) Papertrey Ink *Accent:* (brown flower die cut) Lily Bee Design *Rub-on:* (happy holidays) Lily Bee Design *Stickers:* (Santa, red frame, holly from Noel collection) Making Memories *Fibers:* (aqua/white twine) The Twinery *Dies:* (circles) Spellbinders

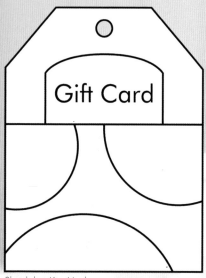

Sketch by: Kim Hughes

⁵ₛₜₑₚₛ Bee in My Pocket

Designer: Kim Howard

❶ Make card from cardstock; trim front to create pocket. Trim back into tag shape. Punch hole from cardstock and adhere.

❷ Die-cut circles from cardstock; stamp Honeycomb background and adhere. Trim off excess; zigzag-stitch edges.

❸ Die-cut circle edge on cardstock panel; insert in pocket.

❹ Stamp Medium Bee on cardstock; color with markers. Apply glaze and cut out. Adhere with foam tape.

❺ Stamp Tiny Bee on cardstock; color with markers. Punch into circle and adhere with foam tape.

Finished size: 3½" x 5½"

SUPPLIES: *Cardstock:* (Lemon Tart) Papertrey Ink; (Perfect Little Black Dress, white) Clear & Simple Stamps *Rubber stamps:* (Honeycomb background, Medium Bee with Tiny Bee Mounted on side) Stampotique *Specialty ink:* (Perfect Little Black Dress hybrid) Clear & Simple Stamps *Color medium:* (yellow, gray markers) Copic *Finish:* (dimensional glaze) Sakura *Dies:* (circles) Spellbinders *Tools:* (circle punches) Marvy Uchida

DESIGNER TIP

While you're at it, why not make several gift card holders for quick holiday gifts?

DESIGNER TIP

Adhere pink panel at three sides to create a pocket for a gift card.

Merry Gift Tag

Designer: Rae Barthel

① Make tag from patterned paper. ② Adhere block of patterned paper on sides and bottom. Adhere patterned paper strip. ③ Cut ticket from patterned paper; adhere with foam tape. ④ Punch hole; thread ribbon through. Tie on floss. ⑤ Adhere pearls.

Finished size: 3½" x 5"

SUPPLIES: *Patterned paper:* (Red Damask, Red Dots, Stripes from Noel collection) Teresa Collins Designs *Accents:* (silver pearls) Hobby Lobby *Fibers:* (cream ribbon) Hobby Lobby; (black floss)

Sailboat Birthday

Designer: Kim Kesti

① Make tag from cardstock. ② Punch half circle from patterned paper; adhere. Punch hole and tie on ribbon. ③ Fold under three edges of patterned paper; stitch three sides to create pocket. ④ Punch circle from cardstock; adhere. Cut sailboat and sails from cardstock and patterned paper, following patterns on p. 284. Adhere. ⑤ Stamp happy birthday on cardstock; trim. Attach brads. Adhere with foam tape.

Finished size: 4" x 6"

SUPPLIES: *Cardstock:* (Grenadine, Admiral, white) Bazzill Basics Paper *Patterned paper:* (Awesome Dots, In the Clouds from Little Boy collection) Echo Park Paper; (Buttercup Dot from Double Dot collection) BoBunny Press *Clear stamp:* (happy birthday) Hampton Art *Pigment ink:* (Not Quite Navy) Stampin' Up! *Accents:* (red brads) Doodlebug Design *Fibers:* (navy stitch ribbon) May Arts *Tools:* (circle punches) Marvy Uchida

Lacy Birthday

Designer: Lucy Abrams

① Make card from cardstock; trim into tag shape. Stitch edges. ② Create project in software. Stamp Lace Star repeatedly. Print on cardstock. ③ Stamp Graph Background on panel; stitch edges and adhere. ④ Stamp happy birthday. Adhere ribbon bow.

Finished size: 3¾" x 5"

SUPPLIES: *Cardstock:* (Chocolate, Carnation) Hero Arts *Rubber stamp:* (Graph Background) Hero Arts *Clear stamps:* (happy birthday from Find Joy set) Hero Arts *Dye ink:* (Soft Blossom, Black) Hero Arts *Digital element:* (Lace Star stamp) www.twopeasinabucket.com *Fibers:* (pink ribbon) Creative Impressions

Sketch by: Betsy Veldman

INSIDE

It's Your Day!

DESIGNER TIPS

Allow liquid appliqué to air dry overnight for a smooth finish. Use a heat tool for a puffy effect.

Brads are very useful for attaching shaped cards. The two identical shapes will be able to slide apart to reveal the card interior.

BONUS IDEAS

Attach twine or string to tiny cards and secure to a gift bag.

Pack tiny cards in your child's lunch box for a fun surprise.

5 STEPS Ice Cream Greetings

Designer: Julie Campbell

❶ Stamp cone on cardstock; color with markers and cut out.

❷ Stamp ice cream on cardstock; cut out and adhere.

❸ Trace card front on cardstock; trim. Stamp inside sentiment; attach pieces with brad.

❹ Adhere liquid appliqué.

❺ Stamp cherry on cardstock; color with markers, cut out, and adhere.

Finished size: 2" x 4½"

SUPPLIES: *Cardstock:* (kraft, white) Papertrey Ink *Rubber stamps:* (cone, ice cream, cherry, sentiment from Sweet Life set) Unity Stamp Co. *Dye ink:* (Fountain Pen, Cough Syrup) Ranger Industries *Color medium:* (brown, green, red markers) Copic *Accents:* (white liquid appliqué) Marvy Uchida; (brad)

WHAT:
WHEN:
WHERE:

INSIDE

FIND IT

Pattern on p. 283

you're invited

USA

INSIDE

FIND IT

Pattern on p. 283

DESIGNER TIP

Flip your sketch for a new and unique inspiration.

cheese...

Cheese & Thank You

Designer: Betsy Veldman

1 Cut cheese card base from cardstock and cheese top pieces from patterned paper, following patterns on p. 283. Punch holes in cheese top pieces with circle punches. Assemble and stitch edges to form pocket. **2** Adhere cardstock strip; affix stickers to spell "Cheese...". **3** Tie on twine; thread button with twine and adhere. **4** Die-cut mouse from cardstock; adhere patterned paper to ears. **5** Stamp & on cardstock; affix stickers to spell "Thank you". Adhere. **6** Punch flower from patterned paper; adhere. **7** Thread button with twine and adhere. Adhere rhinestone. Insert mouse into cheese.

Finished size: 6¾" x 3¼"

Rocket Invitation

Designer: Michelle Liimatainen

1 Die-cut rockets and flames from cardstock. **2** Stamp and emboss rocket body with Envelope Background. **3** Stitch rocket bodies together, leaving base open. Color tip with pen. **4** Stamp you're invited. Color rocket pieces with markers and attach. *Note: Use foam tape on orange pieces.* **5** Affix stickers to spell "USA". **6** Stamp robot on cardstock; punch into circle. Adhere with foam tape. Punch round frame with circle punches; color with pen and adhere. **7** Ink flames. **8** Stamp sentiment on cardstock; ink edges and adhere between flame pieces. Slip inside rocket body.

Finished size: 2½" x 8¼"

Mr. Gnome

Designer: Beth Opel

1 Cut gnome body from cardstock and hat from felt, following patterns on p. 283. **2** Make card from cardstock. Adhere body to card base; adhere felt hat. **3** Punch cheek and nose circles from cardstock; adhere with foam tape. **4** Draw mouth with pen. **5** Cut hair, mustache, and eyebrows from chipboard swirls; adhere flocking and adhere. **6** Adhere wiggle eyes. **7** Thread ribbon through slide and adhere.

Finished size: 4¾" x 6¾"

SUPPLIES: *Cardstock:* (Harvest Gold) Papertrey Ink; (gray) Core'dinations *Patterned paper:* (Gertie Sweet Stripe, Blossom from Stella & Rose pad) My Mind's Eye *Clear stamp:* (& from Get to the Point set) Papertrey Ink *Specialty ink:* (Smokey Shadow) Papertrey Ink *Accents:* (yellow, green buttons) Papertrey Ink; (black rhinestone) Kaisercraft *Stickers:* (Micro Monogram alphabet) BasicGrey *Fibers:* (natural twine) Papertrey Ink *Die:* (mouse) Provo Craft *Tools:* (circle punches, flower punch) EK Success

SUPPLIES: *Cardstock:* (Navy Blue) Bazzill Basics Paper; (white) *Rubber stamp:* (Envelope Pattern) Hero Arts *Clear stamps:* (you're invited) Hampton Art; (robot) BasicGrey *(sentiment from Monkey Birthday set)* Rubber Soul *Dye ink:* (Fired Brick, Dried Marigold, Spiced Marmalade, Barn Door, Mustard Seed) Ranger Industries; (black) Stewart Superior Corp. *Pigment ink:* (white) Clearsnap *Embossing powder:* (clear) Ranger Industries *Color media:* (silver leafing pen) Krylon; (assorted markers) Copic *Stickers:* (white alphabet) *Dies:* (rocket, flames) Silhouette America *Tools:* (circle punches) Carl Manufacturing

SUPPLIES: *Cardstock:* (tan) Bazzill Basics Paper *Color medium:* (burgundy pen) Bic *Accents:* (wiggle eyes) Darice; (gold ribbon slide) We R Memory Keepers *Stickers:* (white chipboard swirls) American Crafts; (white flocking) Hampton Art *Fibers:* (green ribbon) Making Memories *Tools:* (circle punches) EK Success, Marvy Uchida *Other:* (burgundy felt) Kunin

Pull out tag

⟨5 STEPS⟩ Holiday Ornament Card

Designer: Betsy Veldman

❶ Cut corners from cardstock squares, adhere patterned paper, and stitch bottom and left edges to form pocket. Ink edges.

❷ Stamp sentiment on journaling tag; ink edges and adhere with foam tape.

❸ Tie twine on stickers; adhere with foam tape. Adhere rhinestones.

❹ Die-cut ornament from cardstock; stamp circle and ink edges.

❺ Tie on ribbon and insert in pocket.

Finished size: 5½" x 6"

SUPPLIES: *Cardstock:* (Vintage Cream) Papertrey Ink *Patterned paper:* (Woodland from Eskimo Kisses collection) BasicGrey *Clear stamp:* (sentiment from Tree Trimming Trio set) Papertrey Ink; (circle from Distressing Round set) Glitz Design *Chalk ink:* (Creamy Brown) Clearsnap *Specialty ink:* (Ripe Avocado, Spring Moss hybrid) Papertrey Ink *Accents:* (blue rhinestones) BasicGrey; (red journaling tag) My Mind's Eye; (pink glitter brads) Doodlebug Design *Stickers:* (ornaments) BasicGrey *Fibers:* (burgundy ribbon, cream twine) Papertrey Ink *Die:* (ornament) Provo Craft

FIND IT

Patterns on p. 282

Peeking Pumpkin Card

Designer: Maren Benedict

SUPPLIES: *Cardstock:* (True Black) Papertrey Ink; (orange) American Crafts *Patterned paper:* (Creepy Crawlers from Boo to You collection) My Mind's Eye *Dye ink:* (Black Soot) Ranger Industries *Accent:* (green button) BasicGrey *Stickers:* (Tiny Alpha alphabet) Making Memories *Fibers:* (green ribbon) Papertrey Ink; (black pompom trim) Michaels; (black twine) Canvas Corp. *Die:* (circle) Spellbinders

Finished size: 4¾" x 4¾"

Adore Card

Designer: Kim Hughes

SUPPLIES: *Patterned paper:* (Dearest Dots, Smitten Stripes from Be-Loved collection) My Mind's Eye; (orange lined from Orange Memo notebook) Jenni Bowlin Studio *Accents:* (blue button) Creative Café; (pink heart, blue adore circle, pink scalloped circle die cuts) My Mind's Eye *Fibers:* (tan, pink floss) DMC; (tan ribbon) American Crafts

Finished size: 4½" x 4¾"

Hanukkah Card

Designer: Teri Anderson

SUPPLIES: *Cardstock:* (Bluebonnet, Lemon Yellow, Dark Blue, white) WorldWin *Patterned paper:* (Gingerbread House from Merrymint collection) American Crafts *Accents:* (clear rhinestones) Imaginisce *Fibers:* (white twill) Papertrey Ink *Font:* (CK Sassy) Creating Keepsakes *Die:* (circle) Spellbinders

Finished size: 4¼" x 4¼"

Sketch by: Maren Benedict

DESIGNER TIP

Make multiple tags and tie together to create a holiday garland.

Festive Monogram Tag

Designer: Kimberly Crawford

Ink all edges.

❶ Stamp triangle on patterned paper; trim.

❷ Die-cut star and inverted scalloped circles from patterned paper.

❸ Stamp music circle on patterned paper; trim.

❹ Paint sticker. Adhere to music circle.

❺ Adhere all layers together using foam tape.

❻ Punch top corners and tie on ribbon bows.

Finished size: 3¼" x 3¾"

SUPPLIES: *Patterned paper:* (Mitten Mitten, Merry & Bright, Yuletide, Wrapping Paper from Oh Joy collection) Cosmo Cricket *Clear stamps:* (music circle, triangle banner from Big Banner with Rosettes set) Pink Persimmon *Dye ink:* (Tuxedo Black) Tsukineko *Chalk ink:* (Creamy Brown) Clearsnap *Paint:* (white) Making Memories *Sticker:* (e from Eva alphabet) BasicGrey *Fibers:* (gold wired ribbon) Michaels *Dies:* (inverted scalloped circle, star) Spellbinders *Tool:* (⅛" circle punch)

Baby Boy Gift Bag
Designer: Becky Olsen

SUPPLIES: *Patterned paper:* (Tweet Tweet from Best Friends collection, Bright Moons from Chloé Lynn collection, Plaid Sky from Big Attitude collection) My Mind's Eye *Rubber stamps:* (stork from Vintage Baby Expressions set, sentiment from Baby Dear set) Cornish Heritage Farms *Dye ink:* (Cobalt) Ranger Industries *Accents:* (chrome eyelet) Making Memories; (small brass safety pin) Li'l Davis Designs *Fibers:* (white floss) DMC; (white ribbon) Creative Impressions *Tool:* (2" circle punch) Marvy Uchida *Other:* (white gift bag) Roberts Crafts

Finished size: 5½" x 8½"

Baby Bib Card
Designer: Betsy Veldman

SUPPLIES: *Cardstock:* (Vintage Cream, Sweet Blush) Papertrey Ink *Clear stamps:* (sentiment from Scattered Showers set, polka dots from Polka Dot Basics set) Papertrey Ink *Chalk ink:* (Creamy Brown) Clearsnap *Specialty ink:* (Sweet Blush, Dark Chocolate hybrid) Papertrey Ink *Accents:* (pink, yellow, white buttons) Papertrey Ink; (silver eyelets) Provo Craft; (pig tag) October Afternoon *Fibers:* (white twine, pink twill) Papertrey Ink *Tools:* (scalloped circle punch) The Paper Studio; (decorative-edge scissors) Provo Craft; (circle punch) Marvy Uchida

Finished size: 5½" x 4¾"

Greetings Earthling Card
Designer: Laura O'Donnell

SUPPLIES: *Cardstock:* (Natural White) Stampin' Up! *Patterned paper:* (red bicycles, pink hearts, green dots, blue numbers, cream grid from Daydreams pad; gold glitter from Christmas Cheer pad) K&Company *Rubber stamps:* (Rocket, Greetings Earthling) Just Johanna Rubber Stamps *Dye ink:* (Tuxedo Black) Tsukineko *Tools:* (circle cutter) Creative Memories; (1⅜" circle punch) EK Success

Finished size: 4" x 5"

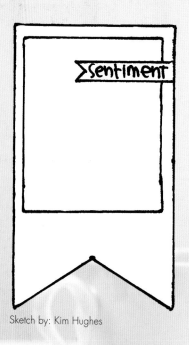

Sketch by: Kim Hughes

Teacher's Apple Card

Designer: Betsy Veldman

❶ Make card from cardstock; cut triangle from bottom edge.

❷ Cut patterned paper slightly smaller than card front; ink edges and adhere.

❸ Cut rectangle of patterned paper; ink edges, stitch border, and adhere.

❹ Stamp teacher on patterned paper; trim and ink edges.

❺ Stamp apples on cardstock; cut out. Adhere teacher piece and apples.
   Note: Adhere one apple with foam tape.

❻ Wrap ribbon around card front; tie bow. Attach button with twine.

Finished size: 3½" x 6½"

SUPPLIES: *Cardstock:* (Pure Poppy, white) Papertrey Ink *Patterned paper:* (Number Cruncher from Teacher's Pet collection) Imaginisce; (Wouldn't It Be Nice from Blue Skies collection) American Crafts; (Daydream from Grayson Hall collection) Collage Press *Clear stamps:* (apples, teacher from Teacher's Apple set) Papertrey Ink *Chalk ink:* (Creamy Brown) Clearsnap *Specialty ink:* (Pure Poppy, Ripe Avocado hybrid) Papertrey Ink *Accent:* (blue button) Papertrey Ink *Fibers:* (apple ribbon) Imaginisce; (white twine)

DESIGNER TIP

If you use double-sided patterned paper as your card base, the inside will have some color as well!

Golden Thanks Card
Designer: Teri Anderson

SUPPLIES: *Cardstock:* (Vintage Cream) Papertrey Ink; (white) WorldWin *Patterned paper:* (yellow floral, small script, green flourish from Autumn Splendor pad) Making Memories *Clear stamps:* (thanks sentiment from Autumn Abundance set) Papertrey Ink *Dye ink:* (Tuxedo Black) Tsukineko *Accent:* (brown brad) Oriental Trading Co.

Finished size: 4¼" x 5½"

Christmas Joy Card
Designer: Beatriz Jennings

SUPPLIES: *Cardstock:* (Rustic Cream) Papertrey Ink *Patterned paper:* (Laurel Leaves, Noel from Wassail collection) BasicGrey *Dye ink:* (Vintage Photo) Ranger Industries *Accents:* (white glitter chipboard snowflake) Melissa Frances; (chipboard alphabet) Tattered Angels; (burgundy, green flower buttons; red glitter, white pearl) Digital element: (vintage Santa stamp from Posted Santa Postage Stamps No. 02 kit) www.designerdigitals.com *Rub-ons:* (flourishes) Glitz Design *Fibers:* (white ribbon, jute twine)

Finished size: 4" x 5½"

Be Mine Gingham Card
Designer: Danielle Flanders

SUPPLIES: *Patterned paper:* (Hearts Bloom, Bow and Arrow, Bullseye from Cupid collection) Pink Paislee *Accents:* (love you tag die cut) Pink Paislee; (white pearl) Melissa Frances *Rub-on:* (be mine) Pink Paislee *Fibers:* (blue twill)

Finished size: 5¼" x 3¼"

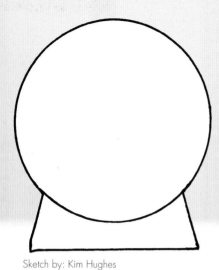

Sketch by: Kim Hughes

FIND IT

Pattern on p. 282

5 STEPS Bee Happy Card

Designer: Teri Anderson

1 Cut card base, following pattern on p. 282.

2 Cut circle from patterned paper; adhere.

3 Adhere die cuts and rhinestone swirl.

Finished size: 3½" x 3¾"

SUPPLIES: *Cardstock:* (gray) Bazzill Basics Paper; (white) WorldWin *Patterned paper:* (Picking Pumpkins from Weathervane collection) October Afternoon *Accents:* (clear rhinestone swirl) Zva Creative; (bee, happy die cuts) October Afternoon

DESIGNER TIP

Trace cups and bowls for fun circle sizes.

BONUS IDEA

This sketch is the perfect shape for a snowglobe-themed card or even a bubble-gum machine with bright button gumballs.

Let It Snow Card
Designer: Lisa Johnson

SUPPLIES: *Cardstock:* (Spring Rain, Soft Stone, white) Papertrey Ink *Clear stamps:* (let it snow from Winter Swirls set; snowman, snowflake from Holiday Tree set) ~~Papertrey Ink~~ *Pigment ink:* (Fresh Snow) Papertrey Ink *Specialty ink:* (Pure Poppy, True Black, Smokey Shadow hybrid) Papertrey Ink *Accent:* (white glitter) Stewart Superior Corp. *Fibers:* (red gingham ribbon) Creative Impressions *Tools:* (1/8" circle punch, large circle punch) Marvy Uchida

Finished size: 3" x 3½"

Get Well Flowers Card
Designer: Debbie Olson

SUPPLIES: *Cardstock:* (Vintage Cream, Spring Moss) Papertrey Ink *Patterned paper:* (floral, polka dot from Autumn Abundance collection) Papertrey Ink *Clear stamps:* (pitcher with flowers from Autumn Abundance set, get well from Tea for Two set) Papertrey Ink *Dye ink:* (Tuxedo Black) Tsukineko; (Chamomile) Papertrey Ink *Specialty ink:* (Ripe Avocado hybrid) Papertrey Ink *Color medium:* (assorted markers) Copic *Fibers:* (yellow ribbon) Papertrey Ink *Dies:* (circles) Spellbinders

Finished size: 4" x 4½"

Stinkin' Cute Card
Designer: Kim Hughes

SUPPLIES: *Cardstock:* (Vanilla Cream, Restful Blue) Prism; (Butter embossed) Bazzill Basics Paper *Color medium:* (brown pen) Sakura *Accents:* (white flowers) Making Memories; (brown, green glitter brads) We R Memory Keepers *Rub-on:* (so stinkin' cute) American Crafts

Finished size: 5¼" x 5"

Sketch by: Kim Hughes

FIND IT

Pattern on p. 282

Girly Girl Purse Card

Designer: Kim Hughes

❶ Cut purse, following pattern on p. 282.

❷ Punch circles from patterned paper; adhere along flap edge.

❸ Cut patterned paper to fit flap twice; adhere on front and inside flap.

❹ Make handle by cutting slits in purse top; thread ribbon ends through and adhere.

❺ Attach brad to felt flower; adhere.

❻ Apply rub-on.

Finished size: 5½" x 4"

SUPPLIES: *Patterned paper:* (Nutmeg from Kitchen Spice collection) BoBunny Press; (Soiree from Ooh La La For Him collection) My Mind's Eye *Accents:* (purple flower epoxy brad) BasicGrey; (orange felt flower) Making Memories *Rub-on:* (girly girl) Melissa Frances *Fibers:* (tan ribbon) American Crafts *Tool:* (½" circle punch) EK Success

DESIGNER TIP

Stamp the main sentiment first, then mask that portion of the bag when stamping your background.

Grateful For You Card

Designer: Jessica Witty

SUPPLIES: *Clear stamps:* (type from Background Basics: Text Style; grateful for you from Friends 'Til the End set) Papertrey Ink *Dye ink:* (Black Soot) Ranger Industries; *Buttons:* (red, grey) buttons) Papertrey Ink; (vintage book page) *Fibers:* (white floss) DMC *Other:* (gusseted glassine bag)

Finished size: 4½" square

Happy Bird-Day Bag

Designer: Kim Hughes

SUPPLIES: *Cardstock:* (yellow, pink embossed; dark yellow, white) Bazzill Basics Paper *Patterned paper:* (Honor Roll from Teen collection) American Crafts *Color Medium:* (brown pen) Sakura *Sticker:* (red) American Crafts *Fibers:* (pink polka dot ribbon) American Crafts *Other:* (kraft gift bag)

Finished size: 3¼" x 5¼"

Birthday Cupcake Card

Designer: Latisha Yoast

SUPPLIES: *Cardstock:* (pink) Prism; (white) Flourishes *Patterned paper:* (Bundt Pan from Nook & Pantry collection) BasicGrey *Clear stamp:* (happy birthday from Sweet Nothings set) Flourishes *Dye ink:* (Tuxedo Black) Tsukineko *Accents:* (pink pompoms) May Arts *Sticker:* (felt cupcake) BasicGrey *Fibers:* (clear plastic thread) *Die:* (scalloped oval) Spellbinders

Finished size: 4¼" x 4"

Sketch by: Betsy Veldman

FIND IT

Patterns on p. 282

5 STEPS Easter Basket Card

Designer: Heidi Van Laar

1. Make basket and handle card, following pattern on p. 282.

2. Cut kraft cardstock panel to fit card front. Weave cardstock strips, adhere to panel, trim, and adhere panel to card.

3. Punch edge of cardstock and patterned paper strips; layer and adhere together. Stamp sentiment and flower; color flower with pen.

4. Stitch stamped piece with twine, spell "Easter" with stickers, and adhere.

5. Tie tag sticker to handle; adhere flower. Thread button with twine and adhere.

Finished size: 5" x 7"

SUPPLIES: *Cardstock:* (white) American Crafts; (kraft) The Paper Company *Patterned paper:* (Nutmeg from Kitchen Spice Collection) BoBunny Press *Clear stamps:* (happy, flower from All Occasion Messages set) Hero Arts *Chalk ink:* (Chestnut Roan) Clearsnap *Color medium:* (pink pen) Sakura *Accents:* (aqua flower) Prima; (white button) *Stickers:* (chipboard bunny tag) Cosmo Cricket; (Delight Alphabet) American Crafts *Fibers:* (natural jute twine) Darice *Tool:* (embossing border punch) EK Success

Merry & Bright Santa Card

Designer: Kim Hughes

SUPPLIES: *Cardstock:* (Cream Puff) Bazzill Basics Paper; (Tawny Light) Prism *Patterned paper:* (Floating Flowers from Blossom collection) My Mind's Eye; (Deck the Halls from Christmas Past collection) Graphic 45 *Rubber stamp:* (Merry & Bright) Stamping Bella *Dye ink:* (Grassroots) Storage Units, Ink *Color medium:* (black pen) Sakura *Accents:* (ivory buttons) SEI *Fibers:* (cream twine) Creative Impressions *Tool:* (circle punch) EK Success

Finished size: 4¾" x 5½"

Sweet Cupcake Card

Designer: Betsy Veldman

SUPPLIES: *Cardstock:* (Vintage Cream, Dark Chocolate) Papertrey Ink *Specialty paper:* (Pink Swiss Dot Doily die cut from June Bug collection) BasicGrey *Clear stamps:* (sentiment from Cupcake Collection set; heart from Heart Prints set) Papertrey Ink *Chalk ink:* (Creamy Brown) Clearsnap *Specialty ink:* (Sweet Blush, Dark Chocolate hybrid) Papertrey Ink *Accents:* (cupcake epoxy brad, white glitter) Doodlebug Design *Sticker:* (pink glitter lace) We R Memory Keepers *Fibers:* (natural twine, ivory ribbon) Papertrey Ink *Die:* (cupcake) Provo Craft *Tool:* (heart punch) EK Success

Finished size: 5¾" x 4¾"

Melt with You Card

Designer: Lisa Johnson

SUPPLIES: All supplies from Papertrey Ink unless otherwise noted. *Cardstock:* (Hibiscus Burst, kraft) *Vellum; Clear stamps:* (sentiment, heart from Love Songs set; dots from Background Basics: Spots & Dots set) *Dye ink:* (Creamy Caramel) Stampin' Up! *Specialty ink:* (True Black, Hibiscus Burst, Raspberry Fizz hybrid) *Accent:* (iridescent glitter) Stewart Superior Corp. *Fibers:* (pink polka dot ribbon) *Template:* (Argyle embossing) Provo Craft *Tool:* (circle punch) Marvy Uchida

Finished size: 3" x 5¾"

Sketch by: Betsy Veldman

⁵⁵ Smiling Frog Card

Designer: Teri Anderson

❶ Cut circles from patterned paper and cardstock. Adhere top of circles to form card; sand edges.

❷ Trim and adhere cardstock. Stamp sentiment.

❸ Adhere frog and wiggle eyes.

❹ Trim patterned paper squares; adhere. Attach brad.

Finished size: 7" diameter

SUPPLIES: *Cardstock:* (white) WorldWin *Patterned paper:* (Tweet Tweet, Scattered Flowers from Best Friends collection; Spunky Spots from Shine collection; Hot Wheels from Nice Ride collection) My Mind's Eye *Clear stamps:* (sentiment, smile from Favorite Memories set) Technique Tuesday *Dye ink:* (Tuxedo Black) Tsukineko *Accents:* (chipboard frog, pink brad) Colorbok; (wiggle eyes) Darice

Best Friend Tin

Designer: Lisa Johnson

SUPPLIES: All supplies by Papertrey Ink unless otherwise noted. *Cardstock:* (Melon Berry, Shimmer White, Enchanted Evening) *Clear stamps:* (flower, sentiment from Out of the Box set; large, small polka dots from Polka Dot Basics II set) *Pigment ink:* (Fresh Snow) *Specialty ink:* (Enchanted Evening hybrid) *Accents:* (silver metal dots) Michaels (peach button) *Fibers:* (blue polka dot ribbon) *Tool:* (circle punch) Marvy Uchida *Other:* (tin)

Finished size: 3¼" diameter x 2¼" height

80s Mix CD Case

Designer: Kim Hughes

SUPPLIES: *Cardstock:* (green glitter) Doodlebug Design *Patterned paper:* (Pleasantly Puzzled from Vintage Yummy collection) Sassafras Lass *Stickers:* (Daydream alphabet; black glitter bracket, music note) American Crafts *Tool:* (star punch) EK Success *Other:* (CD case)

Finished size: 5½" x 5"

Sunflower Thank You Tag

Designer: Kim Kesti

SUPPLIES: *Cardstock:* (Lily White, Limeade, Sea Water, Pauly Poo) Bazzill Basics Paper *Accent:* (yellow button) Doodlebug Design *Stickers:* (loopy Lou Alphabet) Doodlebug Design *Fibers:* (striped ribbon) Strano Designs *Tool:* (decorative-edge scissors) Fiskars *Other:* (photo)

Finished size: 5" diameter

Sketch by: Betsy Veldman

5 STEPS New Home Card

Designer: Maile Belles

1 Make card from cardstock.

2 Cut half circle from cardstock rectangle, stamp Wood Grain Background, and adhere.

3 Stamp sentiment on cardstock strip, punch holes, and tie on with floss.

4 Cut triangle from cardstock; adhere torn cardstock strips. Adhere to card.

5 Thread buttons with floss and adhere.

Finished size: 5¾" x 7½"

SUPPLIES: *Cardstock:* (Raspberry Fizz, Dark Chocolate, kraft) Papertrey Ink *Rubber stamp:* (Wood Grain Background) Plaid *Clear stamp:* (sentiment from Boards & Beams set) Papertrey Ink *Watermark ink:* Tsukineko *Specialty ink:* (Dark Chocolate hybrid) Papertrey Ink *Accents:* (pink, brown buttons) Papertrey Ink *Fibers:* (brown floss) DMC *Tool:* (circle cutter) Provo Craft

Highest Star Card

Designer: Betsy Veldman

SUPPLIES: *Cardstock:* (Pure Poppy, Rustic Cream) Papertrey Ink *Patterned paper:* (Content Beads from Peace collection, Bonded from My Friend collection) My Mind's Eye *Clear stamps:* (polka dot star, sentiment from Star Prints set) Papertrey Ink *Chalk ink:* (Creamy Brown, orange) Clearsnap *Specialty ink:* (Pure Poppy hybrid) Papertrey Ink *Accents:* (assorted buttons) Papertrey Ink; (red brad) BasicGrey; (green/cream tag) My Mind's Eye *Fibers:* (cream twine) Papertrey Ink *Tools:* (star, corner rounder punches) Fiskars

Finished size: 3" x 6¼"

From the Dog Card

Designer: Rae Barthel

SUPPLIES: *Cardstock:* (white) *Patterned paper:* (Pearl Bobbinhauser, Elanore Battington, Faye Needleworth, Ethel Dartsmith from Craft Fair collection) American Crafts *Accents:* (red heart buttons) *Fibers:* (white floss) DMC *Font:* (Wish I Were Taller) www.kevinandamanda.com *Tool:* (corner rounder punch) EK Success

Finished size: 5¼" x 7"

Happily Ever After Card

Designer: Lisa Johnson

SUPPLIES: *Cardstock:* (Smokey Shadow, Soft Stone, Lemon Tart, white) Papertrey Ink *Clear stamps:* (door, windows from Home Made set; sentiment from Wedding Day set; scallops from Background Basics: Retro set) Papertrey Ink *Specialty ink:* (Noir hybrid) Stewart Superior Corp.; (True Black, Smokey Shadow hybrid) Papertrey Ink *Color media:* (assorted markers) Copic; (white gel pen) Marvy Uchida *Accents:* (clear rhinestones) Zva Creative; (white flowers) Michaels *Fibers:* (green leaf ribbon) May Arts *Tool:* (decorative-edge scissors) Fiskars

Finished size: 4¼" x 7½"

Sketch by: Betsy Veldman

5 STEPS Spooky Spider Card

Designer: Rebecca Oehlers

1 Make card from cardstock. Die-cut into pinked circle.

2 Die-cut pinked circle from cardstock, stitch line, and adhere with foam tape.

3 Color chipboard letter with marker; adhere, using foam tape at top.

4 Stamp spooky and spider on cardstock. Trim. *Note: Trim sentiment with decorative-edge scissors. Adhere, using foam tape for sentiment.*

5 Adhere buttons.

Finished size: 4" diameter

SUPPLIES: *Cardstock:* (True Black, Orange Zest, white) Papertrey Ink *Clear stamps:* (spooky, spider from Spooky Sweets set) Papertrey Ink *Specialty ink:* (True Black hybrid) Papertrey Ink *Color medium:* (black marker) Copic *Accents:* (orange buttons) Papertrey Ink; (chipboard letter) *Dies:* (pinked circles) Spellbinders *Tool:* (decorative-edge scissors) Fiskars

Elegant Mother Card
Designer: Betsy Veldman

SUPPLIES: *Cardstock:* (Vintage Cream) Papertrey Ink *Patterned paper:* (Tea Cakes from Nook & Pantry collection) BasicGrey *Clear stamp:* (mother from Mother set) Papertrey Ink *Chalk ink:* (Creamy Brown) Clearsnap *Specialty ink:* (Pure Poppy hybrid) Papertrey Ink *Accents:* (floral chipboard circle) BasicGrey; (white pearls) Zva Creative; (printed monogram) Creative Imaginations; (assorted buttons) Papertrey Ink *Fibers:* (cream twine) Papertrey Ink *Die:* (scalloped card base) Provo Craft

Finished size: 5" diameter

Have a Ball Card
Designer: Beth Opel

SUPPLIES: *Cardstock:* (Light Blue) Bazzill Basics Paper; (Charcoal) WorldWin; (blue) *Patterned paper:* (Decaf Dot from Double Dot collection) BoBunny Press; (Edith Fitzbolt, Myrtle O'Seam from Craft Fair collection; Red Rover from Kids collection) American Crafts; (Harbor View from Bridgeport collection) SEI; (Moonlight from The Night Owl collection, yellow grid from MODsheets collection) Scrap In Style TV; (Pearl Crocodile) Fibermark *Stickers:* (Typo alphabet) American Crafts *Font:* (Rockwell) www.fonts.com

Finished size: 5" diameter

Wood Grain Thanks Card
Designer: Tiffany Johnson

SUPPLIES: *Cardstock:* (Vintage Cream, Hibiscus Burst) Papertrey Ink *Rubber stamp:* (Wood Grain Background) Plaid *Clear stamp:* (thanks from Thank You set) Close To My Heart *Dye ink:* (Outdoor Denim, Grey Wool) Close To My Heart *Pigment ink:* (Fresh Snow) Papertrey Ink *Embossing powder:* (White Daisy) Close To My Heart *Accents:* (silver brads) American Crafts *Stickers:* (Dolce alphabet) American Crafts *Dies:* (circles) Spellbinders

Finished size: 3¾" diameter

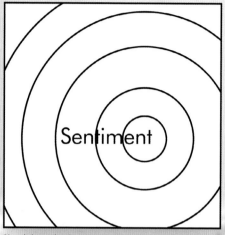

Sketch by: Julia Stainton

5 STEPS You Did It!

Designer: Lindsay Amrhein

❶ Make card from cardstock.

❷ Die-cut circles from cardstock.

❸ Layer and adhere circles; trim.

❹ Stamp sentiment on cardstock, trim, and adhere.

❺ Thread buttons and adhere.

Finished size: 3½" square

SUPPLIES: *Cardstock:* (Terracotta Tile, Orange Zest, Harvest Gold, Simply Chartreuse, Aqua Mist) Papertrey Ink; (white) *Clear stamp:* (sentiment from Enjoy the Ride set) Papertrey Ink *Specialty ink:* (True Black hybrid) Papertrey Ink *Accents:* (black buttons) Papertrey Ink *Fibers:* (black floss) DMC *Dies:* (circles) Spellbinders

DESIGNER TIP

When using multiple nested dies, use a thin magnetic sheet to hold the dies in place, or use removable tape.

DESIGNER TIPS

When piercing holes for stitching, be careful not to pierce too close to the edge of the cardstock or it may rip when stitching.

Use tape to secure loose stitches on the back of your work.

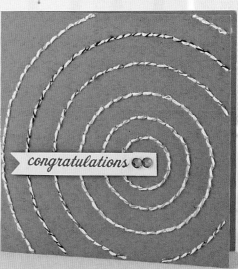

I {heart} You

Designer: Stephanie Johnson

❶ Make card from cardstock. ❷ Trim hearts from cardstock; adhere. ❸ Affix "I" and "u" stickers. ❹ Trim heart from cardstock and adhere with foam tape.

Finished size: 5" square

Ripple of Hope

Designer: Regina Mangum

❶ Make card from cardstock. ❷ Print sentiment on cardstock panel. ❸ Dry-emboss panel and trim. ❹ Adhere ribbon, attach brad, and adhere panel with foam tape.

Finished size: 5" square

Rainbow Congratulations

Designer: Joscelyne Cutchens

❶ Make card from cardstock. ❷ Draw circles with pencil and compass. ❸ Pierce holes and stitch assorted twine. ❹ Stamp congratulations, die-cut into banner, trim, and adhere rhinestones. Adhere with foam tape.

Finished size: 5½" square

SUPPLIES: *Cardstock:* (white) American Crafts; (pink, blue, yellow, green) Michaels *Stickers:* (Sprinkles alphabet) American Crafts

SUPPLIES: *Cardstock:* (Solar White) Neenah Paper; (Aqua Mist) Papertrey Ink *Accent:* (pearl brad) My Mind's Eye *Fibers:* (aqua woven ribbon) American Crafts *Font:* (Londonderry Air) www.fonts101.com *Templates:* (embossing circles) Spellbinders

SUPPLIES: *Cardstock:* (Solar White) Neenah Paper; (kraft) Papertrey Ink *Clear stamp:* (congratulations from Enjoy the Ride set) Papertrey Ink *Dye ink:* (Bahama Blue) Tsukineko *Accents:* (blue rhinestones) Creative Charms *Fibers:* (pink/white, red/white, orange/white, yellow/white, green/white, aqua/white twine) Divine Twine *Die:* (double ended banner) Papertrey Ink *Tool:* (compass)

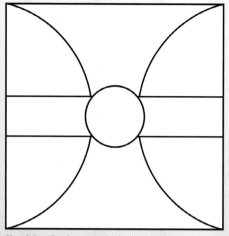

Sketch by: Stephanie Halinski

You're Amazing

Designer: Natalie Dever

1 Make card from cardstock.

2 Trim patterned paper, mat with cardstock, and stitch.

3 Die-cut doilies from cardstock, trim, and adhere.

4 Circle-punch patterned paper, trim, and adhere.

5 Stamp you're amazing on cardstock, circle-punch, and ink edges. Adhere.

6 Affix sticker and tie on ribbon. Adhere panel.

Finished size: 4¼" x 5½"

SUPPLIES: *Cardstock:* (black) The Paper Cut; (Vintage Cream) Papertrey Ink; (red) *Patterned paper:* (Apron Strings, Advertisement from For the Record collection) Echo Park Paper *Clear stamp:* (you're amazing from Sentimental set) There She Goes Clear Stamps *Dye ink:* (Jet Black) Tsukineko; (Old Paper) Ranger Industries *Sticker:* (blue doily) Echo Park Paper *Fibers:* (black stitched ribbon) *Die:* (doily) Cheery Lynn Designs *Tool:* (2½" circle punch) Marvy Uchida

DESIGNER TIP

It's easy to remove the attachment loop from a charm by using needle nose pliers. Remember, the product you have can always be altered!

just a note to say hello

Congratulations

The Sweet Life
Designer: Melissa Phillips

❶ Make card from cardstock. Cover with patterned paper and ink edges. ❷ Stamp newspaper on cardstock, die-cut into doily, and ink edges. Trim and adhere. ❸ Stitch top and bottom card edges. ❹ Paint bookplate and adhere. Die-cut doily from patterned paper and adhere. ❺ Adhere velvet leaves and affix sticker. ❻ Adhere rhinestones and flowers.

Finished size: 4" x 4¼"

5 STEPS Tea Hello
Designer: Lesley Langdon

❶ Make card from patterned paper. ❷ Die-cut label from patterned paper, cut in half, and adhere to cardstock square. ❸ Adhere trim and ribbon. Die-cut medallion from cardstock and adhere. ❹ Stamp sentiment on tag, tie on floss, and adhere with foam tape. ❺ Adhere tea kettle and adhere panel with foam tape.

Finished size: 5" square

5 STEPS Elegant Congratulations
Designer: Susan R. Opel

❶ Make card from cardstock. Cover with patterned paper. ❷ Cut circle from patterned paper, trim, and adhere. ❸ Stamp congratulations on patterned paper, trim, and adhere with foam tape. ❹ Tie on ribbon and adhere charm.

Finished size: 5¼" square

SUPPLIES: *Cardstock:* (Spring Moss, Lavender Moon) Papertrey Ink *Patterned paper:* (Dreamland from Lullaby Lane collection) Webster's Pages; (Glossary) BasicGrey *Clear stamp:* (newspaper from Background Basics: Newsprint set) Papertrey Ink *Specialty ink:* (Smokey Shadow, Lavender Moon hybrid) Papertrey Ink *Paint:* (white) DecoArt *Accents:* (copper bookplate) American Crafts; (clear rhinestones, yellow flowers) The Little Pink Studio; (yellow leaves) *Sticker:* (label) K&Company *Dies:* (doilies) Papertrey Ink

SUPPLIES: *Cardstock:* (Corner Hutch) Core'dinations *Patterned paper:* (Heirloom from Restoration collection) Crate Paper; (Mary Mary Wonderful from Quite Contrary collection) My Mind's Eye *Rubber stamp:* (sentiment from My Type set) Hero Arts *Dye ink:* (black) Stewart Superior Corp. *Accents:* (white tag) Staples; (tea pot chipboard) Crate Paper *Fibers:* (pink velvet ribbon) May Arts; (cream trim, white floss) *Dies:* (medallion, label) Spellbinders

SUPPLIES: *Cardstock:* (white) *Patterned paper:* (Diamond from White Elegance collection) SEI; (Mint Chocolate Chip from Summer collection) Nikki Sivils Scrapbooker *Clear stamp:* (congratulations from Fancy Phrases set) Waltzingmouse Stamps *Dye ink:* (brown) Hero Arts *Accent:* (clear rhinestone charm) Teresa Collins Design *Fibers:* (green ribbon) May Arts *Tool:* (circle cutter) Creative Memories

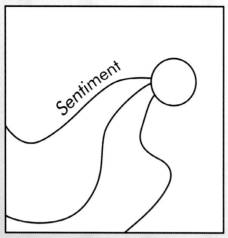

Sketch by: Julia Stainton

DESIGNER TIP

This sentiment set is also available from Stampin' Up! in English under the set name "Picture This". The sentiment reads, "A Star is Born."

A Star is Born

Designer: Cindy Major

1 Make card from cardstock.

2 Stamp stars and cloud on cardstock.

3 Stamp starburst and emboss.

4 Stamp sentiment and emboss. Mat with cardstock and adhere.

5 Cover cardstock with watermark ink and emboss with Iridescent Ice. Circle-punch moon from cardstock and adhere. Die-cut stars and adhere. Adhere sentiment star with foam tape.

6 Stamp rocket on cardstock, emboss, and color using blender pen. Trim and adhere with foam tape.

Finished size: 5¼" square

SUPPLIES: All supplies from Stampin' Up! unless otherwise noted. *Cardstock:* (Night of Navy, So Saffron, Soft Suede, Pacific Point) *Specialty paper:* (watercolor) *Rubber stamps:* (sentiment, star from Messages Illustres set; starburst, cloud from Extreme Elements set; rocket from Pun Fun set) *Dye ink:* (Night of Navy, So Saffron, Whisper White, Soft Suede) *Watermark ink:* Tsukineko *Embossing powder:* (Iridescent Ice, gold, white) *Color medium:* (blender pen) *Dies:* (stars) Provo Craft *Tool:* (2½" circle punch)

DESIGNER TIP

Create depth to the house by cutting out the same image twice and layering one house on top of the other using foam tape.

DESIGNER TIP

Create depth to the house by cutting out the same image twice and layering one house on top of the other using foam tape.

DESIGNER TIP

When using curves on a project, sketch them out in pencil before cutting to make completely smooth edges.

Wish Upon a Star
Designer: Maggie Haas

❶ Make card from cardstock. ❷ Trim patterned paper pieces to create wavy pattern. Adhere to cardstock and stitch. ❸ Mat panel with cardstock and adhere. ❹ Stamp sentiment. ❺ Die-cut star from felt and adhere. ❻ Thread button with twine and adhere.

Finished size: 4¼" square

New Home Congrats
Designer: Charity Hassel

❶ Make card from cardstock. ❷ Trim cardstock, attach brads, and adhere. Trim patterned paper pieces and adhere. ❸ Trim house, trees, and cloud from patterned paper and adhere. ❹ Trim house from patterned paper and adhere with foam tape. ❺ Apply rub-on, adhere buttons, and attach brads.

Finished size: 4¼" x 4½"

Way to Go
Designer: Julia Stainton

❶ Make card from cardstock. Cover with patterned paper. ❷ Trim patterned paper pieces to create wavy design and adhere. ❸ Affix "A" sticker. ❹ Affix stickers to spell "Way to go". ❺ Attach staples and library clip.

Finished size: 4¼"

SUPPLIES: *Cardstock:* (Harvest Gold, Dark Chocolate, kraft) Papertrey Ink *Patterned paper:* (Gable, Chaplin from Circa 1934 collection) Cosmo Cricket *Clear stamp:* (sentiment from Star Prints set) Papertrey Ink *Dye ink:* (Early Espresso) Stampin' Up! *Accent:* (brown button) Papertrey Ink *Fibers:* (natural twine) Papertrey Ink; *Die:* (star) Papertrey Ink *Other:* (gold felt)

SUPPLIES: *Cardstock:* (light blue) BoBunny Press; (kraft) Jo-Ann Stores *Patterned paper:* (Green Acres, Sunnyside Lane from Hometown Summer collection) Pink Paislee *Accents:* (brown buttons) BasicGrey; (brown brad) Bazzill Basics Paper; (brown glitter brads) We R Memory Keepers *Rub-on:* (congrats) Doodlebug Design

SUPPLIES: *Cardstock:* (kraft) Bazzill Basics Paper *Patterned paper:* (Steve's Keys, Borders N' Blocks, Pep Rally from Midterm collection) Bella Blvd *Accent:* (silver library clip) Tim Holtz *Stickers:* (Weathered Wood alphabet) Pink Paislee; (Tiny Type alphabet) Cosmo Cricket

Sentiment

Sketch by: Julia Stainton

DESIGNER TIP

Kalyn's color inspiration for this project came from a winter sweater. The combination of rich patterned papers gives great texture. Mix your favorite fonts to design your own unique sentiments!

5 STEPS Joyeux Noel

Designer: Kalyn Kepner

1. Make card from cardstock.

2. Print sentiment on patterned paper. Trim, ink edges, and adhere.

3. Trim patterned paper pieces and layer; adhere.

4. Stitch edges and tie on twine.

Finished size: 4¼" square

SUPPLIES: *Cardstock:* (kraft) Bazzill Basics Paper *Patterned paper:* (Flannel Pajamas, Coal, Tartan Plaid, Shopkeeper from Jovial collection; Prima Donna from Cappella collection) BasicGrey *Chalk ink:* (Creamy Brown) Clearsnap *Fibers:* (natural twine) Westrim Crafts *Fonts:* (American Typewriter) Adobe; (Jane Austen) www.dafont.com

DESIGNER TIP

Collect your favorite Peanuts sayings and swap out the sentiments to create a card set in no time.

DESIGNER TIP

Repeatedly stamping images is a great way to create your own patterns or backgrounds.

Life is like an ice-cream cone, you have to lick it one day at a time.
Charles M. Schulz

Happy Day
Designer: Kimberly Crawford

❶ Make card from cardstock. ❷ Stamp friend definition. ❸ Stamp zigzag repeatedly on cardstock. Trim and adhere. ❹ Affix sticker with foam tape. ❺ Adhere pearls.

Finished size: 4¼" x 5½"

One Day At a Time
Designer: Terri Davenport

❶ Make card from cardstock. ❷ Print quote on cardstock, trim, and adhere. ❸ Trim cardstock chevron and adhere.

Finished size: 5½" x 4¼"

Chevron Hello
Designer: Betsy Veldman

❶ Make card from cardstock; ink edges. ❷ Trim four 1" strips of patterned paper; adhere. ❸ Trim ½" strips of patterned paper and adhere to create chevron pattern. Stitch. ❹ Affix stickers. Adhere pearls. ❺ Wrap twine around card. Thread button with twine and tie bow.

Finished size: 4¼" x 5½"

SUPPLIES: *Cardstock:* (Rustic Cream, kraft) Papertrey Ink *Clear stamps:* (zigzag from Beyond Borders set) I {heart} papers; (Friend Definition) Hero Arts *Dye ink:* (Frayed Burlap) Ranger Industries *Specialty ink:* (Charcoal hybrid) Stewart Superior Corp. *Accents:* (yellow pearls) Hero Arts *Sticker:* (happy day label) My Mind's Eye

SUPPLIES: *Cardstock:* (Grandma's Rocker from Whitewash collection) Core'dinations; (Ebony) Bazzill Basics Paper *Font:* (Times New Roman) Microsoft

SUPPLIES: *Cardstock:* (Rustic Cream) Papertrey Ink *Patterned paper:* (Blissful, Sparkling from Hello Luscious collection) BasicGrey *Chalk ink:* (Creamy Brown) Clearsnap *Accents:* (red pearls) Kaisercraft; (green button) Papertrey Ink *Stickers:* (flowers) BasicGrey; (sentiment tag) Crate Paper *Fibers:* (cream twine) Papertrey Ink

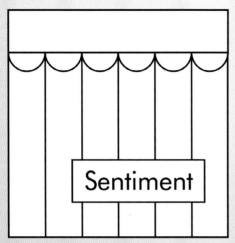

Sketch by: Vanessa Menhorn

DESIGNER TIP

Lining up alphabet stamps on a gridline block makes stamping words a breeze.

5 STEPS Bravo

Designer: Paula Laird

1. Make card from cardstock.

2. Cut, score, and pleat cardstock. Adhere.

3. Die-cut border from cardstock and adhere with foam tape.

4. Stamp "Bravo" on cardstock, trim, and mat with cardstock. Adhere rhinestones and adhere to card.

Finished size: 5½" square

SUPPLIES: *Cardstock:* (white) Papertrey Ink; (Cherry Cobbler, More Mustard, Basic Black) Stampin' Up! *Clear stamps:* (Trajan Monogram Edition set) Papertrey Ink *Dye ink:* (Tuxedo Black) Tsukineko *Accents:* (clear rhinestones) The Paper Studio *Die:* (scalloped border) Papertrey Ink

Green Best Wishes
Designer: Colleen Dietrich

❶ Make card from cardstock. ❷ Trim strips of patterned paper and adhere. ❸ Border-punch patterned paper strip and adhere. ❹ Adhere lace and line of pearls. ❺ Stamp best wishes on cardstock, emboss, and die-cut into tag. Ink oval with sponge. Adhere pearls and adhere with foam tape. ❻ Tie on ribbon.

Finished size: 5¼" square

With Sympathy
Designer: Susan R. Opel

❶ Make card from cardstock. ❷ Trim strips of patterned paper and adhere. ❸ Affix border sticker. ❹ Stamp with sympathy on cardstock, die-cut into label, and adhere with foam tape. ❺ Adhere flower.

Finished size: 5½" square

Button & Bows Birthday
Designer: Dana Ford

❶ Make card from cardstock. ❷ Trim strips from patterned paper, punch bottom edge, and adhere. ❸ Stamp sentiment and frame on cardstock. ❹ Die-cut into label, ink edges, and adhere with foam tape. ❺ Thread buttons with twine and adhere. ❻ Adhere rhinestone flourish.

Finished size: 6" square

SUPPLIES: *Cardstock:* (Vintage Cream) Papertrey Ink *Patterned paper:* (Green Plumes, Cream Pattern) Anna Griffin *Rubber stamp:* (best wishes from Vintage Labels set) Stampin' Up! *Dye ink:* (Mellow Moss) Stampin' Up! *Watermark ink:* Tsukineko *Embossing powder:* (gold) Rubber Stampede *Accents:* (white pearls) Michaels *Fibers:* (green ribbon) Offray; (cream lace) *Die:* (tag) Spellbinders *Tool:* (border punch) Martha Stewart Crafts

SUPPLIES: *Cardstock:* (Gingerbread Dot from Double Dot collection) BoBunny Press *Patterned paper:* (Gabrielle from Gabrielle collection; Timepiece Moments from Timepiece collection) BoBunny Press; (Mittens from Max & Whiskers collection) BasicGrey *Clear stamp:* (with sympathy from All Year Greetings set) Fiskars *Dye ink:* (brown) Hero Arts *Accent:* (teal flower) Hero Arts *Sticker:* (gold border) EK Success *Die:* (label) Spellbinders

SUPPLIES: *Cardstock:* (Whisper White) Stampin' Up! *Patterned paper:* (Kisa, Fiona, Elsa, Sonia, Julia from Perhaps collection) BasicGrey *Clear stamps:* (sentiment from Fillable Frames #1 set; frame from Fillable Frames #4 set) Papertrey Ink *Dye ink:* (Early Espresso, Always Artichoke) Stampin' Up! *Accents:* (assorted buttons) BasicGrey; (rhinestone flourish) Michaels *Fibers:* (natural twine) Papertrey Ink *Die:* (frame) Papertrey Ink *Tool:* (square punch) Marvy Uchida

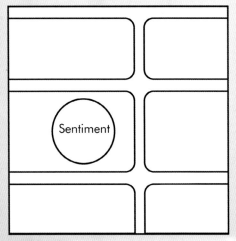

Sketch by: Kim Kesti

Welcome to the Neighborhood

Designer: Sarah Jane Moerman

1 Make card from cardstock.

2 Print sentiment on cardstock. Stamp Envelope Pattern, trim into rectangles, and round corners. Adhere.

3 Die-cut circle, house, and heart from cardstock. Adhere.

Finished size: 4¼" square

SUPPLIES: *Cardstock:* (tan) Bazzill Basics Paper; (white) Michaels; (Pure Poppy, New Leaf, Dark Chocolate) Papertrey Ink *Rubber stamp:* (Envelope Pattern) Hero Arts *Chalk ink:* (Grass) Hero Arts *Font:* (Calibri Body) Microsoft *Dies:* (heart, house) Silhouette America; (circle) Spellbinders *Tool:* (corner rounder punch) We R Memory Keepers

DESIGNER TIP

If you don't like the color coverage of the shimmer spray on the flower once you have rolled it, spray the completed flower until you reach the desired color.

DESIGNER TIP

Using two coordinating colors mixed with neutrals is an easy way to create a well balanced card.

I Adore You

Designer: Erin Taylor

❶ Make card from cardstock. ❷ Stamp music notes on cardstock, round corners, and adhere. ❸ Trim rectangles from cardstock, round corners, and adhere. ❹ Tie on ribbon. ❺ Stamp sentiment circle and heart on cardstock. Circle-punch and adhere with foam tape.

Finished size: 4¼" x 5½"

Colorful Hi

Designer: Lynn Reaney

❶ Make card from cardstock. ❷ Die-cut labels from patterned paper, trim, and adhere. ❸ Affix stickers to spell "Hi". ❹ Spray fabric stem with shimmer spray. Tie knot on end and wrap flower. ❺ Trim leaf from fabric, spray with shimmer spray, and adhere. Adhere flower. ❻ Thread button with floss and adhere.

Finished size: 5" square

It's All About You

Designer: Beth Opel

❶ Make card from patterned paper. ❷ Trim rectangles from patterned paper, round corners, and adhere with foam tape. ❸ Affix sticker. ❹ Adhere rhinestone.

Finished size: 4¼" x 5"

SUPPLIES: *Cardstock:* (Aqua Mist, Ocean Tides, kraft, white) Papertrey Ink *Clear stamps:* (small heart from Love Lives Here set; music notes from Background Basics: Sheet Music set) Papertrey Ink; (sentiment circle from Adored by Ali set) Technique Tuesday *Dye ink:* (Early Espresso, Baja Breeze) *Fibers:* (white ribbon) Papertrey Ink *Tools:* (1⅜" circle punch) EK Success; (corner rounder punch) Fiskars

SUPPLIES: *Cardstock:* (kraft) Bazzill Basics Paper *Patterned paper:* (Heirloom, Refinish, Slipcover, Lace, Flea Market from Restoration collection) Crate Paper *Specialty ink:* (Red Velvet, Graphite, Forest Green shimmer spray) Tattered Angels *Accents:* (fabric stem) Punky Sprouts; (yellow button) *Stickers:* (yellow alphabet) Crate Paper *Fibers:* (brown floss) DMC *Die:* (label) Spellbinders

SUPPLIES: *Patterned paper:* (Our Home, Damask from Welcome Home collection) Teresa Collins Designs; (pink floral from Peyton collection) Anna Griffin; (Sugar Dot from Back to Basics collection) BoBunny Press; (Trench Coat, Dots from Runway collection) Heidi Swapp; (Zebra Stripes) Hambly Screen Prints *Accent:* (clear rhinestone) Making Memories *Sticker:* (sentiment label) Anna Griffin *Tool:* (corner rounder punch) EK Success

Sentiment

Sketch by: Kim Kesti

Just For You

Designer: Maile Belles

1. Make card from cardstock.

2. Stamp large doily on cardstock, round corners, and adhere.

3. Stamp medium doily on cardstock, die-cut, and adhere with foam tape.

4. Stamp sentiment on cardstock, die-cut into banner, and adhere with foam tape.

5. Die-cut button from cardstock and adhere with foam tape.

6. Stamp doily on coaster board, die-cut into button, and thread with ribbon.

7. Tie bow and adhere.

Finished size: 4½" square

SUPPLIES: All supplies from Papertrey Ink unless otherwise noted. *Cardstock:* (Berry Sorbet, Summer Sunrise, white) *Specialty paper:* (coaster board) *Clear stamps:* (large doily, medium doily from Delightful Doilies set; sentiment from Fillable Frames Additions #1 set) *Specialty ink:* (Berry Sorbet, Pure Poppy, Summer Sunrise, True Black hybrid); (Icicle shimmer spray) Tattered Angels *Fibers:* (white ribbon) *Dies:* (doily, double ended banner, button) *Tool:* (corner rounder punch) EK Success

DESIGNER TIP

This quick and easy design would be perfect for a thank you card!

⟨5 STEPS⟩ Fabulous Flower

Designer: Lindsay Amrhein

❶ Make card from cardstock. ❷ Stamp absolutely fabulous on patterned paper, trim, and adhere. ❸ Tie on twine. ❹ Adhere flower.

Finished size: 4¼" square

⟨5 STEPS⟩ Butterfly Ever After

Designer: Vanessa Menhorn

❶ Make card from cardstock. ❷ Create 5" x 3¼" project in software; stamp butterfly. Print on cardstock, trim, ink edges, and adhere. ❸ Stamp sentiment. ❹ Adhere pearls.

Finished size: 4¾" square

⟨5 STEPS⟩ Hey Bloom

Designer: Chan Vuong

❶ Make card from cardstock. ❷ Trim flower from patterned paper and adhere. ❸ Thread button with twine and adhere. ❹ Affix stickers to spell "Hey!".

Finished size: 4¼" square

SUPPLIES: *Cardstock:* (Vintage Cream) Papertrey Ink *Patterned paper:* (Rule from Basic Kraft collection) BasicGrey *Clear stamp:* (absolutely fabulous from Mega Mixed Messages set) Papertrey Ink *Specialty ink:* (True Black hybrid) Papertrey Ink *Accent:* (crinkled rose) Petaloo *Fibers:* (natural twine) Westrim Crafts

SUPPLIES: *Cardstock:* (Sweet Blush, Rustic Cream) Papertrey Ink *Clear stamp:* (sentiment from Love Lives Here set) Papertrey Ink *Dye ink:* (Rich Cocoa) Tsukineko *Accents:* (pink pearls) Prima *Digital element:* (butterfly stamp from Apple of My Eye collection) www.twopeasinabucket.com

SUPPLIES: *Cardstock:* (Aqua Mist) Papertrey Ink *Patterned paper:* (Dots from 72 & Sunny collection) We R Memory Keepers *Accent:* (orange button) *Stickers:* (Blue Line alphabet) Cosmo Cricket *Fibers:* (green twine) Martha Stewart Crafts

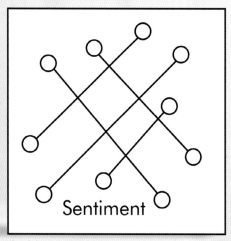

Sentiment

Sketch by: Kim Hughes

DESIGNER TIPS

Cover the back of your card front with cardstock to hide stitching.

Pierce stitching holes first with a paper piercer to prevent your cardstock from buckling.

⁵ Baker's Twine Hi

Designer: Julia Stainton

1 Make card from cardstock.

2 Stitch twine to card.

3 Attach brads and adhere buttons over twine ends.

4 Affix stickers to spell "Hi".

Finished size: 4¼" square

SUPPLIES: *Cardstock:* (black) Bazzill Basics Paper *Accents:* (orange, green, yellow brads) Making Memories; (red, blue buttons) *Stickers:* (Bliss alphabet) American Crafts *Fibers:* (red/white twine) Jillibean Soup; (blue/white twine)

DESIGNER TIPS

Use a repositionable note cut to the size of the card to use as a template of where to pierce holes in order to not draw lines on the font of the card.

Use a piece of foam under the card so the paper piercer will go through the cardstock more easily.

FOLLOW YOUR *dreams*

Celebrate Bows

Designer: Amy Abad

❶ Make card from cardstock. ❷ Pierce holes. Thread twine and tie bows. ❸ Stamp celebrate.

Finished size: 4" square

Follow Your Dreams

Designer: Jessica Witty

❶ Make card from cardstock. ❷ Stamp globe, seal, and postage stamp. ❸ Stamp sentiment on strip of patterned paper and adhere. ❹ Adhere floss. ❺ Punch circles from patterned paper and adhere with foam tape.

Finished size: 5" square

Just Be You

Designer: Lesley Langdon

❶ Make card from cardstock. Cover with patterned paper. ❷ Stamp sentiment on cardstock, mat with cardstock, and adhere. ❸ Draw lines; color. ❹ Circle-punch dots from patterned paper and adhere. ❺ Apply glitter glue.

Finished size: 4¾" square

SUPPLIES: *Cardstock:* (kraft) Papertrey Ink *Clear stamp:* (celebrate from Fillable Frames #5 set) Papertrey Ink *Dye ink:* (Tuxedo Black) Tsukineko *Fibers:* (purple/white, teal/white, pink/white twine) The Twinery

SUPPLIES: *Cardstock:* (kraft) Papertrey Ink *Patterned paper:* (Itinerary from Documentary collection) Studio Calico; (Varnish Passport from Great Escape collection) Making Memories *Clear stamps:* (globe, seal, postage stamp from Time Traveler set) Tattered Angels; (sentiment from Fillable Frames #3 set) Papertrey Ink *Pigment ink:* (Vintage Cream, Dark Chocolate) Papertrey Ink *Fibers:* (brown floss) DMC *Tool:* (pinked circle punch) Martha Stewart Crafts

SUPPLIES: *Cardstock:* (black) Bazzill Basics Paper; (white) Staples *Patterned paper:* (Heirloom, Refinish, Slipcover from Restoration collection) Crate Paper *Rubber stamp:* (Just Be You) Unity Stamp Co. *Dye ink:* (black) Stewart Superior Corp. *Color media:* (yellow, green, blue, pink markers) Copic; (black pen) Sharpie *Accent:* (red glitter glue) Ranger Industries

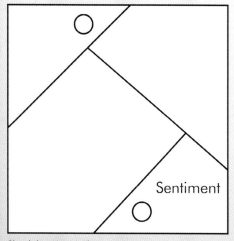

Sentiment

Sketch by: Kim Hughes

Shabby Good Luck

Designer: Emily Branch

1 Make card from cardstock.

2 Trim patterned paper triangles; adhere.

3 Trim striped ribbon and adhere. Zigzag-stitch.

4 Border-punch patterned paper strip and adhere with foam tape.

5 Ink game alphabet stickers and affix stickers to spell "Good luck".

6 Pleat polka dot ribbon and adhere. Adhere twine.

7 Trim circles from patterned paperand adhere behind epoxy dots; adhere. *Note: Use foam tape on one dot.*

Finished size: 4¼" square

SUPPLIES: *Cardstock:* (Vintage Cream) Papertrey Ink *Patterned paper:* (Mama's Dress, Die Cut from Red/Blackline Extension III collection) Jenni Bowlin Studio *Chalk ink:* (Creamy Brown) Clearsnap *Accents:* (epoxy dots) Epiphany Crafts *Stickers:* (For the Record alphabet) Echo Park Paper *Fibers:* (black polka dot ribbon) Offray; (black/white twine) May Arts; (black striped ribbon) My Mind's Eye *Tools:* (button maker) Epiphany Crafts; (border punch) Martha Stewart Crafts

Using a right angle on the back of the patterned paper makes quick work of perfect patchwork shapes.

Friend 4-Ever
Designer: Alicia Thelin

❶ Make card from cardstock. ❷ Trim patterned paper pieces, adhere, and stitch borders. ❸ Stamp 4 ever on cardstock and emboss. ❹ Stamp friend, circle-punch, and adhere with foam tape. ❺ Attach brads and tie on ribbon.

Finished size: 4½" square

SUPPLIES: All supplies from Stampin' Up! unless otherwise noted. *Cardstock:* (kraft) Papertrey Ink *Patterned Paper:* (Rose McGrain from Craft Fair collection) American Crafts *Rubber stamps:* (friend from Word Play set; 4 ever from You're a Gem set) *Dye ink:* (Pixie Pink, Whisper White) *Embossing powder:* (white) *Accents:* (white brads) *Fibers:* (white ribbon) *Tool:* (1" circle punch)

Just a Note
Designer: Kristen Swain

❶ Make card from cardstock. Cover with patterned paper. ❷ Trim patterned paper strips with decorative-scissors and adhere. ❸ Stamp sentiment on cardstock, trim, and adhere with foam tape. ❹ Thread button with twine and adhere. ❺ Tie bow with twine; adhere. Adhere flowers.

Finished size: 5¼" x 5"

SUPPLIES: *Cardstock:* (white) Paper Reflections *Patterned paper:* (Vintage Patchwork from Paper Girl collection) The Girls' Paperie *Clear stamp:* (sentiment from Greetings set) The Paper Company *Dye ink:* (green) Autumn Leaves *Accents:* (cream flower) Petaloo; (pink flower) Prima; (pink button) *Fibers:* (natural twine) The Beadery *Tool:* (decorative-edge scissors) Provo Craft

Everyday Friend
Designer: Kim Kesti

❶ Make card from cardstock. ❷ Trim patterned paper pieces, adhere, and zigzag–stitch seams. ❸ Stamp bike and typewriter. ❹ Affix stickers. ❺ Trim patterned paper strips and adhere to create border.

Finished size: 6" x 5¾"

SUPPLIES: *Cardstock:* (natural) Bazzill Basics Paper *Patterned paper:* (Geranium Stripe, Rose Bouquet from Kitch collection; Picnic Blanket from Jubilee collection) The Girls' Paperie; (Dark from Real Wood collection) Creative Imaginations *Clear stamps:* (bike, typewriter from Kitch set) The Girls' Paperie *Dye ink:* (Tuxedo Black) Tsukineko *Stickers:* (everyday, friend) The Girls' Paperie

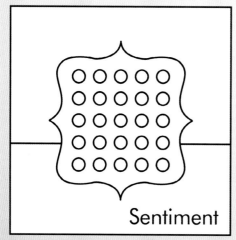

Sentiment

Sketch by: Betsy Veldman

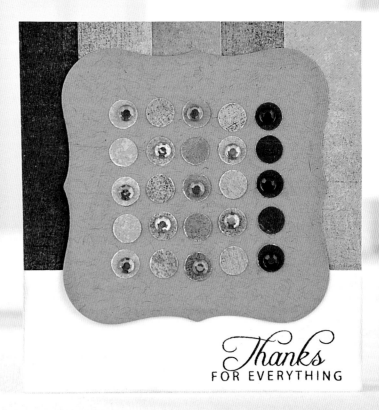

Thanks
FOR EVERYTHING

Thanks for Everything

Designer: Teri Anderson

1. Make card from cardstock.

2. Trim patterned paper strips and adhere.

3. Stamp sentiment on cardstock strip, ink edges, and adhere.

4. Die-cut label from cardstock and adhere.

5. Punch circles from patterned paper and adhere.

6. Adhere rhinestones.

Finished size: 4¼" x 4½"

SUPPLIES: *Cardstock:* (white) Georgia-Pacific; (kraft) Neenah Paper *Patterned paper:* (Raspberry Syrup, Radish, Thrive, Succulent, Honeyed from Hello Luscious collection) BasicGrey *Clear stamps:* (thanks, for everything from Swanky Sentiments set) Technique Tuesday *Dye ink:* (Tuxedo Black) Tsukineko; (Old Paper) Ranger Industries *Accents:* (red, orange, blue, pink, green rhinestones) Kaisercraft *Die:* (label) Spellbinders

DESIGNER TIP

When die-cutting something printed, temporarily attach the die to the paper with tape.

Noel

Designer: Chan Vuong

① Make card from cardstock. ② Trim patterned paper and adhere. ③ Stamp Noel. ④ Tie on twine. ⑤ Die-cut label from cardstock; adhere with foam tape. ⑥ Thread buttons with twine and adhere.

Finished size: 4" square

5 STEPS Missing U

Designer: Sarah Jane Moerman

① Make card from cardstock. ② Print "missing u" on cardstock, stamp Envelope Pattern, and adhere. ③ Stamp Daisy Outline Pattern on cardstock and adhere. ④ Tie on ribbon. ⑤ Print alphabet on cardstock, die-cut into label, and adhere with foam tape.

Finished size: 5¼" x 5"

Cake Happy Party

Designer: Emily Branch

① Make card from cardstock. Cover with patterned paper. ② Adhere strip of patterned paper. Paint edges. ③ Wrap twine around card and adhere. ④ Affix stickers to spell "Birthday". ⑤ Die-cut label from patterned paper, stitch, and ink edges. ⑥ Affix stickers to spell sentiment. *Note: Use foam tape on some.* ⑦ Adhere panel using foam tape.

Finished size: 5¼" square

SUPPLIES: *Cardstock:* (Pure Poppy, kraft) Papertrey Ink *Patterned paper:* (deer print from Scandinavian pad) Martha Stewart Crafts *Clear stamp:* (Noel from Gift Tag set) Martha Stewart Crafts *Dye ink:* (Jumbo Java) Tsukineko *Accents:* (wooden buttons) Martha Stewart Crafts *Fibers:* (green, red twine) Martha Stewart Crafts *Die:* (label) Spellbinders

SUPPLIES: *Cardstock:* (Pure Poppy, Aqua Mist) Papertrey Ink; (white) *Rubber stamps:* (Envelope Pattern, Daisy Outline Pattern) Hero Arts *Dye ink:* (Tumbled Glass) Ranger Industries *Chalk ink:* (Punch) Hero Arts *Fibers:* (pink ribbon) Papertrey Ink *Font:* (LD Remington Portable) Microsoft *Die:* (label) Spellbinders

SUPPLIES: *Cardstock:* (Vintage Cream) Papertrey Ink *Patterned paper:* (Fancy Floral, Picket Fence, Stamp of Approval from For the Record collection) Echo Park Paper *Chalk ink:* (Chestnut Roan) Clearsnap *Paint:* (white) Delta *Stickers:* (For the Record alphabet) Echo Park Paper *Fibers:* (brown twine) May Arts *Die:* (label) Spellbinders

Sketch by: Teri Anderson

5 STEPS Thanks, Dad Card

Designer: Teri Anderson

1. Make card from cardstock; ink edges.

2. Round corners of patterned paper. Ink edges and adhere.

3. Trim patterned paper pieces with corner rounder punch. Adhere cardstock pieces and attach brads; adhere.

4. Stamp sentiment on card.

5. Affix badge and spell "Dad" with stickers.

Finished size: 4¼" square

SUPPLIES: *Cardstock:* (Vintage Cream) Papertrey Ink; (kraft) Provo Craft; (green) Bazzill Basics Paper *Patterned paper:* (Forest Deer from Autumn Forest collection) Reminisce; (Woodgrain) A Muse Artstamps *Clear stamp:* (thank you from Personal Stationery set) A Muse Artstamps *Dye ink:* (Chocolate) Close To My Heart; (Old Paper) Ranger Industries *Accents:* (cream brads) American Crafts *Stickers:* (tree badge, Delight alphabet) American Crafts *Tool:* (corner rounder punch)

Million Dollar Teacher Card
Designer: Ashley Harris

SUPPLIES: *Cardstock:* (white) Bazzill Basics Paper; (cream) American Crafts *Patterned paper:* (Flamingo Dot, Sunflower Dot, Island Mist Dot from Double Dot collection) BoBunny Press *Color medium:* (black marker) Stampin' Up! *Rub-on:* (sentiment) Melissa Frances *Stickers:* (Mini alphabet) My Little Shoebox *Fibers:* (hemp twine) *Tool:* (corner rounder punch)

Finished size: 4½" square

Smile Card
Designer: Heidi Van Laar

SUPPLIES: *Cardstock:* (white) Strathmore Artist Papers *Accents:* (blue, orange flourish die cuts) My Mind's Eye; (blue, orange flowers) Prima *Stickers:* (Rockabye alphabet) American Crafts *Fibers:* (white crochet thread) Coats & Clark *Template:* (Polka Dots embossing) QuicKutz

Finished size: 5½" x 6"

Feel Better Card
Designer: Kim Hughes

SUPPLIES: *Cardstock:* (Katydid, Cardinal) Core'dinations; (Tawny Light) Prism *Rubber stamp:* (Polka Dots) Frog's Whisker's Ink *Dye ink:* (Desert Sand) Close To My Heart *Color medium:* (black marker) Sakura *Tool:* (heart punch) EK Success

Finished size: 3½" square

Sketch by: Maren Benedict

5 STEPS : Happy 4th Birthday Card

Designer: Betsy Veldman

1. Made card from cardstock. Cut patterned paper panel to fit card front.

2. Adhere strips of patterned paper to panel; stitch border. Trim top of patterned paper piece into curve; adhere and zigzag-stitch seam.

3. Tie on twine and adhere panel to card.

4. Ink journaling tag edges; adhere. Affix number and dog stickers.

5. Stamp sentiment on cardstock, trim, and ink edges. Adhere sentiment and buttons.

Finished size: 5" square

SUPPLIES: *Cardstock:* (Vintage Cream) Papertrey Ink *Patterned paper:* (Carbonation, Boardwalk from Snorkel collection; Apron Strings from Early Bird collection; Acorn from Nutmeg collection) Cosmo Cricket *Clear stamp:* (sentiment from Birthday Basics set) Papertrey Ink *Chalk ink:* (Creamy Brown) Clearsnap *Specialty ink:* (Pure Poppy hybrid) Papertrey Ink *Accents:* (round journaling tag) Jillibean Soup; (red, green buttons) Papertrey Ink *Stickers:* (felt dog) BasicGrey; (4 from Delight alphabet) American Crafts *Fibers:* (natural twine) Papertrey Ink

Thank You Tree Card

Designer: Maile Belles

SUPPLIES: All supplies from Papertrey Ink unless
otherwise indicated. *Cardstock:* (Vintage Cream,
Spring Moss, kraft) *Clear stamps:* (tree, sentiment from
Beyond Basic Borders set); (Houndstooth) Studio Calico
Specialty ink: (Dark Chocolate hybrid) *Accents:* (pink
buttons) *Fibers:* (melon floss) DMC *Tool:* (2" circle
punch) Marvy Uchida

Finished size: 3½" x 7"

Floral Wish Card

Designer: Rae Barthel

SUPPLIES: *Cardstock:* (white) Hobby Lobby *Patterned
paper:* (Placemats, Tea Cakes, Cookbook from Nook
& Pantry collection) BasicGrey; (scallop from Rouge
Paperie collection notebook) Making Memories
Accents: (green rhinestones) Michaels *Stickers:* (Nook
& Pantry alphabet) BasicGrey *Fibers:* (green striped
ribbon) Cosmo Cricket

Finished size: 5" square

Enjoy the Small
Stuff Card

Designer: Kim Kesti

SUPPLIES: All supplies from Cosmo Cricket unless
otherwise indicated. *Cardstock:* (Arizona, Adobe)
Bazzill Basics Paper *Patterned paper:* (Rethink, Reuse
from Earth Love collection) *Rub-on:* (sentiment) *Stickers:*
(chipboard mushrooms) *Fibers:* (green scalloped
ribbon)

Finished size: 6" x 4½"

Sketch by: Maren Benedict

DESIGNER TIP

Save the other half of your die cut to use on another card, or make two of the same card to keep in your stash!

5 STEPS Thank You Flowers Card

Designer: Debbie Seyer

1 Make card from cardstock.

2 Cut patterned paper panel, adhere patterned paper strips, tie on ribbon, and adhere panel.

3 Die-cut and emboss labels from cardstock, stamp sentiment on one, and adhere together. Cut in half and adhere.

4 Stamp flowers on cardstock, fussy-cut, and attach brads. Adhere with foam tape.

Finished size: 5¼" square

SUPPLIES: *Cardstock:* (Dark Chocolate) Papertrey Ink; (Rain) Bazzill Basics Paper; (white) Stampin' Up! *Patterned paper:* (Chilly Mornings, Sweater Weather from Weathervane collection) October Afternoon *Clear stamps:* (sentiment from Thankful Blossoms set, flowers from Grateful Elegance set) Verve Stamps *Dye ink:* (Chocolate Chip) Stampin' Up! *Accents:* (orange, blue rhinestone brads) Stampin' Up! *Fibers:* (yellow decorative ribbon) Stampin' Up! *Dies:* (labels) Spellbinders

Best Wishes Card

Designer: Kim Hughes

SUPPLIES: *Cardstock:* (Katydid) Core'dinations; (Vanilla Cream) Prism *Patterned paper:* (Mellow Yellow Dot from Double Dot collection) BoBunny Press; (Repeat from Earth Love collection) Cosmo Cricket; (Simple as Pie from Domestic Goddess collection) Graphic 45 *Accents:* (rust paper flower) Hero Arts; (green button) Creative Café *Rub-on:* (sentiment) Imaginisce *Fibers:* (twine) Creative Impressions

Finished size: 5¼" x 4¼"

Orange Miss You Card

Designer: Kim Kesti

SUPPLIES: *Cardstock:* (white) Bazzill Basics Paper *Patterned paper:* (Here Comes the Sun, Sunny Day, Walking on Sunshine, What a Feelin' from Blue Skies collection) American Crafts *Sticker:* (miss you badge) American Crafts *Fibers:* (orange pompom trim) Awesome Albums *Tool:* (corner rounder punch) We R Memory Keepers

Finished size: 5" square

Birthday Wishes Card

Designer: Lisa Johnson

SUPPLIES: All supplies from Papertrey Ink unless otherwise noted. *Cardstock:* (Raspberry Fizz, Summer Sunrise, white) *Clear stamps:* (medallion, sentiment from Giga Guide Lines set) *Specialty ink:* (Raspberry Fizz, Orange Zest hybrid) *Color medium:* (white pen) Marvy Uchida *Accent:* (pink button) *Fibers:* (orange ribbon, natural twine) *Tools:* (corner rounder punch) Marvy Uchida; (decorative-edge scissors) Fiskars

Finished size: 4" square

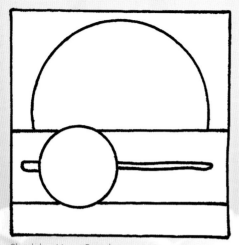

Sketch by: Maren Benedict

5 STEPS Thank You Sunshine Card

Designer: Betsy Veldman

Ink all edges.

1. Make card from cardstock. Cut patterned paper panel to fit card front.
2. Adhere patterned paper strip to panel; stitch edges.
3. Adhere journaling card. Tie on ribbon.
4. Stamp cloud and sun on cardstock, trim, and adhere, using foam tape for sun.
5. Stamp branch and sentiment on cardstock and adhere. Affix badge.

Finished size: 5″ square

SUPPLIES: *Cardstock:* (white) *Patterned paper:* (Wouldn't It Be Nice, Daydream Believer from Blue Skies collection) American Crafts *Clear stamps:* (cloud, sun, branch from Blue Skies Laughter set) American Crafts; (sentiment from Vintage Picnic set) Papertrey Ink *Chalk ink:* (Creamy Brown) Clearsnap *Specialty ink:* (Raspberry Fizz, Dark Chocolate, Summer Sunrise, Aqua Mist hybrid) Papertrey Ink *Accent:* (orange scalloped journaling card) Little Yellow Bicycle *Sticker:* (bird badge) American Crafts *Fibers:* (pink ribbon) Papertrey Ink

DESIGNER TIP

Use a sewing machine to poke holes for hand stitching. Just remove the thread from the sewing machine first!

DESIGNER TIP

Sliders and other interactive elements are perfect for kid cards! Adhere ribbon along a slider to add a pull element to this card.

Enjoy the Journey Card
Designer: Kim Hughes

SUPPLIES: *Cardstock:* (Argos, Nightfall, Snowflake) Core'dinations *Patterned paper:* (Bright Stripes from Colorful Christmas collection; Beautiful Morning from Ooh La La for Her collection; Soiree from Ooh La La for Him collection) My Mind's Eye *Accent:* (chipboard car) My Mind's Eye *Sticker:* (sentiment) Making Memories *Fibers:* (white floss) DMC

Finished size: 6" x 4¼"

Rocket Birthday Card
Designer: Maren Benedict

SUPPLIES: *Cardstock:* (Pure Poppy) Papertrey Ink *Patterned paper:* (Drivers Ed, Study Hall, Tube Socks, Appreciation from The Boyfriend collection) Cosmo Cricket *Rubber stamps:* (rocket from Sketchy Little Boy set; sentiment from Another Sweet Day set) Unity Stamp Co. *Dye ink:* (Black Soot, Vintage Photo) Ranger Industries *Color medium:* (red marker) Copic *Accent:* (chipboard 4) Sassafras Lass *Fibers:* (red twill) Papertrey Ink *Die:* (large circle) Spellbinders *Tool:* (rounded rectangle punch) Stampin' Up!

Finished size: 5" square

Just for You Card
Designer: Lisa Johnson

SUPPLIES: All supplies from Papertrey Ink unless otherwise indicated. *Cardstock:* (True Black, Raspberry Fizz, Summer Sunrise, white) *Patterned paper:* (black polka dots from Black & White Basics collection; yellow polka dots from 2008 Bitty Dot Basics collection) *Clear stamps:* (thank you, just for you, small flower from Around & About Sentiments set) *Specialty ink:* (Raspberry Fizz, Summer Sunrise, True Black hybrid) *Accents:* (green button); (pewter brads) Creative Impressions *Fibers:* (green stitched, black polka dot ribbon) *Tools:* (large, small circle punches; large, small flower punches; scallop trimmer, corner rounder punch) Marvy Uchida

Finished size: 4¼" square

Draw a dashed line with pens on your projects to create faux stitching.

Apply rub-on sentiments in sections to perfectly align on a journaling block.

Sketch by: Kim Hughes

Thoughts & Prayers Gift Box

5 STEPS

Designer: Julie Campbell

1 Cover box with patterned paper.

2 Adhere cardstock square. Wrap ribbon around box and adhere.

3 Stamp journaling block on cardstock; trim, color, and draw stitches. Apply rub-on and adhere to box.

4 Tie ribbon on handle.

Finished size: 4¼" x 5¾" x 2"

SUPPLIES: *Cardstock:* (Birchtone Dark, kraft) Prism *Patterned paper:* (Moss Winter Berries) Paper Source *Rubber stamp:* (journaling block from Following My Heart set) Unity Stamp Co. *Chalk ink:* (Dark Brown) Clearsnap *Color media:* (green, brown markers) Copic; (green colored pencil) Sanford; (white gel pen) Ranger Industries *Rub-on:* (sentiment) Melissa Frances *Fibers:* (green stitched ribbon) Papertrey Ink *Other:* (wood box with handles)

DESIGNER TIP

Once you cut out your first bracket, trace it in reverse on patterned paper to make the second bracket exactly the same size and shape.

DESIGNER TIP

When using a neutral card base, choose vividly colored accents for a bold splash of color.

Baby & Parents Card
Designer: Laura O'Donnell

SUPPLIES: *Cardstock:* (Vanilla) Cornish Heritage Farms *Patterned paper:* (Die-Cut Lattice from Poolside Paperie collection; Big Dot, Large Floral, Fabric Brocade from Rouge Paperie collection; stripes from Noteworthy collection notebook) Making Memories *Rubber stamps:* (stork, flowers, sentiment from Vintage Baby Expressions set) Cornish Heritage Farms *Dye ink:* (Tuxedo Black) Tsukineko *Accents:* (gray, pink, burgundy buttons) Autumn Leaves *Fibers:* (white string) *Tool:* (oval cutter) Creative Memories

Finished size: 5" square

Many Thanks, Teacher Card
Designer: Jessica Witty

SUPPLIES: *Cardstock:* (white, kraft) Papertrey Ink *Patterned paper:* (Wipe That Up!, My New Pencil Box from Teacher's Pet collection) Imaginisce *Clear stamp:* (thanks from Mega Mixed Messages set) Papertrey Ink *Dye ink:* (Going Gray) Stampin' Up! *Accents:* (red, blue, green buttons) Papertrey Ink *Stickers:* (chipboard apple, best teacher) Imaginisce; (bracket label) *Fibers:* (blue polka dot ribbon) American Crafts; (blue, yellow floss) DMC

Finished size: 4" square

Graphic Flowers Hi Card
Designer: Rae Barthel

SUPPLIES: *Cardstock:* (white, black) Bazzill Basics Paper *Clear stamp:* (bracketed journaling block from Journaling set) Autumn Leaves *Pigment ink:* (Onyx Black) Tsukineko *Accents:* (pink, green flowers) Prima; (clear rhinestones) *Stickers:* (Vera alphabet) American Crafts *Tool:* (corner rounder punch) EK Success

Finished size: 3½" square

Sketch by: Kim Kesti

5 STEPS You Rock Card

Designer: Ryann Salamon

1. Make card from cardstock.

2. Cut patterned paper and mat with cardstock. Cut photo corners from cardstock and adhere. Adhere to card.

3. Affix stereo and thought bubble. Spell sentiment with stickers.

Finished size: 4¼" square

SUPPLIES: *Cardstock:* (Dark Chocolate) Papertrey Ink; (Classic Red) Prism *Patterned paper:* (Tube Socks from The Boyfriend collection) Cosmo Cricket *Stickers:* (chipboard stereo, thought bubble) Cosmo Cricket; (Wonderful alphabet) My Little Shoebox

DESIGNER TIP

Use dye ink markers when coloring directly on the stamp so that it doesn't permanently stain the rubber.

Hey Chick Card
Designer: Ashley C. Newell

SUPPLIES: *Cardstock:* (Aqua Mist, Dark Chocolate, Hibiscus Burst, Lavender Moon, Lemon Tart, white) Papertrey Ink *Patterned paper:* (yellow grid from 2008 Bitty Box Basics collection) Papertrey Ink *Clear stamps:* (sentiment from Everyday Button Bits set; birds, legs from Bird Watching Additions set) Papertrey Ink *Dye ink:* (Chocolate Chip) Stampin' Up! *Specialty ink:* (Aqua Mist, Plum Pudding, Summer Sunrise hybrid) Papertrey Ink *Accents:* (pink, yellow, blue rhinestones) Kaisercraft *Other:* (yellow felt) Heather Bailey

Finished size: 5" square

Woof Card
Designer: Angie Tieman

SUPPLIES: *Cardstock:* (kraft) Stampin' Up! *Patterned paper:* (Admiral from June Bug collection) BasicGrey; (Elements from Jolly By Golly) Cosmo Cricket *Stickers:* (chipboard dog) BasicGrey; (Playroom alphabet) American Crafts *Template:* (Houndstooth embossing) Provo Craft

Finished size: 5¼" square

Really Ruff You Card
Designer: Laura O'Donnell

SUPPLIES: *Cardstock:* (white) Cornish Heritage Farms *Rubber stamps:* (sentiment from Doggie Expressions set, The Honeymooners, Vintage Text Scrapblock) Cornish Heritage Farms *Dye ink:* (black, Summer Sky) Tsukineko *Color medium:* (black, red markers) Tsukineko

Finished size: 5" square

Sketch by: Kim Kesti

DESIGNER TIP

Use both sides of double-sided paper for a good, quick match.

Shabby Baby Card

Designer: Julia Stainton

1 Make card from cardstock.

2 Cut patterned paper square, sand edges, and adhere. Stitch edges.

3 Die-cut scalloped square from patterned paper, sand edges, and adhere. Zigzag-stitch border.

4 Adhere ribbon and flower. Attach safety pin.

5 Spell "Baby" with stickers.

Finished size: 5¼" square

SUPPLIES: *Cardstock:* (kraft) Bazzill Basics Paper *Patterned paper:* (Baby's Breath from Little Sprout collection) Fancy Pants Designs *Accents:* (brown flower) Pink Paislee; (gold safety pin) Tim Holtz *Stickers:* (Sprinkles alphabet) American Crafts *Fibers:* (pink ribbon) Making Memories *Die:* (scalloped square) Spellbinders

DESIGNER TIP

Add stitching before adhering the piece to the front of the card, so it doesn't show on the inside.

Thank You Teacher Card

Designer: Kim Hughes

SUPPLIES: *Cardstock:* (white) Bazzill Basics Paper *Patterned paper:* (Whirlybird from Shine collection) My Mind's Eye *Paint:* (Blank Canvas) Ranger Industries *Rub-on:* (thank you) American Crafts *Stickers:* (apple) American Crafts; (pencil) Imaginisce *Fibers:* (twine) Creative Impressions

Finished size: 3½" square

Jack-O-Lantern Halloween Card

Designer: Latisha Yoast

SUPPLIES: *Cardstock:* (Ivory) Flourishes; (kraft) Papertrey Ink *Rubber stamps:* (Halloween, pumpkins from Vintage Halloween set) Artistic Outpost *Dye ink:* (Spiced Marmalade) Ranger Industries; (Tuxedo Black) Tsukineko *Fibers:* (orange stitched ribbon) Papertrey Ink *Die:* (scalloped square) Spellbinders

Finished size: 4¼" square

Yellow Hi Card

Designer: Courtney Kelley

SUPPLIES: *Cardstock:* (Raven) Bazzill Basics Paper *Patterned paper:* (Bus Route from Report Card collection) October Afternoon *Accents:* (journaling square) Jillibean Soup; (red, blue flowers) Prima; (green brad) Sassafras Lass *Stickers:* (Typo alphabet) American Crafts *Fibers:* (dark blue floss) DMC

Finished size: 4½" square

Sketch by: Kim Kesti

DESIGNER TIP

This sketch follows a simple layout that allows patterned papers to take center stage.

5 STEPS Lacy Thank You Card

Designer: Jessica Witty

1. Make card from cardstock.

2. Cut patterned paper and transparency sheet squares and adhere.

3. Stamp sentiment.

4. Stitch border.

Finished size: 5¼" square

SUPPLIES: *Cardstock:* (kraft) Papertrey Ink *Patterned paper:* (pink, turquoise, gold from Old Lace collection) Hambly Screen Prints *Transparency sheet:* (Old Lace White) Hambly Screen Prints *Clear stamp:* (thank you from Damask Designs set) Papertrey Ink *Pigment ink:* (Pink Passion) Stampin' Up!

Twine Ribbon Birthday Card

Designer: Debbie Seyer

SUPPLIES: *Cardstock:* (Shimmery White) Stampin' Up!; (Soft Sand, Chocolate Kiss) Gina K Designs *Patterned paper:* (Oilcloth, Red Circle Flower, Lemonade, Green Crosshatch from Front Porch collection) Jenni Bowlin Studio *Rubber stamp:* (happy birthday from Eclectic Summer Sayings set) Gina K Designs *Chalk ink:* (Warm Red) Clearsnap *Accents:* (brown brads) Stampin' Up! *Fibers:* (twine ribbon) May Arts *Dies:* (oval, tag) Spellbinders

Finished size: 5¼" square

Stacked Birthday Cake Card

Designer: Kim Kesti

SUPPLIES: *Cardstock:* (Candy Apple, Festive, Ladybug, Lemonade, Lily White, Ocean, Parakeet, kraft) Bazzill Basics Paper *Accent:* (red brad) *Stickers:* (birthday tag, cake) Karen Foster Design

Finished size: 5" x 6½"

Knew You Could Card

Designer: Beth Opel

SUPPLIES: *Cardstock:* (Aqua, Candy Apple, Festive, Jade, Raven) Bazzill Basics Paper *Patterned paper:* (Rebel Teal from Rebel collection) Glitz Design *Accent:* (white chipboard star) American Crafts *Stickers:* (Bold alphabet) Close To My Heart

Finished size: 6" square

Sketch by: Betsy Veldman

5 STEPS Mushroom Hi Card

Designer: Teri Anderson

1. Make card from cardstock.

2. Adhere patterned paper squares.

3. Affix alphabet stickers to cardstock square, ink edges, and adhere.

4. Affix mushrooms.

Finished size: 5" square

SUPPLIES: *Cardstock:* (Vintage Cream) Papertrey Ink; (white) WorldWin *Patterned paper:* (Relive from Earth Love collection) Cosmo Cricket *Dye ink:* (Old Paper) Ranger Industries *Stickers:* (Daydream alphabet) American Crafts; (chipboard mushrooms) Cosmo Cricket

Soaring By to Say Card
Designer: Betsy Veldman

SUPPLIES: *Cardstock:* (Vintage Cream, white) Papertrey Ink *Patterned paper:* (Alpine from Eskimo Kisses collection, Bundt Pan from Nook & Pantry collection) BasicGrey; (Christine from Madame Royale collection) We R Memory Keepers; (Notebook Doodles from Chassé collection) My Mind's Eye; (Farm Yard from Farm Fresh collection) October Afternoon; (Saturday from Girl Friday collection) Cosmo Cricket *Clear stamps:* (balloon baskets, sentiment from Everyday Button Bits set; thank you from Vintage Picnic set) Papertrey Ink *Chalk ink:* (Creamy Brown) Clearsnap *Specialty ink:* Hibiscus Burst, Dark Chocolate hybrid) Papertrey Ink *Accents:* (pink, green, orange buttons) Papertrey Ink; (green rhinestone) Zva Creative; (white glitter) Doodlebug Design *Stickers:* (pink photo corners) Doodlebug Design *Fibers:* (cream twine) Papertrey Ink *Dies:* (clouds) Provo Craft *Tool:* (½" circle punch)

Finished size: 5" square

Mama Said Card
Designer: Latisha Yoast

SUPPLIES: *Cardstock:* (cream) *Patterned paper:* (Cinnamon from Nutmeg collection) Cosmo Cricket *Clear stamps:* (sentiment from Feeling Groovy set) Verve Stamps *Dye ink:* (Tuxedo Black) Tsukineko *Stickers:* (chipboard trees, clouds) Cosmo Cricket

Finished size: 5" square

Flowering Hugs Card
Designer: Roree Rumph

SUPPLIES: *Cardstock:* (Guacamole) Bazzill Basics Paper; (Angel Orchid) Core'dinations *Patterned paper:* (Splish Splash from Ducks in a Row collection) October Afternoon *Accents:* (printed chipboard buttons) Jenni Bowlin Studio; (blue hugs) KI Memories; (purple, green, blue buttons) BasicGrey *Fibers:* (blue, purple, green floss) DMC *Tool:* (decorative-edge scissors) Fiskars *Other:* (green, purple, blue felt)

Finished size: 5½" square

Sketch by: Jessica Witty

DESIGNER TIP

When stamping objects, give them a shadow underneath so they don't appear to be floating.

5 STEPS Love Conquers All Card

Designer: Kimberly Crawford

1. Make card from cardstock.

2. Die-cut and emboss label from cardstock, emboss using template, and adhere.

3. Trim patterned paper and adhere; tie on twine.

4. Die-cut and emboss rectangle from cardstock; stamp Knight Shield and color. Adhere with foam tape.

5. Adhere buttons to card; stamp sentiment.

Finished size: 4¾" x 4¼"

SUPPLIES: *Cardstock:* (Stormy, Poinsettia) Core'dinations; (Solar White) Neenah Paper *Patterned paper:* (Sunday Dishes from Cherry Hill collection) October Afternoon *Rubber stamps:* (Knight Shield, Love Conquers) Stampendous! *Dye ink:* (Tuxedo Black) Tsukineko *Color medium:* (assorted markers) Copic *Accents:* (red heart buttons) Jesse James & Co. *Fibers:* (cream twine) May Arts *Template:* (Floral & Stone embossing) Spellbinders *Dies:* (bracketed label, rectangle) Spellbinders

Miss You Birdie Card
Designer: Jessica Witty

SUPPLIES: *Cardstock:* (white, kraft) Papertrey Ink *Patterned paper:* (Sunrise from Early Bird collection) Cosmo Cricket; (Nutmeg from Kitchen Spice collection) BoBunny Press *Clear stamp:* (branch from Blue Skies Laughter set) American Crafts *Color medium:* (Old Olive, Chocolate Chip markers) Stampin Up! *Accents:* (white eyelets) Making Memories *Sticker:* (bird badge) American Crafts *Fibers:* (yellow polka dot ribbon) American Crafts *Font:* (Too Much Paper) www. fontcubes.com *Dies:* (label) Spellbinders

Finished size: 4½" square

Just Because Cherries Card
Designer: Betsy Veldman

SUPPLIES: *Cardstock:* (Summer Sunrise, white) Papertrey Ink *Patterned paper:* (blue grid from 2008 Bitty Box Basics collection; red polka dots from 2008 Bitty Dot Basics collection) Papertrey Ink; (Cut Outs from Calypso collection) BoBunny Press *Clear stamps:* (cherry stems from Everyday Button Bits set, sentiment from Mega Mixed Messages set) Papertrey Ink *Chalk ink:* (Creamy Brown) Clearsnap *Specialty ink:* (Ripe Avocado, Dark Chocolate hybrid) Papertrey Ink *Accents:* (red buttons) Papertrey Ink; (red rhinestones) Kaisercraft *Fibers:* (Summer Sunrise ribbon) Papertrey Ink *Tool:* (border punch) Fiskars

Finished size: 4¼" x 5½"

Green Monster Birthday Card
Designer: Maren Benedict

SUPPLIES: *Cardstock:* (Summer Sun) Papertrey Ink *Patterned paper:* (green from Nutmeg pad) Cosmo Cricket; (Farm House from Farm Fresh collection, Bus Route from Report Card collection) October Afternoon *Rubber stamp:* (sentiment from Sketched Sentiments set) Lizzie Anne Designs *Clear stamp:* (monster from M set) Bam Pop *Dye ink:* (Black Soot) Ranger Industries *Color medium:* (black) American Crafts; (white gel pen) Sanford *Accents:* (journaling card) Cosmo Cricket; (red brads) BasicGrey *Fibers:* (red ribbon) Papertrey Ink

Finished size: 5" square

Sketch by: Jessica Witty

5 STEPS Button Birdies Card

Designer: Alli Miles

1. Make card from cardstock.

2. Trim journaling card. Stamp birds and color. Mat with patterned paper and adhere.

3. Adhere buttons. Stamp wings on patterned paper, trim, and adhere. Draw eyes.

4. Ink edges of patterned paper strip and adhere. Stamp sentiment on journaling card strip and adhere.

5. Attach brad to flower; adhere.

Finished size: 4¼" x 5"

SUPPLIES: *Cardstock:* (Vintage Cream) Papertrey Ink *Patterned paper:* (This Little Piggy from Ducks in a Row collection) October Afternoon *Clear stamps:* (sentiment, birds from Everyday Button Bits set) Papertrey Ink *Dye ink:* (cream) *Specialty ink:* (Dark Chocolate hybrid) Papertrey Ink *Color medium:* (yellow, gray, black markers) Copic *Accents:* (journaling card) Jenni Bowlin Studio; (pink flower) Prima; (white, pink buttons) Papertrey Ink; (white button brad) Imaginisce

Joy Filled Day Card

Gretchen Clark

SUPPLIES: *Cardstock:* (Ocean Tides, Ripe Avocado) Papertrey Ink; (Whisper White, Chocolate Chip) Stampin' Up! *Clear stamps:* (sentiment from Everyday Button Bits set; flower, leafy stem from Life set) Papertrey Ink *Dye ink:* (Chocolate Chip) Stampin' Up! *Specialty ink:* (Ocean Tides, Ripe Avocado hybrid) Papertrey Ink *Accents:* (olive button) Stampin' Up! (iridescent glitter glue) Ranger Industries *Fibers:* (blue ribbon) Papertrey Ink; (natural twine) Stampin' Up! *Die:* (tag) Spellbinders

Finished size: 4¼" x 5½"

To Comfort You Card

Designer: Beth Opel

SUPPLIES: *Cardstock:* (Cinnamon) WorldWin *Patterned paper:* (Flax from Granola collection) BasicGrey *Specialty paper:* (glossy photo) *Accents:* (black rhinestones) Glitz Design *Fibers:* (black ribbon) *Fonts:* (Times New Roman) Microsoft; (Black Jack, Tagettes) www.dafont.com *Software:* (photo editing) *Other:* (digital photo)

Finished size: 6½" x 5"

Hospitality Thanks Card

Designer: Julie Masse

SUPPLIES: *Cardstock:* (Not Quite Navy) Stampin' Up! (ivory) Gina K Designs *Patterned paper:* (Brunch, Sunrise from Early Bird collection) Cosmo Cricket *Clear stamps:* (sentiment, house from Blessed By You set) Waltzingmouse Stamps *Dye ink:* (Rhubarb Stalk) Tsukineko; (Chamomile) Papertrey Ink *Accents:* (cream, green, red buttons) Papertrey Ink *Fibers:* (green ribbon, cream twine) Papertrey Ink

Finished size: 4¼" square

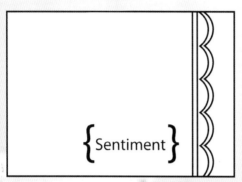

{Sentiment}

Sketch by: Lucy Abrams

Thank You Bird

Designer: Julie Lacey

❶ Make card from cardstock.

❷ Cut cardstock panel; adhere patterned paper.

❸ Punch edge of cardstock strip; adhere. Zigzag-stitch.

❹ Stamp Thank You.

❺ Adhere ribbon around panel. Tie ribbon bow, tie on twine, and adhere. Adhere flower.

❻ Adhere panel with foam tape.

Finished size: 5½" x 4¼"

SUPPLIES: *Cardstock:* (Early Espresso) Stampin' Up!; (Vintage Cream, Berry Sorbet) Papertrey Ink *Patterned paper:* (Little One Darling Dots from Stella & Rose Gertie collection) My Mind's Eye *Rubber stamp:* (Thank You) Unity Stamp Co. *Dye ink:* (Early Espresso) Stampin' Up! *Accent:* (orange flower) Prima *Fibers:* (ivory ribbon) May Arts; (natural twine) Papertrey Ink *Tool:* (border punch) Stampin' Up!

DESIGNER TIP

Make a coordinating set of cards, changing the patterned paper and trim. It's a great way to use ribbon and paper scraps in your stash!

5 STEPS Call Me
Designer: Latisha Yoast

1 Make card from cardstock. **2** Trim cardstock panel. Adhere patterned paper strip. **3** Stamp Call Me. **4** Punch edge of cardstock strip; adhere. **5** Tie on ribbon, adhere rhinestones, and adhere panel to card with foam tape.

Finished size: 6" x 3¾"

5 STEPS Live Life Loud
Designer: Valerie Stangle

1 Make card from cardstock; round one corner. **2** Adhere patterned paper piece. Cut patterned paper strip, round one corner, and adhere. Sand card edges. **3** Border-punch edge of cardstock strip; adhere. Tie on ribbon. **4** Die-cut circle from cardstock. Stamp flower. Stamp sentiment; emboss. **5** Attach brad and adhere to card with foam tape.

Finished size: 5½" x 3¾"

5 STEPS Laugh a Little
Designer: Kelly Rasmussen

1 Make card from cardstock; round one corner. **2** Cut cardstock panel. Punch six circles from vintage book page, fold in half, and adhere to panel. **3** Adhere patterned paper strip. Adhere trim and twine. **4** Stamp sentiment. **5** Round one corner of panel and adhere to card with foam tape.

Finished size: 4¼" x 5½"

SUPPLIES: *Cardstock:* (Royal Velvet, Lemon Tart, white) Papertrey Ink *Patterned paper:* (Your Life from Life's Portrait collection) Webster's Pages *Rubber stamp:* (Call Me) Unity Stamp Co. *Dye ink:* (Tuxedo Black) Tsukineko *Accents:* (black rhinestones) Kaisercraft *Fibers:* (yellow stitched ribbon) Papertrey Ink *Tool:* (embossing border punch) EK Success

SUPPLIES: *Cardstock:* (white, black) Gina K Designs *Patterned paper:* (Coastline, Grass Stain from Lauderdale collection) BasicGrey *Rubber stamps:* (flower, sentiment from Live Life Loud set) Gina K Designs *Dye ink:* (Bahama Blue) Tsukineko *Pigment ink:* (Onyx Black) Tsukineko *Embossing powder:* (clear) *Accent:* (green rhinestone brad) Stampin' Up! *Fibers:* (black gingham ribbon) Gina K Designs *Die:* (circle) Spellbinders *Tools:* (embossing border punch) EK Success; (corner rounder punch) Stampin' Up!

SUPPLIES: *Cardstock:* (Dark Chocolate, kraft) Papertrey Ink *Patterned paper:* (Lace from Restoration collection) Crate Paper *Clear stamp:* (sentiment from Type set) Hero Arts *Dye ink:* (Vintage Photo) Ranger Industries *Fibers:* (green trim) Making Memories; (brown/white twine) The Twinery *Tools:* (corner rounder punch) We R Memory Keepers; (¾" circle punch) EK Success *Other:* (vintage book page)

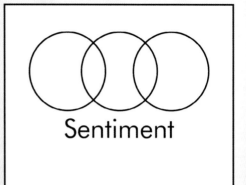

Sentiment

Sketch by: Julia Stainton

DESIGNER TIP

The stamp used in this project has been discontinued. A good substitute is happy birthday from the Type set by Hero Arts.

5 STEPS Happy Birthday Circles

Designer: Kristin K. Tierney

1. Make card from cardstock; tie on twine.

2. Stamp birthday and emboss.

3. Punch circles from cardstock; piece together and adhere to cardstock strip.

4. Stamp happy and emboss. Stamp happy repeatedly across circles.

5. Adhere circles to card with foam tape.

Finished size: 5½" x 4¼"

SUPPLIES: *Cardstock:* (Real Red, Pumpkin Pie, Daffodil Delight, Old Olive, Tempting Turquoise, Crumb Cake) Stampin' Up! *Clear stamp:* (Happy Birthday) Studio Calico *Pigment ink:* (white) Stampin' Up! *Watermark ink:* Tsukineko *Embossing powder:* (Winter White) Stampin' Up! *Fibers:* (natural hemp twine) *Tool:* (circle punch) Marvy Uchida

DESIGNER TIP

Feel safe using many of the fun stick pin embellishments available by pushing pin ends into the edge of foam tape.

Happy Foreverness

Designer: Anabelle O'Malley

❶ Make card from cardstock. ❷ Cut patterned paper panel; emboss. Stitch edges. ❸ Cut flowers from necklace; adhere to panel, wrapping ribbon around edges. Remove center from one flower; adhere pearl center. ❹ Adhere panel to card. Adhere remaining necklace ribbon. ❺ Die-cut tag from patterned paper; stamp happy foreverness. Adhere with foam tape.

Finished size: 5¼" x 4¼"

Three Trees

Designer: Lucy Abrams

❶ Make card from cardstock. ❷ Cut patterned paper panel; stitch edges and adhere to card. ❸ Stamp sentiment. ❹ Adhere trees with foam tape. ❺ Tie twine bow; adhere. Adhere pearls.

Finished size: 5½" x 4¼"

Vintage Easter

Designer: Vivian Masket

❶ Make card from cardstock; cover with patterned paper. ❷ Punch three circles from patterned paper; insert into memo pins. ❸ Cut cardstock strip. Adhere ribbon. Spell "Happy Easter" and adhere to card with foam tape. ❹ Insert memo pins behind sentiment strip; adhere circles with foam tape.

Finished size: 4¼" x 5½"

SUPPLIES: *Cardstock:* (white) Papertrey Ink *Patterned paper:* (blue from Celebrate Jack & Jill pad) Prima *Clear stamp:* (happy foreverness from Fancy Phrases set) Waltzingmouse Stamps *Specialty ink:* (Smokey Shadow hybrid) Papertrey Ink *Accents:* (white flower/ribbon necklace, silver/blue pearl center) Prima *Template:* (embossing brocade) Provo Craft *Die:* (tag) Spellbinders

SUPPLIES: *Cardstock:* (Grass) Hero Arts *Patterned paper:* (Swimming Pool Dot Grid from Petite Prints collection) Doodlebug Design *Clear stamp:* (sentiment from Find Joy set) Hero Arts *Dye ink:* (black) Hero Arts *Accents:* (red heart pearls) Hero Arts *Stickers:* (trees) Doodlebug Design *Fibers:* (cream twine)

SUPPLIES: *Cardstock:* (Atlantic) Bazzill Basics Paper; (white) *Patterned paper:* (Butterscotch, Root Beer Barrels from 5 & Dime collection) October Afternoon *Accents:* (metal memo pins) Tim Holtz *Stickers:* (Hello Luscious alphabet) BasicGrey *Fibers:* (brown ribbon) American Crafts *Tool:* (circle punch) Fiskars

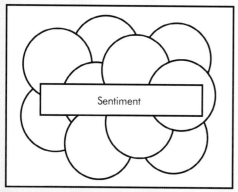

Sketch by: Stephanie Halinski

5 Steps: Orange You Sweet!

Designer: Laura O'Donnell

❶ Make card from cardstock.

❷ Cut cardstock to fit card front; deboss and ink. Distress edges and adhere to card.

❸ Stamp orange slice ten times on cardstock; emboss. Cut out and adhere to card.

❹ Stamp sentiment on cardstock; emboss. Distress edges and adhere with foam tape.

Finished size: 5½" x 4¼"

SUPPLIES: *Cardstock:* (white) Neenah Paper; (Enchanted Evening) Papertrey Ink; (Madero Beach) French Paper *Clear stamp:* (orange slice, sentiment from Fruit Stand set) Technique Tuesday *Dye ink:* (Antique Linen) Ranger Industries *Watermark ink:* Tsukineko *Embossing powder:* (Carnelian, Detail White) Stampendous! *Template:* (debossing woodgrain) Papertrey Ink

DESIGNER TIPS

A spectrum ink pad works well when using multiple colors on the same project as they will complement each other nicely.

For a fresh sentiment idea, use a popular song lyric, which can be especially fun for teens.

you're a firework LET YOUR COLORS BURST -Katy Perry

DESIGNER TIP

Keep the sunny theme but change the sentiment to "Sending You Sunshine" for a warm get-well card.

happy birthday to you

YOU ARE MY SUNSHINE

Several Circles Birthday

Designer: Julie Lacey

❶ Make card from cardstock. ❷ Punch circles from patterned paper. Adhere several circles; stitch around circle edges. ❸ Adhere remaining circles with foam tape. ❹ Affix sticker to cardstock strip; adhere to card.

Finished size: 5½" x 4¼"

You're a Firework

Designer: Stephanie Halinski

❶ Make card from cardstock. ❷ Stamp sunburst repeatedly across card. ❸ Print sentiment on paper, trim, and adhere to card with foam tape. ❹ Adhere rhinestones.

Finished size: 5½" x 4¼"

You are My Sunshine

Designer: Stephanie Halinski

❶ Make card from patterned paper. ❷ Punch circle from cardstock, trim cardstock strips, and adhere. ❸ Fussy-cut clouds from patterned paper; adhere. ❹ Thread button with floss; adhere. ❺ Cut fabric paper strip, spell "You are my" with stickers, and affix. Affix sunshine sticker.

Finished size: 5½" x 4¼"

SUPPLIES: *Cardstock:* (Vintage Cream) Papertrey Ink *Patterned paper:* (Mother Ledger, Happy Polka Dots, Fancy Doily, Lovely Bouquet Die-cut, So Sweet Plaid Die-cut, Remember Buttercup from Stella & Rose pads; yellow polka dot, blue mini floral, pink polka dot) My Mind's Eye *Sticker:* (sentiment) SRM Press *Tools:* (circle punches) Stampin' Up!

SUPPLIES: *Cardstock:* (white) Bazzill Basics *Paper:* (white) *Clear stamp:* (sunburst from Awesome Days of Summer set) Technique Tuesday *Chalk ink:* (Ocean Breeze spectrum) Clearsnap *Accents:* (clear rhinestones) Dreamtime Creations *Font:* (Trebuchet) Microsoft

SUPPLIES: *Cardstock:* (yellow, orange, red glitter) DCWV Inc. *Patterned paper:* (Kahuna Kiwi from Heat Wave collection; Howdy from Everyday collection) American Crafts *Specialty paper:* (Fountain adhesive fabric from Dear Lizzy Spring collection) American Crafts *Accent:* (yellow button) BasicGrey *Stickers:* (Mini Shimmer alphabet) Making Memories; (chipboard sunshine) American Crafts *Fibers:* (yellow floss) *Tool:* (circle punch) Stampin' Up!

Sentiment

Sketch by: Stephanie Halinksi

sorry for your loss

5 STEPS Sorry for Your Loss

Designer: Vanessa Menhorn

❶ Make card from cardstock.

❷ Cut cardstock panel. Stamp flourish and sentiment.

❸ Mat panel with cardstock; adhere.

❹ Adhere pearls and flower.

Finished size: 5½" x 4¼"

SUPPLIES: *Cardstock:* (Vintage Cream, Dark Chocolate, Spring Moss) Papertrey Ink *Clear stamps:* (flourish from Embellishments set) Papertrey Ink; (sentiment from Everyday Sayings set) Hero Arts *Dye ink:* (Bamboo Leaves) Tsukineko *Accents:* (cream pearls) Hero Arts; (cream flower) Prima

DESIGNER TIP

Do you have a rub-on that you love but are afraid to use? Rub it on cardstock, trim, and then adhere it anywhere you would like. It makes placement easier and takes the stress out of getting it perfect.

happy new home.

love always

thanks, dad

Love Always

Designer: Angeline Yong Jeet Leen

❶ Make card from cardstock. ❷ Cut cardstock panel; stamp love always and plaid. ❸ Attach brad. ❹ Mat panel with cardstock and adhere to card.

Finished size: 5½" x 4"

Happy New Home

Designer: Lynn Ghahary

❶ Make card from patterned paper. ❷ Print sentiment on cardstock; trim and adhere. ❸ Cut patterned paper strips; adhere. ❹ Adhere felt house.

Finished size: 5" x 4¼"

Thanks, Dad

Designer: Becky Olsen

❶ Make card from cardstock. ❷ Adhere strips of transparency sheet; stitch. ❸ Apply mustache rub-on to cardstock, trim, and adhere to card with foam tape. ❹ Spell "Thanks, dad" with rub-ons.

Finished size: 5½" x 4¼"

SUPPLIES: *Cardstock:* (black, white) Bazzill Basics Paper; (kraft) *Clear stamps:* (love always, plaid from Sweet Nothings set) Wplus9 Design Studio *Pigment ink:* (brown, sepia) Kaisercraft *Accent:* (red heart brad) Doodlebug Design

SUPPLIES: *Cardstock:* (white) American Crafts *Patterned paper:* (Aspen Ridge Road from Adobe collection) American Crafts; (Club from Tree House collection) Pebbles in My Pocket *Accents:* (felt house) Pebbles *Font:* (Traveling Typewriter) www.dafont.com

SUPPLIES: *Cardstock:* (kraft) Bazzill Basics Paper *Transparency sheet:* (Mini Moustaches) Hambly Screen Prints *Rub-ons:* (black moustache) Hambly Screen Prints; (Holly alphabet) American Crafts

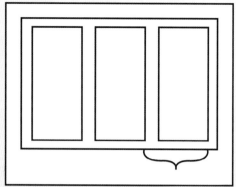

Sketch by: Emily Branch

DESIGNER TIP

This sketch lends itself well to using repetitive icons and stamps.

5 STEPS ❦ Together Chairs

Designer: Kimberly Crawford

1. Make card from cardstock; adhere patterned paper.

2. Trim patterned paper panel; ink edges and adhere to card.

3. Die-cut rectangles from patterned paper. Stamp chair on each piece; ink edges. Adhere to card with foam tape.

4. Affix together sticker.

5. Color twine with marker and tie on.

Finished size: 5½" x 4¼"

SUPPLIES: *Cardstock:* (kraft) Papertrey Ink *Patterned paper:* (Joy Woodgrain, Play Damask, So Sweet Herringbone from Stella & Rose pad) My Mind's Eye *Clear stamp:* (chair from Stella & Rose Memories set) My Mind's Eye *Dye ink:* (Tuxedo Black) Tsukineko; (Frayed Burlap) Ranger Industries *Color medium:* (green marker) Copic *Sticker:* (together chipboard) My Mind's Eye *Fibers:* (cream twine) May Arts *Dies:* (rectangles) Spellbinders

⁵ STEPS Reeds of Sympathy

Designer: Korin Sutherland

❶ Make card from cardstock. ❷ Stamp reeds and birds on cardstock; trim into three strips and ink edges. Mat with cardstock and adhere to card with foam tape. ❸ Stamp with sympathy.

Finished size: 5½" x 4¼"

⁵ STEPS Dress Form Thanks

Designer: Rachael Burdick

❶ Make card from cardstock; cover with patterned paper. ❷ Cut cardstock panel. Stamp Mini Dressform on cardstock three times, trim, and adhere to panel. Adhere panel to card. ❸ Adhere flower and insert pins. ❹ Die-cut and emboss label from cardstock. Stamp thanks and adhere.

Finished size: 3½" x 5"

⁵ STEPS Missing You Couches

Designer: Nina Brackett

❶ Make card from cardstock. ❷ Cut cardstock panel; stamp couches and missing you. ❸ Mat panel with cardstock; border-punch one mat edge. Adhere to card. ❹ Stamp pillows on cardstock; trim and adhere with foam tape. ❺ Tie on ribbon; trim with decorative-edge scissors. Thread button with twine and adhere.

Finished size: 4¼" x 5½"

SUPPLIES: *Cardstock:* (kraft) Marco's Paper; (brown) Michaels; (white) Georgia-Pacific *Clear stamps:* (reeds, birds from Serene Silhouettes set; with sympathy from Peaceful Swans set) Sweet 'n Sassy Stamps *Dye ink:* (Sweet Leaf, Desert Sand) Close To My Heart

SUPPLIES: *Cardstock:* (Sugar, Onyx) A Muse Studio *Patterned paper:* (Last One from The Thrift Shop pad) October Afternoon *Rubber stamp:* (Mini Dressform) Invoke Arts *Clear stamp:* (thanks from Mixed Messages set) Papertrey Ink *Dye ink:* (black) A Muse Studio *Accents:* (cream pearl stick pins) Jenni Bowlin Studio; (pink flower) Michaels *Die:* (label) Spellbinders

SUPPLIES: *Cardstock:* (Rocket Red, Black Onyx, Ivory) Gina K Designs *Rubber stamps:* (couch, missing you from Fine Furnishings Additions set; pillow from Fine Furnishings set) Gina K Designs *Dye ink:* (Aqua, Brick, Straw) Clearsnap; (Tuxedo Black) Tsukineko *Accent:* (red button) *Fibers:* (blue stitched ribbon) Papertrey Ink; (yellow/white twine) The Twinery *Tools:* (border punch, decorative-edge scissors) Fiskars

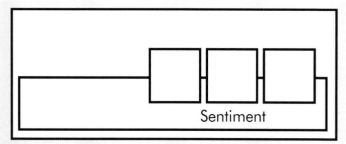

Sentiment

Sketch by: Ryann Salamon

5 STEPS Bee Happy

Designer: Regina Mangum

❶ Make card from cardstock.

❷ Adhere patterned paper piece. Stamp sentiment and tie on twill.

❸ Punch small and medium squares from cardstock.

❹ Stamp bees on small squares; color. Mat squares with medium squares and adhere to card with foam tape.

❺ Stamp bees on cardstock, color, and fussy-cut. Adhere with foam tape. Accent with glitter glue.

Finished size: 6¼" x 2¾"

SUPPLIES: *Cardstock:* (Aqua Mist, Vintage Cream, kraft) Papertrey Ink *Patterned paper:* (Blue Damask from Lush collection) My Mind's Eye *Rubber stamps:* (bee, sentiment from Garden Party Critters set) Taylored Expressions *Dye ink:* (Tuxedo Black) Tsukineko *Color medium:* (blue, yellow markers) Copic *Accent:* (iridescent glitter glue) Ranger Industries *Fibers:* (aqua twill) Papertrey Ink *Tool:* (small, medium square punches) EK Success

DESIGNER TIP

When coloring fall leaves, use the darkest color in the middle and vary the amount of color for more realism.

DESIGNER TIP

Using patterned papers from the same collection makes coordination of colors and patterns a breeze!

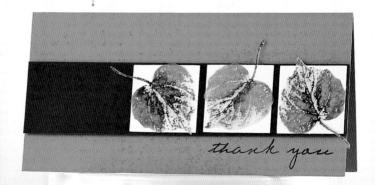

⑤ I Thought of You

Designer: Emily Leiphart

❶ Make card from cardstock; cover with patterned paper. ❷ Stamp sentiment on patterned paper strip; adhere. ❸ Stamp International Skyline on patterned paper; punch into squares. Mat squares with patterned paper and adhere with foam tape.

Finished size: 6" x 3¼"

⑤ Fall Thank You

Designer: Jaydee

❶ Make card from cardstock. ❷ Stamp Wonderfully Worn on card. Stamp thank you. ❸ Cut cardstock strip. Stamp Wonderfully Worn on strip. Punch squares from cardstock, adhere to strip, and adhere to card with foam tape. ❹ Stamp French Foliage on vellum; let dry. Fussy-cut leaves and adhere to card.

Finished size: 6" x 3"

⑤ Superstar

Designer: Alicia Thelin

❶ Make card from cardstock. ❷ Dry-emboss cardstock strip; adhere. ❸ Stamp images on cardstock; punch into squares, trim, and adhere with foam tape. ❹ Apply superstar rub-on to card. Attach brad.

Finished size: 5½" x 2¾"

SUPPLIES: *Cardstock:* (white) Gina K Designs *Patterned paper:* (Metropolis, Lost Luggage, Hub, Lightrail from Wander collection) BasicGrey *Rubber stamps:* (International Skyline) Hero Arts; (sentiment from Fly… Free set) Unity Stamp Co. *Dye ink:* (Rich Cocoa) Tsukineko *Tool:* (square punch) McGill

SUPPLIES: *Cardstock:* (Cajun Craze, More Mustard, Very Vanilla) Stampin' Up! *Vellum:* Stampin' Up! *Rubber stamps:* (leaf from French Foliage set; Wonderfully Worn) Stampin' Up! *Clear stamp:* (thank you from Inside & Out: Thank You set) Papertrey Ink *Dye ink:* (Cajun Craze) Stampin' Up! *Watermark ink:* Tsukineko *Color medium:* (More Mustard, Bravo Burgundy markers) Stampin' Up! *Tool:* (square punch) Stampin' Up!

SUPPLIES: All supplies from Stampin' Up! unless otherwise noted. *Cardstock:* (Naturals Ivory, Old Olive, Pumpkin Pie, Tempting Turquoise, Basic Black) *Clear stamps:* (hand, MP3 player, headphones from Rock On set) We R Memory Keepers *Pigment ink:* (Basic Black) *Embossing powder:* (clear) *Accent:* (olive brad) *Rub-on:* (superstar) *Template:* (embossing Tiny Bubbles) Provo Craft *Tool:* (square punch)

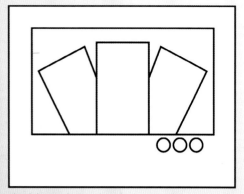

Sketch by: Emily Branch

5 STEPS Scooting By to Say Hi

Designer: Teri Anderson

1. Make card from cardstock.

2. Cut cardstock panel; draw border. Stamp sentiment.

3. Stamp clouds on cardstock, trim, and adhere to panel. Mat panel with cardstock and adhere to card.

4. Trim building stickers and affix. Affix car and dots.

5. Adhere rhinestones.

Finished size: 6" x 5½"

SUPPLIES: *Cardstock:* (blue) Bazzill Basics Paper; (white) Georgia-Pacific *Patterned paper:* (Tarmac from Wander collection) BasicGrey *Clear stamps:* (clouds from Make a Scene set) A Muse Studio; (sentiment from Spiffy Scooters set) Paper Smooches *Dye ink:* (Tuxedo Black) Tsukineko *Color medium:* (black pen) American Crafts *Accents:* (black rhinestones) Kaisercraft *Stickers:* (chipboard buildings, car, circles) BasicGrey

DESIGNER TIP

Use sketch as inspiration for a completely different look and layout.

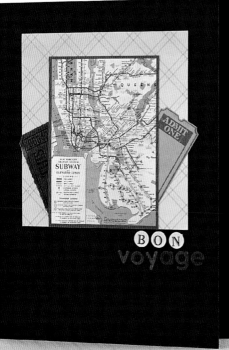

5 STEPS · Masterpiece of Nature

Designer: Julia Stainton

Ink all paper edges. ❶ Make card from cardstock. ❷ Trim patterned paper; adhere. Attach staples. ❸ Adhere bird and floral cards. Adhere friend label. ❹ Adhere feather. Tie twine bow, adhere, and attach staples. ❺ Attach brads.

Finished size: 4¼" x 5½"

5 STEPS · Under the Big Top

Designer: Jennifer Cuthbertson

❶ Make card from cardstock. ❷ Cut patterned paper panel. Adhere patterned paper piece. ❸ Stamp Circus Ticket on cardstock, trim, and ink edges. Distress edges and adhere to panel. ❹ Tie ribbon around panel and adhere panel to card. ❺ Adhere star with foam tape.

Finished size: 5½" x 4¼"

5 STEPS · Bon Voyage

Designer: Angie Tieman

❶ Make card from cardstock. ❷ Cut patterned paper piece; adhere. Adhere tickets and road map card. ❸ Spell "Bon" with stickers, adhering with foam tape. Spell "Voyage" with stickers.

Finished size: 5" x 7"

SUPPLIES: *Cardstock:* (kraft) Bazzill Basics Paper *Patterned paper:* (ledger from Flora & Fauna collection notebook) K&Company *Dye ink:* (Brushed Corduroy) Ranger Industries *Accents:* (friend label, bird card, floral card, black spotted feather) K&Company; (purple brads) Making Memories; (silver mini staples) Tim Holtz *Fibers:* (natural twine) Westrim Crafts

SUPPLIES: *Cardstock:* (Riding Hood Red) Stampin' Up!; (Vintage Cream) Papertrey Ink *Patterned paper:* (Under the Big Top, Greatest Show on Earth from Le Cirque collection) Graphic 45 *Rubber stamp:* (Circus Ticket) Stampin' D'Amour *Dye ink:* (Basic Black) Stampin' Up!; (Chamomile, Chai) Papertrey Ink *Accent:* (silver glitter star) MemrieMare *Fibers:* (black ribbon) MemrieMare

SUPPLIES: *Cardstock:* (Basic Black) Stampin' Up! *Patterned paper:* (Pinwheels from Togetherness collection) Cosmo Cricket *Accents:* (road map card) October Afternoon; (green ticket) K&Company; (red ticket) *Stickers:* (Star Banner alphabet) Jenni Bowlin Studio; (Curio alphabet) BasicGrey

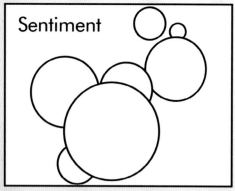

Sentiment

Sketch by: Vanessa Menhorn

DESIGNER TIP

For even more dimension, stamp some doilies a second time on cardstock, fussy-cut, and adhere with foam tape.

⑤ Doily Birthday

Designer: Karolyn Loncon

❶ Make card from cardstock.

❷ Cut cardstock panel. Mat with cardstock and zigzag-stitch edges.

❸ Stamp doilies and happy birthday.

❹ Thread buttons with twine; adhere.

❺ Adhere panel with foam tape.

Finished size: 5½" x 4¼"

SUPPLIES: *Cardstock:* (Spring Moss, Sweet Blush, Vintage Cream) Papertrey Ink *Rubber stamp:* (happy birthday from Nana's Needlework Sentiments set) Gina K Designs *Clear stamps:* (doilies from Stella & Rose Girly set) My Mind's Eye; (doilies from Doilies set) Maya Road *Pigment ink:* (Celery, Fuchsia, Pink Lemonade, Chocolate) Impress Rubber Stamps *Accents:* (pink, green buttons) Papertrey Ink *Fibers:* (cream twine) Papertrey Ink

5 STEPS Birthday Collage

Designer: Vanessa Menhorn

Ink all edges. ❶ Make card from cardstock; stamp happy birthday. ❷ Die-cut circles and scalloped circle from patterned paper; adhere. ❸ Die-cut and punch butterflies from patterned paper. Bend wings up slightly and adhere. ❹ Adhere pearls, buttons, and flower. Insert pins.

Finished size: 5½" x 4¼"

5 STEPS Pinwheel Get Well

Designer: Teri Anderson

❶ Make card from cardstock; ink edges. ❷ Punch circles from patterned paper, ink edges, and adhere. ❸ Adhere doily, affix flower stickers, and adhere pearls. ❹ Stamp sentiment.

Finished size: 5½" x 4¼"

5 STEPS Happy for You!

Designer: Lindsay Amrhein

❶ Make card from cardstock; round right corners. ❷ Stamp flowers; ink centers. ❸ Stamp sentiment on cardstock and adhere with foam tape. ❹ Adhere rhinestones.

Finished size: 5½" x 4¼"

SUPPLIES: *Cardstock:* (white) Papertrey Ink *Patterned paper:* (Great Find, Needs Paint, Collectors Item from The Thrift Shop collection; Lemonade, Front Porch from Fly a Kite collection) October Afternoon; (white polka dot from Basics White pad) BasicGrey *Clear stamp:* (happy birthday from Communique Curves Sentiments set) Papertrey Ink *Dye ink:* (Tuxedo Black) Tsukineko; (Walnut Stain, Tea Dye) Ranger Industries *Accents:* (cream pearl stick pins) Jenni Bowlin Studio; (blue pearls, cream flower) Prima; (cream buttons) Papertrey Ink *Dies:* (circles) Spellbinders; (medium, large butterflies; scalloped circle) Papertrey Ink *Tool:* (butterfly punch) Martha Stewart Crafts

SUPPLIES: *Cardstock:* (white) Georgia-Pacific *Patterned paper:* (Rosemary, Succulent from Hello Luscious collection) BasicGrey *Clear stamp:* (sentiment from Sophie's Sentiments set) Lawn Fawn *Dye ink:* (Tuxedo Black) Tsukineko; (Old Paper) Ranger Industries *Accents:* (white pearls) Kaisercraft; (white doily) Martha Stewart Crafts *Stickers:* (flowers) BasicGrey *Tools:* (circle punches) Fiskars

SUPPLIES: *Cardstock:* (kraft) Papertrey Ink *Clear stamps:* (flowers from Layered Flowers set) Hero Arts; (sentiment from Enjoy the Ride set) Papertrey Ink *Pigment ink:* (Fresh Snow) Papertrey Ink *Specialty ink:* (True Black hybrid) Papertrey Ink *Accents:* (red rhinestones) Kaisercraft *Tool:* (corner rounder punch) We R Memory Keepers

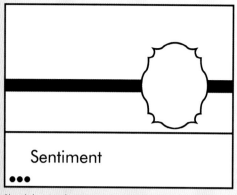

Sentiment

Sketch by: Latisha Yoast

Happily EVER AFTER

Rhapsody in Orange

Designer: Latisha Yoast

1. Make card from cardstock.

2. Adhere patterned paper strip. Adhere ribbon.

3. Stamp sentiment. Adhere rhinestones.

4. Die-cut and emboss label from cardstock; adhere with foam tape.

5. Affix butterfly.

Finished size: 5½" x 4¼"

SUPPLIES: *Cardstock:* (ivory) Flourishes *Patterned paper:* (Orange Damask from Lush collection) My Mind's Eye *Rubber stamp:* (sentiment from Fanciful Tags set) Gina K Designs *Dye ink:* (Tuxedo Black) Tsukineko *Accents:* (orange rhinestones) Kaisercraft *Sticker:* (embellished orange butterfly) Jenni Bowlin Studio *Fibers:* (orange ribbon) Papertrey Ink *Die:* (label) Spellbinders

⟨5 STEPS⟩ Graduation Day

Designer: Tanisha Long

❶ Make card from cardstock; emboss card front. **❷** Trim patterned paper strip; punch edge and adhere. Adhere patterned paper strip. **❸** Die-cut circle from patterned paper. Mat with cardstock and trim with decorative-edge scissors. **❹** Die-cut graduation cap from cardstock; adhere to circle with foam tape. Adhere rhinestones and adhere circle to card with foam tape. **❺** Apply graduation day rub-on. Adhere glitter dots.

Finished size: 5½" x 4¼"

⟨5 STEPS⟩ My Life is Rich

Designer: Jessica Witty

❶ Make card from cardstock. **❷** Adhere patterned paper panel and strip. Adhere ribbon. **❸** Stamp cameo on frame sticker. Adhere frame and flowers with foam tape. Tie ribbon bow and adhere. **❹** Stamp sentiment. Adhere rhinestones.

Finished size: 5½" x 4¼"

⟨5 STEPS⟩ Mitten Wishes

Designer: Katie Stilwater

❶ Make card from cardstock; emboss card front. Trim 1" from front flap. **❷** Stamp sentiment and adhere rhinestones. Punch edge of cardstock strip; adhere inside front flap. **❸** Tie on twine. Thread button with twine and adhere. **❹** Die-cut label from cardstock; stamp frame. Stamp mittens and color. Adhere with foam tape.

Finished size: 4¼" x 5½"

SUPPLIES: *Cardstock:* (black, white) Bazzill Basics Paper *Patterned paper:* (Stars from Magic collection) Queen & Co.; (Advertisement from For the Record collection) Echo Park Paper *Accents:* (clear rhinestones) Bazzill Basics Paper; (black glitter dots) Mark Richards *Rub-on:* (graduation day) Karen Foster Design *Template:* (embossing lines) Cheery Lynn Designs *Die:* (graduation cap, circle) Cheery Lynn Designs *Tools:* (border punch) Fiskars; (decorative-edge scissors) Provo Craft

SUPPLIES: *Cardstock:* (kraft) Papertrey Ink *Patterned paper:* (Heirloom, Textile from Curio collection) BasicGrey *Clear stamps:* (cameo from Toil & Trouble set) The Girls' Paperie; (sentiment from Mama=Love set) Technique Tuesday *Specialty ink:* (Dark Chocolate hybrid) Papertrey Ink *Accents:* (yellow rhinestones) Kaisercraft *Stickers:* (flower, frame) BasicGrey *Fibers:* (yellow ribbon) 7gypsies; (brown floss) DMC

SUPPLIES: *Cardstock:* (Lichen, Bermuda) A Muse Studio; (white) Neenah Paper *Rubber stamps:* (sentiment, mittens from Winter Wishes set; frame from Vintage Labels set) A Muse Studio *Dye ink:* (Tuxedo Black) Tsukineko *Chalk ink:* (Warm Red) Clearsnap *Color medium:* (assorted markers) Copic *Accents:* (pink rhinestones, red button) A Muse Studio *Fibers:* (pink/white twine) Martha Stewart Crafts *Template:* (embossing polka dots) A Muse Studio *Die:* (label) A Muse Studio *Tool:* (border punch) Martha Stewart Crafts

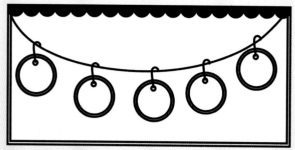

Sketch by: Rebecca Oehlers

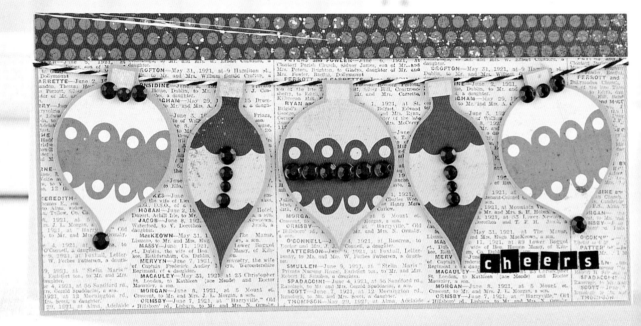

5 STEPS · Cheerful Ornaments

Designer: Teri Anderson

1. Make card from cardstock; cover with cardstock.

2. Cut patterned paper panel; adhere. Adhere patterned paper strip.

3. Adhere twine.

4. Trim ornaments from patterned paper, adhere rhinestones, and adhere with foam tape.

5. Spell "Cheers" with stickers.

Finished size: 8½" x 4"

SUPPLIES: *Cardstock:* (pink) Bazzill Basics Paper; (white) Georgia-Pacific *Patterned paper:* (Newsprint from For the Record collection; Bright Stripe, Ornaments from Everybody Loves Christmas collection) Echo Park Paper *Accents:* (red rhinestones) Kaisercraft *Stickers:* (Tiny Type alphabet) Cosmo Cricket *Fibers:* (red/white twine) The Twinery

DESIGNER TIP

Trace the curve of a small plate as a guide for adhering the twine.

shine brightly

Birthday Stars

Designer: Angie Tieman

❶ Make card from cardstock. ❷ Cut patterned paper panel, adhere to chipboard, and adhere to card with foam tape. ❸ Tear fabric strip; tie on. ❹ Punch star stickers, string on linen thread and adhere to card. Tie ends of thread to safety pins; pin to fabric. ❺ Spell "Happy" on stars with stickers; adhere with foam tape. Spell "Birthday" with stickers.

Finished size: 6½" x 3¼"

Little Girl Clothesline

Designer: Becky Olsen

❶ Make card from cardstock; cover with patterned paper. ❷ Cut border from patterned paper and adhere with foam tape. ❸ Staple twine to card. Tie twine bows and adhere. ❹ Adhere chipboard dresses.

Finished size: 8" x 4"

Shine Brightly

Designer: Lea Lawson

❶ Make card from cardstock; round bottom corners. ❷ Adhere border. Adhere twine; tie twine bows and adhere. ❸ Stamp lanterns. Stamp shine brightly. ❹ Adhere rhinestones.

Finished size: 7" x 3¾"

SUPPLIES: *Cardstock:* (Early Espresso) Stampin' Up! *Patterned paper:* (ledger from Basics Kraft pad) BasicGrey *Accents:* (antique copper safety pins) Stampin' Up! *Stickers:* (stars, Star Banner alphabet) Jenni Bowlin Studio; (Toil & Trouble alphabet) The Girls' Paperie *Fibers:* (linen thread) Stampin' Up! *Tool:* (1/16" circle punch) Fiskars *Other:* (cream linen fabric, chipboard)

SUPPLIES: *Cardstock:* (white) Bazzill Basics Paper *Patterned paper:* (Dainty Sketch from Sweetly Smitten collection) Sassafras Lass *Accents:* (chipboard dresses) American Crafts; (silver mini staples) Tim Holtz *Fibers:* (brown twine)

SUPPLIES: *Cardstock:* (white) Papertrey Ink *Clear stamps:* (lanterns, shine brightly from Lunar Lights set) Lawn Fawn *Pigment ink:* (Scarlet, Orange, Canary, Lime, Turquoise, Heliotrope, Violet, Black) Clearsnap *Accents:* (red scalloped border, assorted rhinestones) Doodlebug Design *Fibers:* (natural twine) Darice *Tool:* (corner rounder punch)

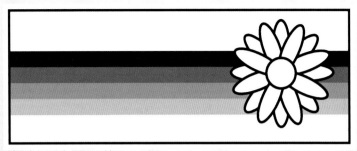

Sketch by: Rebecca Oehlers

⟨5 STEPS⟩ Gradient Blues

Designer: Julia Stainton

❶ Make card from cardstock.

❷ Trim cardstock strips; adhere.

❸ Affix flowers and leaves. Adhere button.

Finished size: 8" x 4"

SUPPLIES: *Cardstock:* (Starmist, Jacaranda, Typhoon, Whirlpool, kraft) Bazzill Basics Paper *Accent:* (blue button) BasicGrey *Stickers:* (chipboard flowers, leaves) Sassafras Lass

Happy Hello

Designer: Marisa Gunn

❶ Make card from cardstock. ❷ Affix tape strips. ❸ Die-cut flower from cardstock; stamp polka dots and ink edges. ❹ Layer flowers and button; stitch with crochet thread. ❺ Die-cut tag from cardstock. Stamp sentiment; adhere with foam tape. Adhere layered flower with foam tape.

Finished size: 8½" x 3¾"

Mermaid Wish

Designer: Beth Opel

❶ Make card from cardstock. ❷ Adhere ribbon. ❸ Apply sentiment rub-on. ❹ Cut mermaid pieces, following patterns at on p. 284. Assemble. ❺ Draw face, adhere pearls, and adhere specialty paper pieces to mermaid and card. ❻ Adhere mermaid to card with foam tape. Affix heart sticker.

Finished size: 7" x 4"

Wishing You a Rainbow

Designer: Mary Dawn Quirindongo

❶ Make card from cardstock. ❷ Tie on twine. ❸ Die-cut rectangle and scalloped rectangle from cardstock. Stamp sentiment on rectangle, mat with scalloped rectangle, and adhere with foam tape. ❹ Thread buttons with twine and adhere.

Finished size: 6¼" x 3¼"

SUPPLIES: *Cardstock:* (white) Neenah Paper; (Summer Sun) Stampin' Up! *Clear stamps:* (sentiment from Everyday Classics set; polka dots from Polka Dot Basics set) Papertrey Ink *Dye ink:* (Tuxedo Black) Tsukineko; (Real Red) Stampin' Up! *Accents:* (red flower button) Creative Café; (yellow foam flower) American Crafts *Stickers:* (red dotted, red pattern, pink floral, yellow dotted tape) Cu-te-Ta-pe *Fibers:* (white crochet thread) *Dies:* (flower, tag) Stampin' Up!

SUPPLIES: *Cardstock:* (white) American Crafts; (orange) Bazzill Basics Paper *Patterned paper:* (Souvenir from Documentary collection) Studio Calico; (Sunflower Dot from Double Dot collection) Bo-Bunny Press *Specialty paper:* (Twirl Hazard die cut from Bloom collection) KI Memories *Color medium:* (black pen) Sakura *Accents:* (white pearls) Mark Richards *Rub-on:* (sentiment) American Crafts *Sticker:* (orange heart epoxy) Heidi Grace Designs *Fibers:* (green, teal scalloped ribbon) Fancy Pants Designs; (aqua, light blue scalloped ribbon) American Crafts

SUPPLIES: *Cardstock:* (Spring Rain, Pure Poppy, white) Papertrey Ink *Clear stamp:* (sentiment from Huge Hugs set) Hero Arts *Dye ink:* (black) Hero Arts *Accents:* (blue, red, white buttons) Papertrey Ink *Fibers:* (red/white, orange/white, yellow/white, green/white, blue/white twine) Divine Twine *Dies:* (rectangle, scalloped rectangle) Spellbinders

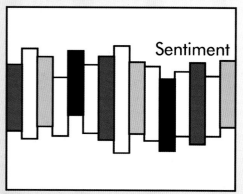

Sentiment

Sketch by: Chan Vuong

DESIGNER TIP

Stick to no more than two colors on a neutral background to make your patterned papers feel coordinated.

baby GIRL

5 STEPS Baby Girl

Designer: Cristina Kowalczyk

❶ Make card from cardstock.

❷ Cut patterned paper strips; adhere.

❸ Apply baby girl rub-on.

Finished size: 5½" x 4¼"

SUPPLIES: *Cardstock:* (white) Papertrey Ink *Patterned paper:* (Betty Bird, Chloe Crowns, Madison Plaid from Little Girl collection) Echo Park Paper; (Ice Cream from Fly a Kite collection) October Afternoon; (Off to Work from Tool Time collection) Three Bugs in a Rug *Rub-on:* (baby girl) American Crafts

DESIGNER TIP

Roll your paper pieces around a wood skewer for nice, even rolls.

⑤ Candle Wish

Designer: Beth Matson

❶ Make card from cardstock. ❷ Trim patterned paper panel, ink edges, and adhere. ❸ Cut patterned paper rectangles; roll. Insert floss strips into rolls to form candles. ❹ Apply sentiment rub-on. Adhere candles.

Finished size: 5½" x 4¼"

⑤ Rainbow Hello

Designer: Cheiron Brandon

❶ Stamp hello on card. ❷ Affix tape strips.

Finished size: 5½" x 4¼"

⑤ Celebrate with Style

Designer: Karolyn Loncon

❶ Make card from cardstock; round bottom corners. ❷ Cut cardstock panel; round bottom corners. ❸ Stamp City Skyline on panel; emboss. Stamp sentiment; emboss. ❹ Punch circle from patterned paper; punch again to form moon. Adhere to panel. ❺ Tie on ribbon. Adhere panel with foam tape. Adhere rhinestones.

Finished size: 5½" x 4¼"

SUPPLIES: *Cardstock:* (kraft) Papertrey Ink *Patterned paper:* (Pattern Stripe from Great Escape collection) Making Memories *Dye ink:* (Vintage Photo) Ranger Industries *Rub-on:* (sentiment) Deja Views *Fibers:* (white waxed floss) Karen Foster Design

SUPPLIES: *Clear stamp:* (hello from Essential Messages set) Hero Arts *Pigment ink:* (Onyx Black) Tsukineko *Stickers:* (assorted tape) Happy Tape, Cu-te-Ta-pe *Other:* (ivory card) Hero Arts

SUPPLIES: *Cardstock:* (Black Licorice) French Paper; (gray) Bazzill Basics Paper *Patterned paper:* (yellow paisley from Isabelle collection) Anna Griffin *Rubber stamp:* (City Skyline) Stampabilities *Clear stamp:* (sentiment from Big & Bold Wishes set) Papertrey Ink *Watermark ink:* Tsukineko *Embossing powder:* (black, aqua) American Crafts *Accents:* (clear rhinestones) Stampin' Up! *Fibers:* (black ribbon) Papertrey Ink *Tools:* (corner rounder punch) We R Memory Keepers; (circle punch) EK Success

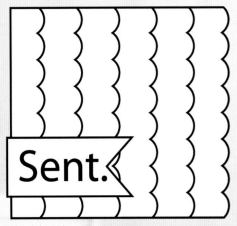

Sketch by: Chan Vuong

⁵Steps Mother's Day Scallops

Designer: Latisha Yoast

❶ Make card from cardstock. Cover with patterned paper and punch right edge.

❷ Cut patterned paper strips, punch right edges, and adhere to card.

❸ Tie on ribbon. Adhere rhinestone.

❹ Die-cut and emboss pennant from cardstock. Stamp sentiment, adhere rhinestones, and adhere to card with foam tape.

Finished size: 4¾" x 4½"

SUPPLIES: *Cardstock:* (white) Papertrey Ink *Patterned paper:* (Blowing Kisses from Sweet Fairy collection; Spring Tide from Madeline collection) Prima *Clear stamp:* (sentiment from Pond Life set) Papertrey Ink *Dye ink:* (Tuxedo Black) Tsukineko *Accents:* (white, pink rhinestones) Teresa Collins Designs *Fibers:* (pink ribbon) Papertrey Ink *Die:* (pennant) Spellbinders *Tool:* (embossing border punch)

DESIGNER TIP

Don't forget when die-cutting your scallop borders to alternate where the scallops are placed so they will be offset on the card.

5 STEPS Elegant Sunshine

Designer: Nerina Hoffe

❶ Make card from cardstock. ❷ Cut cardstock strips; die-cut scallop border from bottom edges. ❸ Emboss strips and adhere to card. ❹ Die-cut label from cardstock. Stamp label and sentiment, punch top, and tie on twine. Adhere. ❺ Tie on ribbon and adhere brad. Adhere pearls.

Finished size: 4¼" x 5½"

SUPPLIES: *Cardstock:* (Vintage Cream, Lemon Tart, Vintage Gold, Summer Sunrise) Papertrey Ink *Clear stamps:* (label from Holiday Labels No. 14 set; sentiment from Compliments of the Season set) Waltzingmouse Stamps *Specialty ink:* (True Black, Summer Sunrise hybrid) Papertrey Ink *Accents:* (cream pearls) Kaisercraft; (decorative metal brad) Stampin' Up! *Fibers:* (cream ribbon) Michaels; (cream twine) Papertrey Ink *Templates:* (embossing Swiss Dots) Provo Craft; (embossing Square Lattice) Sizzix; (embossing Retro Diamonds) QuicKutz; (debossing Sunshine) Papertrey Ink *Dies:* (label) Spellbinders; (scallop border) Papertrey Ink *Tool:* (1/8" circle punch) McGill

5 STEPS Gradient Boo

Designer: Nicky Hsu

❶ Make card from cardstock. ❷ Cut cardstock pieces, die-cut rickrack border from right edges, and adhere to card. ❸ Stamp frame and boo! on cardstock; emboss. Fussy-cut and adhere with foam tape. ❹ Adhere pearls.

Finished size: 4¾" x 4"

SUPPLIES: *Cardstock:* (True Black, Pure Poppy, Orange Zest, Summer Sunrise) Papertrey Ink *Clear stamps:* (frame, boo! from Toil & Trouble set) Making Memories *Watermark ink:* Tsukineko *Embossing powder:* (Disco Black) Stampendous! *Accents:* (orange pearls) Michaels *Die:* (rickrack border) Papertrey Ink

5 STEPS Charming Hello

Designer: Windy Robinson

❶ Make card from cardstock. ❷ Cut patterned paper panels. Punch bottom edges and adhere to card. Distress edges. ❸ Cut tag from cardstock, stamp hello, and adhere. ❹ Tie on ribbon. Thread buttons with twine; adhere.

Finished size: 4¼" x 5½"

SUPPLIES: *Cardstock:* (Vintage Cream) Papertrey Ink *Patterned paper:* (Orange Rose Tonal, Pink Rose Tonal, Pink Stripe, Orange Scallop, Yellow Quatrefoil, Floral Pink from Carmen collection) Anna Griffin *Clear stamp:* (hello from Mega Mixed Messages set) Papertrey Ink *Dye ink:* (Walnut Stain) Ranger Industries *Accents:* (silver pearl buttons) Blumenthal Lansing *Fibers:* (orange ribbon) Michaels; (cream twine) Papertrey Ink *Tool:* (border punch) Stampin' Up!

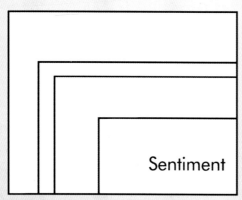

Sentiment

Sketch by: Jessica Witty

DESIGNER TIP

The simplicity and graphic nature of this sketch is fitting for masculine cards.

⑤ Give Thanks

Designer: Lindsay Amrhein

❶ Make card from cardstock.

❷ Cut cardstock and patterned paper pieces, layer, and adhere to card.

❸ Cut cardstock panel. Stamp frame; emboss. Stamp give thanks and acorns.

❹ Tie on twine. Adhere panel with foam tape.

Finished size: 5½" x 4¼"

SUPPLIES: *Cardstock:* (Terracotta Tile, Ripe Avocado, kraft) Papertrey Ink *Patterned paper:* (Maple from Nutmeg collection) Cosmo Cricket *Clear stamps:* (give thanks from Fillable Frames #7 set; frame from Fillable Frames #11 set; acorn from Gobble Gobble set) Papertrey Ink *Watermark ink:* Tsukineko *Chalk ink:* (Chestnut Roan) Clearsnap *Specialty ink:* (Ripe Avocado hybrid) Papertrey Ink *Embossing powder:* (white) Hampton Art *Fibers:* (natural twine) Westrim Crafts

5 STEPS — Bold Hello

Designer: Agnieszka Malyszek

❶ Make card from cardstock; round opposite corners. ❷ Cut two cardstock panels. Round opposite corners and adhere each with foam tape. ❸ Cut cardstock rectangle, round opposite corners, and stamp hello. Adhere ribbon loop and adhere to card with foam tape.

Finished size: 5½" x 4½"

5 STEPS — Daring Adventure

Designer: Anita Hovey

❶ Make card from cardstock. ❷ Cut patterned paper panel and rectangles. Layer rectangles on panel and zigzag-stitch edges. Adhere panel to card. ❸ Stamp Life is Either a Daring Adventure. ❹ Thread some button stickers with string; affix buttons to card.

Finished size: 5½" x 4¼"

5 STEPS — Lacey Easter

Designer: Laurel Seabrook

❶ Make card from cardstock; cover with cardstock. ❷ Cut cardstock strips; border-punch. Cut patterned paper rectangles; layer. Adhere punched strips and zigzag-stitch edges. ❸ Adhere twill to panel. Loop twill, tie on button with cord, and adhere. ❹ Spell "Easter" with stickers. Adhere panel to card. ❺ Adhere buttons.

Finished size: 5½" x 4¼"

SUPPLIES: *Cardstock:* (green) Bazzill Basics Paper; (Raspberry Fizz, Hawaiian Shores, Lemon Tart) Papertrey Ink *Clear stamp:* (hello from Pop Flowers set) My Cute Stamps *Dye ink:* (blue) Studio G *Fibers:* (blue stitched ribbon) Papertrey Ink *Tool:* (corner rounder punch) Fiskars

SUPPLIES: *Cardstock:* (Baja Breeze) Stampin' Up! *Patterned paper:* (Graph, green geometric, yellow lined from Wild Saffron collection) K&Company *Rubber stamp:* (Life is Either a Daring Adventure) Paper Makeup Stamps *Dye ink:* (Early Espresso) Stampin' Up! *Stickers:* (chipboard buttons) K&Company *Fibers:* (white string)

SUPPLIES: *Cardstock:* (White Daisy) Close To My Heart; (kraft) Papertrey Ink *Patterned paper:* (Good Junk, Collector's Item, Needs Paint, One-of-a-Kind from The Thrift Shop collection) October Afternoon *Accents:* (aqua buttons) Papertrey Ink *Stickers:* (Mini Market alphabet) October Afternoon *Fibers:* (aqua twill) Papertrey Ink; (white waxed cord) *Tool:* (border punch) Martha Stewart Crafts

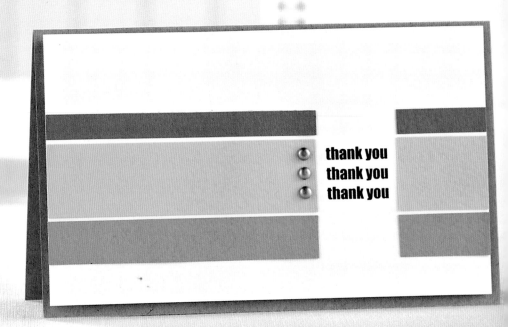

Sketch by: Jessica Witty

Sentiment
Sentiment
Sentiment

thank you
thank you
thank you

🖐5 steps Triple Thank You

Designer: Kim Kesti

❶ Make card from cardstock.

❷ Print sentiment on cardstock; trim.

❸ Adhere cardstock strips and attach brads.

❹ Adhere panel to card with foam tape.

Finished size: 6½" x 4"

SUPPLIES: *Cardstock:* (McIntosh, KI Olive, Stone, white, kraft) Bazzill Basics Paper *Accents:* (silver brads) Making Memories *Font:* (Impact) www.fonts.com

5 STEPS We are All Capable

Designer: Kelley Eubanks

❶ Make card from cardstock. ❷ Adhere butterfly strips. Adhere sentiment card with foam tape. ❸ Adhere rhinestone.

Finished size: 4¼" x 5½"

5 STEPS Father Dad Daddy

Designer: Teri Anderson

❶ Make card from cardstock. ❷ Cut patterned paper to fit card front; adhere patterned paper strip and rectangle. ❸ Stamp father, dad, and daddy. ❹ Die-cut buttons from chipboard; adhere. ❺ Tie on twine and attach brads. Adhere panel to card.

Finished size: 5½" x 4¼"

5 STEPS Navy Flourish

Designer: Cassandra Jones

❶ Make card from cardstock. ❷ Cut cardstock panel; stitch long edges and adhere. ❸ Cut cardstock to fit behind frame, stamp sentiment, and adhere. Tie on ribbon and adhere to card. ❹ Adhere rhinestones.

Finished size: 6¾" x 4¼"

SUPPLIES: *Cardstock:* (white) Papertrey Ink *Accents:* (orange rhinestone) Doodlebug Design; (green sentiment card, butterfly strips) Reminisce

SUPPLIES: *Cardstock:* (white) Georgia-Pacific *Patterned paper:* (Happy Camper, Roughin' It from The Great Outdoors collection) GCD Studios *Clear stamps:* (father, dad, daddy from Dad Rocks set) Technique Tuesday *Dye ink:* (blue) Close To My Heart *Accents:* (screw-head pewter brads) Eyelet Outlet *Fibers:* (natural twine) DCC *Dies:* (butttons) Papertrey Ink *Other:* (white chipboard) Papertrey Ink

SUPPLIES: *Cardstock:* (Night of Navy, Whisper White) Stampin' Up! *Clear stamp:* (sentiment from Inside & Out: Birthday set) Papertrey Ink *Dye ink:* (Night of Navy) Stampin' Up! *Accents:* (wood frame, navy rhinestones) Kaisercraft *Fibers:* (navy ribbon)

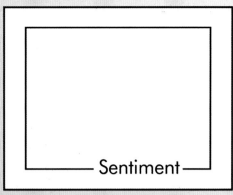

Sentiment

Sketch by: Jessica Witty

DESIGNER TIP

This simple sketch makes for quick and easy cards.

5 STEPS Little Puppy

Designer: Lucy Abrams

1. Make card from cardstock.

2. Create 5¼" x 4¼" project in software. Drop in patterned paper.

3. Drop in sentiment and draw lines. Print on cardstock, trim, and adhere to card.

4. Create 1½" x 1½" project in software, drop in dog, and print on cardstock. Fussy-cut.

5. Tie ribbon bow, adhere to dog, and adhere dog to card with foam tape.

Finished size: 5½" x 4½"

SUPPLIES: *Cardstock:* (kraft) Bazzill Basics Paper; (white) *Digital elements:* (blue polka dot paper from Solid Funky Polkadots kit) www.jessicasprague.com; (dog from HA More Wag kit) www.twopeasinabucket.com; (sentiment from Tiny {New Baby} Sentiments kit) www.pinkpetticoat.co.uk *Fibers:* (blue ribbon) May Arts *Software:* (photo editing)

DESIGNER TIP

Double-stick tape is a wonderful tool for creating frames and other designs with glitter.

DESIGNER TIP

Layering rub-ons to create a larger scene or panel is an easy way to make a big visual impact.

5 STEPS Floral Ever After

Designer: Jessica Witty

❶ Make card from cardstock. ❷ Cut cardstock panel. Apply rub-ons. ❸ Adhere glitter to panel edges. Adhere panel to card with foam tape. ❹ Stamp sentiment on cardstock strip; adhere with foam tape.

Finished size: 5½" x 4¼"

5 STEPS Life is Too Short

Designer: AJ Otto

❶ Make card from cardstock; cover with patterned paper. ❷ Cut cardstock panel. Stamp Matching Socks. Stamp again on patterned paper, cut out socks, and adhere to panel. ❸ Draw border. ❹ Adhere panel to card. Adhere rhinestones.

Finished size: 5½" x 4¼"

5 STEPS Welcome Home

Designer: Jamie Greene

❶ Make card from cardstock. ❷ Cut cardstock rectangle; emboss. ❸ Adhere glitter to card to create frame. Stamp welcome home. ❹ Adhere embossed rectangle with foam tape.

Finished size: 4¼" x 5½"

SUPPLIES: *Cardstock:* (kraft, white) Papertrey Ink *Clear stamp:* (sentiment from Love Lives Here set) Papertrey Ink *Specialty ink:* (Dark Chocolate hybrid) Papertrey Ink *Accent:* (gold glitter) Martha Stewart Crafts *Rub-ons:* (flowers, leaves, butterfly) American Crafts

SUPPLIES: *Cardstock:* (white) Neenah Paper *Patterned paper:* (Connect the Dots, Follow Me from Mr. Boy collection) Bella Blvd *Rubber stamp:* (Matching Socks) Unity Stamp Co. *Dye ink:* (Tuxedo Black) Tsukineko *Color medium:* (black pen) Copic *Accents:* (green rhinestones) Kaisercraft

SUPPLIES: *Cardstock:* (Enchanted Evening, white) Papertrey Ink *Clear stamp:* (welcome home from Boards & Beams set) Papertrey Ink *Specialty ink:* (True Black hybrid) Papertrey Ink *Accent:* (garnet glitter) Martha Stewart Crafts *Template:* (embossing stars) Provo Craft

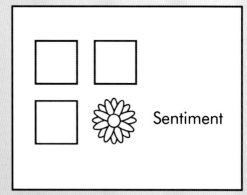

Sketch by: Kim Hughes

Sentiment

⟨5 STEPS⟩ Always on My Mind

Designer: Christina MacLaren

❶ Make card from cardstock; round one corner.

❷ Stamp postage stamps. Stamp leaves and sentiment.

❸ Die-cut scalloped circle from felt. Cut in spiral to center of circle; roll to form flower and adhere.

❹ Adhere flower to card. Adhere pearl.

Finished size: 5½" x 4¼"

SUPPLIES: *Cardstock:* (Fine Linen) Papertrey Ink *Rubber stamps:* (leaves from Baby Blossoms set) Stampin' Up! *Clear stamps:* (postage stamp from Spring Post set) Wplus9 Design Studio; (sentiment from Year of Flowers: Mums set) Papertrey Ink *Specialty ink:* (Dark Chocolate, Ripe Avocado hybrid) Papertrey Ink *Accent:* (white pearl) Queen & Co. *Die:* (scalloped circle) Spellbinders *Tool:* (corner rounder punch) We R Memory Keepers *Other:* (peach felt) Papertrey Ink

DESIGNER TIP

This French sentiments stamp set is also available in English, called "Something to Celebrate". Bonne fete means happy birthday.

Circus Ambition

Designer: Beverly Sizemore

❶ Make card from cardstock. ❷ Cut cardstock panel, mat with cardstock, and adhere. ❸ Apply sentiment rub-on. ❹ Adhere cardstock rectangle. Trim stamps from patterned paper; adhere. ❺ Attach brad to flower; adhere.

Finished size: 6½" x 5"

Look Who's New

Designer: Vanessa Menhorn

❶ Make card from cardstock. ❷ Die-cut three postage stamps from cardstock. Stamp bears, color, and adhere to card. ❸ Stamp bear on cardstock, color, fussy-cut, and adhere with foam tape. ❹ Tie ribbon bow; adhere. Thread buttons with floss and adhere. ❺ Stamp sentiment.

Finished size: 5½" x 4¼"

Queen for a Day

Designer: Cindy Major

❶ Make card from cardstock. ❷ Cut cardstock panel. Stamp background repeatedly. ❸ Punch scalloped squares from patterned paper, ink edges, and adhere to panel. ❹ Stamp background on cardstock, ink, and trim to fit behind acrylic tile. Adhere to card. ❺ Stamp bonne fete; emboss. ❻ Thread ribbon through acrylic tile and tie around panel. Adhere panel to card. ❼ Stamp crown on cardstock; emboss. Cut out and adhere.

Finished size: 5½" x 4¼"

SUPPLIES: *Cardstock:* (Glow) Bazzill Basics Paper; (yellow glitter) DCWV Inc.; (black) The Paper Studio *Patterned paper:* (Wizards of Wonders from Le Cirque collection) Graphic 45 *Accents:* (patterned flower) Prima; (jumbo yellow rhinestone brad) Michaels *Rub-on:* (quote) Royal & Langnickel

SUPPLIES: *Cardstock:* (Vintage Cream, kraft) Papertrey Ink *Clear stamps:* (bear, sentiment from Baby Button Bits set) Papertrey Ink *Dye ink:* (Tuxedo Black) Tsukineko *Color medium:* (turquoise marker) Copic *Accents:* (turquoise buttons) Papertrey Ink *Fibers:* (turquoise ribbon, white floss) *Die:* (postage stamp) Provo Craft

SUPPLIES: All supplies from Stampin' Up! unless otherwise noted. *Cardstock:* (Early Espresso, Pear Pizzazz, Whisper White) *Patterned paper:* (green floral, blue damask, yellow damask from Greenhouse Gala collection) Stampin' Up! *Rubber stamps:* (floral background from Clearly for You set; crown, bonne fete from Quelque Chose à Fêter set) *Dye ink:* (Pear Pizzazz, Baja Breeze, Crumb Cake) *Watermark ink:* Tsukineko *Embossing powder:* (gold) *Accent:* (beveled acrylic tile) *Fibers:* (blue seam binding) *Tool:* (scalloped square punch)

Sentiment

Sketch by: Kim Hughes

5 STEPS : Lovely Mother's Day

Designer: Lesley Langdon

❶ Make card from cardstock; cover with patterned paper.

❷ Cut cardstock panel. Cut cardstock and patterned paper squares; trim bottom edge in wave. Trim strip from bottom of patterned paper piece. Adhere patterned paper piece and strip to cardstock and adhere to panel.

❸ Affix border sticker. Stamp sentiment on cardstock; round corners, ink edges, and adhere.

❹ Adhere panel to card; zigzag-stitch edges.

❺ Tie twine bow; adhere. Adhere chipboard flower and pearl.

Finished size: 6" x 4¾"

SUPPLIES: *Cardstock:* (gray) Bazzill Basics Paper; (white) Staples; (kraft) *Patterned paper:* (Slipcover from Restoration collection) Crate Paper *Rubber stamp:* (sentiment from A Mother's Love set) Unity Stamp Co. *Dye ink:* (black) Stewart Superior Corp.; (gray) *Accents:* (chipboard flower) Crate Paper; (green pearl) *Stickers:* (yellow swirl border) Crate Paper *Fibers:* (yellow twine) *Other:* (corner rounder punch) Marvy Uchida

DESIGNER TIP

See everyday objects in sketches such as this vase.

Take Care

Designer: Andrea Amu

❶ Make card from cardstock. ❷ Cut patterned paper piece, adhere, and stitch. Zigzag-stitch card edges. ❸ Cut patterned paper strip and adhere. ❹ Stamp sentiment on cardstock, ink edges, and adhere. ❺ Adhere flower and text circle.

Finished size: 5½" x 4¼"

Denim Hey

Designer: Charlene Austin

❶ Make card from cardstock; ink edges. ❷ Trim denim, stitch edges, and adhere. ❸ Cut patterned paper strip; adhere. Spell "Hey" with stickers. ❹ Die-cut flowers from felt; adhere. Thread buttons with string and adhere.

Finished size: 5½" x 4¼"

A Moment in Time

Designer: Maria Gurnsey

❶ Make card from cardstock; cover with patterned paper. ❷ Cut cardstock panel. Stamp sentiment. ❸ Cut cardstock strip; adhere. ❹ Cut vellum, curving one side, and adhere to panel. Stitch panel edges. ❺ Stamp flower three times on patterned paper, cut out, and adhere to panel, using foam tape for smaller layers. ❻ Adhere ribbon around panel. Tie ribbon bow and adhere. Adhere panel to card. ❼ Thread button with twine and adhere. Adhere remaining buttons.

Finished size: 4¼" x 6¼"

SUPPLIES: *Cardstock:* (Alabaster Columns White) Couture Cardstock *Patterned paper:* (Free Composition, Fancy Free from Mix & Mend pad) Sassafras Lass *Clear stamp:* (sentiment from Autumn Abundance set) Papertrey Ink *Dye ink:* (Latte) Ranger Industries *Accents:* (green embellished flower, chipboard text circle) Sassafras Lass

SUPPLIES: *Cardstock:* (kraft) Papertrey Ink *Patterned paper:* (blue floral from Springtime Vintage collection) Stampin' Up! *Dye ink:* (Walnut Stain) Ranger Industries *Accents:* (brown buttons) *Stickers:* (Sprinkles alphabet) American Crafts *Fibers:* (white string) Wrights *Dies:* (flowers) Stampin' Up! *Other:* (green felt) Papertrey Ink; (white felt) Michaels; (blue denim)

SUPPLIES: *Cardstock:* (kraft) The Paper Studio; (Simply Chartreuse) Papertrey Ink *Patterned paper:* (Party Line, Cherry Pie, Snickerdoodles from Modern Homemaker collection) October Afternoon *Vellum:* Stampin' Up! *Rubber stamp:* (sentiment from A Moment in Time set; flower from Now & Always set) Ippity by Unity Stamp Co. *Dye ink:* (Tuxedo Black) Tsukineko *Accents:* (green, tan, cream buttons) *Fibers:* (black gingham ribbon, red/white twine) Papertrey Ink

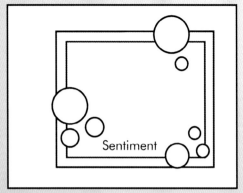

Sentiment

Sketch by: Kim Hughes

Bits & Pieces Hi

Designer: Julia Stainton

❶ Make card from cardstock.

❷ Cut cardstock panel, mat with cardstock, staple, and adhere to card.

❸ Thread one button with twine. Adhere buttons, flower, and flower center. Attach brad.

❹ Spell "Hi" with stickers.

Finished size: 5½" x 4¼"

SUPPLIES: *Cardstock:* (Pomegranate, white) Bazzill Basics Paper; (kraft corrugated) Creative Imaginations *Accents:* (orange buttons) Jenni Bowlin Studio; (red, small orange buttons) BasicGrey; (pink corduroy brad) Zva Creative; (red sequin flower center) Prima; (silver mini staples) Tim Holtz; (pink ribbon flower) *Stickers:* (Bliss alphabet) American Crafts *Fibers:* (natural twine) Westrim Crafts

DESIGNER TIP

Challenge yourself with layered pre-made embellishments. Take them apart and use elements separately, or combine in new ways for a unique look!

Circle Congrats

Designer: Michelle Woerner

❶ Make card from cardstock. ❷ Die-cut rectangle frame from patterned paper; adhere with foam tape. Stamp sentiment. ❸ Die-cut and punch circles from patterned paper; adhere, using foam tape as desired. ❹ Adhere pearls.

Finished size: 5½" x 4¼"

4U

Designer: Teri Anderson

❶ Make card from cardstock; cover with patterned paper. ❷ Trim patterned paper panel, mat with cardstock, and adhere. ❸ Thread buttons with floss. Adhere buttons and circles. ❹ Spell "4u" with stickers.

Finished size: 5½" x 4¼"

Eclectic Adore You

Designer: Melissa Elsner

❶ Make card from cardstock. ❷ Cut patterned paper; adhere. Draw border. ❸ Attach brad. Adhere floral brads with foam tape. ❹ Remove sentiment from sticker; adhere.

Finished size: 5½" x 4¼"

SUPPLIES: *Cardstock:* (white) Gina K Designs *Patterned paper:* (Buddies Argyle, Family Pinstripe, Happy Bouquet, Boy Woven Stripe from Stella & Rose collection) My Mind's Eye *Rubber stamp:* (congratulations! from Tag Lines set) Gina K Designs *Dye ink:* (Tuxedo Black) Tsukineko *Accents:* (silver pearls) Michaels *Dies:* (circles, rectangles) Spellbinders *Tools:* (circle punches) EK Success

SUPPLIES: *Cardstock:* (white) Georgia-Pacific *Patterned paper:* (Adventurer from The Great Outdoors pad; Lovely Garden from Soul Food pad) GCD Studios *Accents:* (yellow buttons) Doodlebug Design; (orange, red chipboard buttons, circles) My Mind's Eye *Stickers:* (Fancy alphabet) American Crafts *Fibers:* (white floss) DMC

SUPPLIES: *Cardstock:* (kraft) Michaels *Patterned paper:* (Favorite Union Station from Lost & Found collection) My Mind's Eye *Color medium:* (black pen) American Crafts *Accents:* (floral epoxy, pearl brads; black epoxy brad) My Mind's Eye *Sticker:* (sentiment) My Mind's Eye

Sketch by: Teri Anderson

5 STEPS Lantern Birthday Card

Designer: Teri Anderson

❶ Cut patterned paper block to finished size.

❷ Punch edge of patterned paper piece; adhere to block on three edges to form pocket. Adhere patterned paper.

❸ Stamp sentiments on cardstock; trim and adhere.

❹ Adhere rhinestones and lanterns.

❺ Cut cardstock to fit in pocket. Punch hole, tie on ribbon, and insert in pocket.

Finished size: 4¾" x 4"

SUPPLIES: *Cardstock:* (Vintage Cream) Papertrey Ink; (white) WorldWin *Patterned paper:* (Spunky Spots from Shine collection; Perfect Plaid from Friends Forever collection; Tweet Tweet from Best Friends collection) My Mind's Eye *Clear stamps:* (sentiments from Birthday Basics set) Papertrey Ink *Dye ink:* (Tuxedo Black) Tsukineko; (Blush) Close To My Heart *Accents:* (clear rhinestones) Imaginisce; (pink, blue chipboard lanterns) My Mind's Eye *Fibers:* (pink polka dot ribbon) Papertrey Ink *Tool:* (1½" circle punch) Fiskars

Monster Celebrate Card

Designer: Rae Barthel

SUPPLIES: *Cardstock:* (Dandelion) Core'dinations; (black) Hobby Lobby *Patterned paper:* (Super Stack, Take Note from Monstrosity collection) Sassafras Lass *Accents:* (blue monster tag) Sassafras Lass; (black, blue rhinestones) Kaisercraft *Stickers:* (stars, circles) Sassafras Lass *Fibers:* (black gingham ribbon) Hobby Lobby *Tool:* (1" circle punch) EK Success

Finished size: 6" x 4"

Cherry Wishes Card

Designer: Maile Belles

SUPPLIES: *Cardstock:* (Berry Sorbet, Spring Moss, Dark Chocolate, white) Papertrey Ink *Clear stamps:* (cherry stems, sentiment from Everyday Button Bits set; polka dots from Polka Dot Basics II set) Papertrey Ink *Specialty ink:* (Ripe Avocado, Dark Chocolate hybrid) Papertrey Ink *Accents:* (melon, cream buttons) Papertrey Ink; (white brads) Making Memories *Fibers:* (green ribbon) Papertrey Ink; (white floss) DMC *Tools:* (1¼", 2" circle punches) Marvy Uchida; (corner rounder punch) EK Success

Finished size: 5½" x 4¼"

Much Appreciated Card

Designer: Ashley Harris

SUPPLIES: *Cardstock:* (Parakeet, white) Bazzill Basics Paper *Patterned paper:* (Daydream Believer from Blue Skies collection) American Crafts; (Flamingo Dot from Double Dot collection) BoBunny Press *Rubber stamp:* (sentiment from Much Appreciated set) Stampin' Up! *Solvent ink:* (Jet Black) Tsukineko *Accents:* (blue, orange, pink rhinestones) Kaisercraft; (silver staple) Tim Holtz *Fibers:* (green polka dot ribbon) BoBunny Press *Tool:* (1¾" circle punch) Fiskars

Finished size: 6" x 4"

Sketch by: Teri Anderson

DESIGNER TIP

Try replacing the patterned paper with coordinating cardstock to achieve a gradient effect.

5 STEPS : Bug Me Card

Designer: Nina Brackett

❶ Make card from cardstock.

❷ Cut cardstock slightly smaller than card front. Cut triangles from piece with craft knife.

❸ Adhere patterned paper behind openings. Mat piece with cardstock and adhere with foam tape.

❹ Stamp sentiment on cardstock; circle-punch. Mat with circle punched from cardstock and adhere to card with foam tape.

❺ Cut bugs from patterned paper; adhere with foam tape.

Finished size: 5½" x 4¼"

SUPPLIES: *Cardstock:* (Certainly Celery, More Mustard) Stampin' Up!; (ivory) Gina K Designs *Patterned paper:* (Rethink, Reuse, Remember, blue floral, brown floral from Earth Love collection) Cosmo Cricket *Rubber stamp:* (sentiment from Bug Me Anytime set) Gina K Designs *Dye ink:* (Rich Cocoa) Tsukineko *Tools:* (1⅜", 1¼" circle punches) EK Success; (craft knife)

DESIGNER TIP

Before stitching with the embroidery floss, draw lines lightly in pencil then pierce holes and erase.

Hello Sunshine! Card

Designer: Maile Belles

SUPPLIES: *Cardstock:* (Summer Sunrise, white) Papertrey Ink *Clear stamps:* (solid circle, patterned circle, hello from Shapes by Design set) Papertrey Ink *Dye ink:* (Barely Banana) Stampin' Up! *Specialty ink:* (Summer Sunrise, True Black hybrid) Papertrey Ink *Accent:* (yellow button) Papertrey Ink *Fibers:* (orange, yellow floss) DMC *Tools:* (corner rounder punch) EK Success; 2", 1⅜" circle punches) Marvy Uchida

Finished size: 5" square

Color My World Card

Designer: Kim Kesti

SUPPLIES: *Cardstock:* (Lily White, Cutie, Beetle Black) Bazzill Basics Paper *Color medium:* (assorted markers) Sanford *Accents:* (assorted brads) BasicGrey *Stickers:* (Loopy Lou alphabet) Doodlebug Design *Tools:* (2¼", 2½" circle punches) EK Success

Finished size: 7" x 5"

It's a SUPER! Card

Designer: Jessica Witty

SUPPLIES: *Cardstock:* (white) Papertrey Ink *Patterned paper:* (Buttercup Dot, Poppy Dot from Double Dot collection) BoBunny Press *Clear stamp:* (super!, stars from Comic Talk set) Michaels *Dye ink:* (Black Soot) Ranger Industries

Finished size: 3" x 5½"

Sketch by: Maren Benedict

DESIGNER TIP

To make this easy wavy cut, use a handheld rotary cutter and a self-healing mat.

5 STEPS Dandelion Wish Card

Designer: Debbie Seyer

1. Make card from cardstock.

2. Adhere patterned paper.

3. Trim cardstock layers, adhere together, and tie on ribbon. Adhere.

4. Ink flower stamp with markers, stamp on cardstock, and stamp wish.

5. Die-cut stamped piece into label, attach brad, and adhere using foam tape.

Finished size: 5½" x 4¼"

SUPPLIES: *Cardstock:* (Melon Berry) Papertrey Ink; (Barely Banana, Certainly Celery, white) Stampin' Up! *Patterned paper:* (Remember from Earth Love collection) Cosmo Cricket *Rubber stamps:* (wish, flower from Go Ahead…Wish set) Unity Stamp Co. *Dye ink:* (Basic Gray) Stampin' Up! *Color medium:* (light green, peach markers) Stampin' Up! *Accent:* (silver brad) Stampin' Up! *Fibers:* (light green twill) Stampin' Up! *Die:* (label) Spellbinders

BONUS IDEA

Substitute feminine patterned paper and create a pleated ruffle with crepe paper to replace the red curve and you have a girlier version!

Day Brightener Card

Designer: Teri Anderson

SUPPLIES: *Cardstock:* (white) Georgia-Pacific *Patterned paper:* (Bewitching from Fascinating collection) Pink Paislee; (Bohemian Vines from Bloom collection; Lots of Dots from Grow collection) My Mind's Eye *Accents:* (green, clear rhinestones) Zva Creative *Stickers:* (bird, flower) American Crafts *Fibers:* (white floss) DMC *Font:* (CK Elsie) Creating Keepsakes *Tool:* (corner rounder punch) Creative Memories

Finished size: 4¼" x 5½"

Let It Rock Card

Designer: Beth Opel

SUPPLIES: *Cardstock:* (Autumn Red) WorldWin; (orange) Bazzill Basics Paper; (black) American Crafts *Patterned paper:* (Guitars from Basics collection) Glitz Design *Accents:* (black rhinestones) Glitz Design *Stickers:* (Bold alphabet) Close To My Heart; (Center of Attention alphabet) Heidi Swapp

Finished size: 7" x 5"

Enjoy the Ride Card

Designer: Gretchen Clark

SUPPLIES: *Cardstock:* (Berry Sorbet) Papertrey Ink; (Chocolate Chip, white) Stampin' Up! *Dye ink:* (Chocolate Chip) Stampin' Up! *Clear stamps:* (bicycle, sentiment from Everyday Button Bits set) Papertrey Ink *Accents:* (pink buttons) Papertrey Ink *Fibers:* (pink ribbon) Papertrey Ink; (twine) Stampin' Up! *Tool:* (border punch) EK Success

Finished size: 5½" x 4¼"

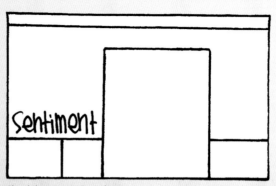

Sentiment

Sketch by: Maren Benedict

I Count You First Card

Designer: Wendy Sue Anderson

1. Make card from cardstock.

2. Adhere patterned papers along bottom.

3. Trim sentiment sticker, affix to patterned paper panel, punch, and tie on crochet thread.

4. Adhere panel; zigzag-stitch seam.

5. Adhere bird sticker using foam tape.

6. Adhere ribbon and tie on thread.

Finished size: 6" x 4¼"

SUPPLIES: *Cardstock:* (white) American Crafts *Patterned paper:* (Clove, Falling Down, Acorn, flower print from Nutmeg collection) Cosmo Cricket *Stickers:* (bird, sentiment) Cosmo Cricket *Fibers:* (tan crochet thread) DMC; (red scalloped ribbon) Cosmo Cricket *Tool:* (1/8" circle punch)

DESIGNER TIP

Choose buttons with slightly different colors and textures to add complexity.

2-Gether Always Card

Designer: Betsy Veldman

SUPPLIES: *Cardstock:* (Vintage Cream) Papertrey Ink *Patterned paper:* (Primrose, Pond from Wisteria collection) BasicGrey; (Umbrellas from Snorkel collection) Cosmo Cricket *Clear stamp:* (happy anniversary, always from Heart Prints set) Papertrey Ink *Specialty ink:* (Dark Chocolate, Spring Rain hybrid) Papertrey Ink *Accents:* (blue button) Papertrey Ink; (white chipboard heart) Scenic Route; (journaling card, border die cut) My Mind's Eye; (iridescent glitter) *Fibers:* (cream ribbon, natural twine) Papertrey Ink

Finished size: 5½" x 4½"

Deck the Halls with Buttons Card

Designer: Debbie Olson

SUPPLIES: *Cardstock:* (Vintage Cream, Pure Poppy) Papertrey Ink *Patterned paper:* (Merry Berry from Jolly by Golly collection) Cosmo Cricket *Clear stamps:* (ornaments, sentiment from Holiday Button Bits set) Papertrey Ink *Dye ink:* (Chamomile) Papertrey Ink *Watermark ink:* Tsukineko *Specialty ink:* (Pure Poppy hybrid) Papertrey Ink *Embossing powder:* (silver) Papertrey Ink *Accents:* (green, red buttons) Papertrey Ink *Fibers:* (green ribbon, white twine) Papertrey Ink *Dies:* (rectangle, scalloped border) Spellbinders

Finished size: 5½" x 4¼"

Gingerbread Card

Designer: Teri Anderson

SUPPLIES: *Cardstock:* (dark red, white) Bazzill Basics Paper *Patterned paper:* (Gingerbread House, Toffee, Pecan Pie from Merrymint collection) American Crafts *Clear stamps:* (sentiment, merry Christmas from Season's Greetings set) Technique Tuesday *Dye ink:* (Tuxedo Black) Tsukineko *Accents:* (antique copper brads) American Tag & Label

Finished size: 5½" x 3¼"

Sketch by: Maren Benedict

DESIGNER TIP

Create your own die cuts by trimming flowers and other design elements from patterned paper.

Sophisticated Get Well Card

Designer: Rae Barthel

1. Make card from patterned paper.

2. Adhere strips of patterned paper. Spell sentiment with stickers.

3. Trim strips of patterned paper; adhere.

4. Trim flower from patterned paper, adhere pearls, and adhere using foam tape.

Finished size: 6" x 4¼"

SUPPLIES: *Patterned paper:* (brown stripes, yellow stripes, blue tiles, yellow mosaic, red small flowers, brown large flower from Mi Casa collection) Die Cuts With a View *Accents:* (white pearls) Zva Creative *Stickers:* (Roosevelt Jr. alphabet) American Crafts

DESIGNER TIP

Cut a small slit at the top of your cards to feed ribbon through when adding ribbon around card folds.

BONUS IDEA

A "Present" card can be created for many different occasions. Make a "Birthday Present" card or a "Bundle of Joy" baby present. The sky's the limit on sentiments!

Friends Crossword Card

Designer: Maren Benedict

SUPPLIES: *Cardstock:* (Aqua Mist, True Black) Papertrey Ink *Patterned paper:* (Vacationer Motel from Road Map collection) October Afternoon *Color media:* (black marker) American Crafts; (silver glitter pen) Copic *Accents:* (black buttons) BasicGrey *Fibers:* (light blue twill) Papertrey Ink *Tool:* (arrow punch) Stampin' Up!

Finished size: 4¼" square

Cherry Thanks Card

Designer: Kim Kesti

SUPPLIES: *Cardstock:* (Vanilla, Ladybug, Java, Lemon Bliss) Bazzill Basics Paper *Patterned paper:* (Tea Towel, Recipe Box from Cherry Hill collection) October Afternoon *Accent:* (brown brad) BasicGrey *Rub-on:* (white stitches) Hambly Screen Prints *Stickers:* (Cherry Hill alphabet) October Afternoon *Other:* (green felt) Michaels

Finished size: 6" x 5"

Christmas Present Card

Designer: Charlene Austin

SUPPLIES: *Cardstock:* (Aqua Mist, Vintage Cream) Papertrey Ink *Patterned paper:* (Merry Berry from Jolly by Golly collection) Cosmo Cricket *Dye ink:* (Walnut Stain) Ranger Industries *Accent:* (red rhinestone) Queen & Co. *Fibers:* (cream ribbon) Papertrey Ink *Font:* (Book Antiqua) Microsoft *Tool:* (corner rounder punch) Stampin' Up!

Finished size: 5½" x 4¼"

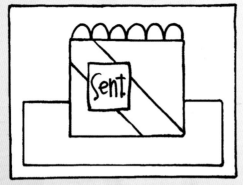

Sketch by: Maren Benedict

DESIGNER TIP

A fabulous way to add a bit of punch to an elegant card is to include vibrant ribbon.

5 STEPS Beautiful Together Card

Designer: Maren Benedict

1 Make card from cardstock. Adhere cardstock.

2 Adhere patterned paper strip.

3 Cut cardstock piece and mat with cardstock. Punch patterned paper strip; adhere to matted piece.

4 Adhere strip of patterned paper. Adhere piece using foam tape.

5 Stamp sentiment on cardstock, attach pin, and adhere using foam tape. Tie on ribbon.

Finished size: 5½" x 4¼"

SUPPLIES: *Cardstock:* (Smokey Shadow) Papertrey Ink; (Glossy White, Whisper White) Stampin' Up! *Patterned paper:* (Black Ink on Onyx Metallic from Old Lace collection) Hambly Screen Prints *Clear stamps:* (beautiful from Beautiful You set; together from Anniversary Birds set) Verve Stamps *Dye ink:* (Black Soot) Ranger Industries *Accent:* (white pearl heart pin) Making Memories *Fibers:* (magenta ribbon) BasicGrey *Tool:* (border punch) Martha Stewart Crafts

Chair-ish You Card
Designer: Gretchen Clark

SUPPLIES: *Cardstock:* (Lemon Tart, New Leaf) Papertrey Ink; (Chocolate Chip, white) Stampin' Up! *Rubber stamp:* (Polka Dot) Stampin' Up! *Clear stamps:* (chair, chair outline, pillow, sentiment from On My Couch set) Papertrey Ink *Dye ink:* (Chocolate Chip) Stampin' Up! *Pigment ink:* (Fresh Snow) Papertrey Ink *Specialty ink:* (Lemon Tart, Berry Sorbet hybrid) Papertrey Ink *Accent:* (green button) Papertrey Ink *Fibers:* (brown polka dot ribbon) Papertrey Ink; (twine) Stampin' Up! *Tool:* (border punch) Stampin' Up!

Finished size: 5½" x 4¼"

Thanks Cupcake Card
Designer: Jessica Witty

SUPPLIES: *Cardstock:* (kraft) Papertrey Ink *Patterned paper:* (Yummy from Raspberry Truffle collection) Webster's Pages; (Addie Pattern Stripe, Delaney Die-Cut Stamp from Noteworthy collection) Making Memories *Clear stamps:* (thanks from Mega Mixed Messages set) Papertrey Ink *Dye ink:* (Chocolate Chip) Stampin' Up! *Accents:* (clear, pink glitter) Martha Stewart Crafts *Fibers:* (cream twine) Papertrey Ink *Template:* (Flourished Frame embossing) Provo Craft *Tools:* (tag punch) Martha Stewart Crafts; (5/8" circle punch) EK Success

Finished size: 5¼" x 4¼"

Greatest Gift Card
Designer: Beatriz Jennings

SUPPLIES: *Cardstock:* (red) *Patterned paper:* (Porch Swing from Old Fashioned Courtship collection; Log from August collection; Flower Bed from English Garden collection) Marks Paper *Dye ink:* (white) *Specialty ink:* (Iridescent Gold shimmer spray) Tattered Angels *Accents:* (flower, leaf die cuts) Marks Paper; (red silk flowers, flower centers, white pearls, cream button) *Sticker:* (sentiment) Melissa Frances *Fibers:* (brown ribbon, twine) *Tool:* (border punch) EK Success

Finished size: 4¾" x 5"

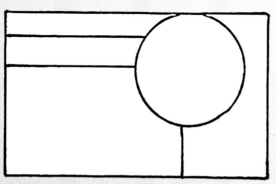

Sketch by: Maren Benedict

DESIGNER TIP

Thread a row of buttons onto a single piece of twine and attach with strong adhesive.

⁵ₛₜₑₚₛ Stylish Celebrate Card

Designer: Maile Belles

❶ Make card from cardstock. Round bottom right corner.

❷ Stamp polka dots on cardstock; adhere. Punch edge of cardstock strip; adhere.

❸ Adhere lace.

❹ Stamp damask and sentiment on cardstock, punch into circle, and adhere using foam tape.

❺ Thread buttons with twine; adhere.

Finished size: 5½" x 4¼"

SUPPLIES: *Cardstock:* (Scarlet Jewel, Dark Chocolate, white, kraft) Papertrey Ink *Clear stamps:* (damask, sentiment from Damask Designs set; polka dots from Polka Dot Basics II set) Papertrey Ink *Specialty ink:* (Dark Chocolate, Scarlet Jewel hybrid) Papertrey Ink *Fibers:* (white lace) Jo-Ann Stores; (cream twine) Michaels *Tools:* (corner rounder punch) EK Success; (2½" circle punch) Marvy Uchida; (border punch) Fiskars

DESIGNER TIP

Save your stamping masks for future use! Store them inside of stamp packaging so you don't have to redo all that intricate cutting.

DESIGNER TIP

Poke a hole for the brads with a push pin or paper piercer before inserting them into the card.

Autumn Celebrate Card

Designer: Tiffany Johnson

SUPPLIES: *Cardstock:* (Pumpkin Spice, white) Gina K Designs; (Scarlet Jewel) Papertrey Ink *Clear stamps:* (polka dots from Spot On Backgrounds set) Close To My Heart; (pumpkin, sentiment, wheat from Happy Harvest set) I Heart Papers *Dye ink:* (Vineyard Berry) Close To My Heart *Specialty ink:* (Dark Chocolate hybrid) Papertrey Ink *Color medium:* (assorted markers) Copic *Accent:* (brass brad) *Fibers:* (maroon ribbon) Papertrey Ink *Template:* (dotted line) Provo Craft *Die:* (circle) Spellbinders

Finished size: 4¼" x 5½"

Love Card

Designer: Maren Benedict

SUPPLIES: *Cardstock:* (cream) Anna Griffin; (pink) *Patterned paper:* (Leaves & Berries, Ivory Paisley, Paisley from Evelyn collection) Anna Griffin *Rubber stamps:* (heart from The Artist In You set; alphabet from Frame This Alpha set) Unity Stamp Co. *Dye ink:* (Black Soot) Ranger Industries *Fibers:* (pink ribbon) Papertrey Ink *Die:* (circle) Spellbinders

Finished size: 5½" x 4¼"

Hi Card

Designer: Teri Anderson

SUPPLIES: *Cardstock:* (blue) Bazzill Basic Paper; (white) WorldWin *Patterned paper:* (Scattered Flowers from Best Friends collection; Spunky Spots from Shine collection) My Mind's Eye *Accents:* (hi die cut) My Mind's Eye; (blue brad) Making Memories; (green brad) Bazzill Basics Paper; (pink brad) Colorbok *Fibers:* (white floss) DMC

Finished size: 5½" x 3½"

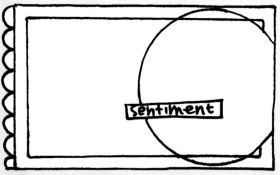

Sketch by: Kim Hughes

(5 STEPS) Warmed by Your Friendship Card

Designer: Julie Masse

1. Make card from cardstock.

2. Adhere ribbon lengths to form tabs along left edge.

3. Cut rectangle of patterned paper; mat with cardstock. Attach lace trim with brads; adhere piece.

4. Die-cut scalloped circle and circle from cardstock; ink circle edge, stamp tree, and mat with scalloped circle. Adhere.

5. Die-cut and emboss tag from cardstock; ink edges, stamp sentiment, attach brad, and adhere with foam tape.

Finished size: 6" x 3½"

SUPPLIES: *Cardstock:* (Dark Chocolate, Ripe Avocado, Vintage Cream) Papertrey Ink *Patterned paper:* (Sonoma Oak Lane) Scenic Route *Clear stamps:* (friendship sentiment, tree from Blessed By You set) Waltzingmouse Stamps *Dye ink:* (Chamomile, Chai) Papertrey Ink *Specialty ink:* (Ripe Avocado, Dark Chocolate hybrid) Papertrey Ink *Accents:* (antique brass brads) Pink Hedgehog *Fibers:* (green ribbon) Papertrey Ink; (vintage lace trim) *Dies:* (scalloped circle, circle, tag) Spellbinders

Vintage Christmas Ornament Card

Designer: Latisha Yoast

SUPPLIES: *Cardstock:* (ivory) Flourishes; (kraft) Papertrey Ink *Patterned paper:* (Merry Berry, reverse sheet music from Jolly by Golly pad) Cosmo Cricket *Clear stamps:* (pine boughs, ornaments from All That Glitters set; merry Christmas from Santa I Believe set) Flourishes *Dye ink:* (Tuxedo Black) Tsukineko *Specialty ink:* (Landscape hybrid) Stewart Superior Corp. *Die:* (circle) Spellbinders *Tool:* (border punch) Stampin' Up!

Finished size: 5¾" x 3½"

Butterfly Wish Card

Designer: Alicia Thelin

SUPPLIES: All supplies from Stampin' Up! unless otherwise noted. *Cardstock:* (white, kraft) *Rubber stamp:* (make a wish from A Little Birthday Cheer set) *Pigment ink:* (Whisper White) *Embossing powder:* (white) *Accent:* (silver craft wire) Michaels *Template:* (branches embossing) Provo Craft *Dies:* (butterflies) *Tools:* (border, corner rounder punches) *Other:* (chipboard, color advertisement) no source

Finished size: 5½" x 4¼"

Glitter Ghost Boo Card

Designer: Windy Robinson

SUPPLIES: *Cardstock:* (kraft) DMD, Inc. *Patterned paper:* (Icon Stripe from Spook Alley collection) Making Memories; (Midnight from The Halloween Collection 2009 collection) Reminisce *Clear stamp:* (boo from Spook Alley set) Making Memories *Chalk ink:* (Charcoal) Clearsnap *Specialty ink:* (black hybrid) Technique Tuesday *Accent:* (glitter foam ghost) Making Memories *Fibers:* (natural twine) May Arts; (brown tulle) Bazzill Basics Paper *Tools:* (border punch) EK Success; (scalloped circle punch)

Finished size: 7½" x 3¾"

Sketch by: Kim Hughes

5 steps Cheery Butterfly Card

Designer: Dawn McVey

❶ Make card from cardstock.

❷ Cut rectangle of cardstock; stamp polka dots, round corners, and adhere.

❸ Cut strip of patterned paper; punch border and adhere. Stamp enjoy.

❹ Die-cut butterfly from cardstock; stamp script and adhere. *Note: Bend wings up slightly for dimension.*

❺ Adhere buttons together; thread with twine, tie bow, and adhere.

Finished size: 5½" x 4¼"

SUPPLIES: *Cardstock:* (Rustic Cream, Vintage Cream, Hibiscus Burst) Papertrey Ink *Patterned paper:* (yellow polka dot from 2008 Bitty Dot Basics collection) Papertrey Ink *Clear stamps:* (enjoy from Spiral Bouquet set; polka dots from Polka Dot Basics II set; script from Background Basics: Text Style set) Papertrey Ink *Watermark ink:* Tsukineko *Specialty ink:* (Dark Chocolate, Summer Sunrise hybrid) Papertrey Ink *Accents:* (orange, pink buttons) Papertrey Ink *Fibers:* (cream twine) Papertrey Ink *Die:* (butterfly) Stampin' Up! *Tools:* (embossing border punch) EK Success; (corner rounder punch) Stampin' Up!

Rest Easy Card
Designer: Betsy Veldman

SUPPLIES: *Cardstock:* (Vintage Cream, Dark Chocolate, Pure Poppy) Papertrey Ink *Clear stamp:* (chair from On My Couch Additions set) Papertrey Ink *Chalk ink:* (Creamy Brown) Clearsnap *Specialty ink:* (Pure Poppy hybrid) Papertrey Ink *Accents:* (brown button) Papertrey Ink; (gingham journaling square) October Afternoon *Fibers:* (jute twine) Papertrey Ink *Fonts:* (Gungsuh) www.ascenderfonts.com; (Script MT Bold) www. myfonts.com *Tools:* (scalloped circle punch) The Paper Studio; (circle punch) Marvy Uchida

Finished size: 4½" x 3"

Amore Card
Designer: Beatriz Jennings

SUPPLIES: *Cardstock:* (Rustic Cream) Papertrey Ink *Patterned paper:* (Butterfly Memories from Cut 'N Paste collection) K&Company *Clear stamp:* (corner flourish from Windsor set) SEI *Dye ink:* (Vintage Photo) Ranger Industries *Pigment ink:* (red) Clearsnap *Specialty ink:* (Candy Apple Red shimmer spray) Tattered Angels *Accents:* (chipboard fleur-de-lis) Tattered Angels; (butterfly, crown die cuts) K&Company; (white pearls, pink flower, white/clear buttons) *Rub-on:* (amore) *Fibers:* (white crocheted trim, jute twine) *Tool:* (border punch)

Finished size: 5½" x 4¼"

Happy Mother's Day Card
Designer: Angie Tieman

SUPPLIES: *Cardstock:* (Old Olive, Naturals Ivory) Stampin' Up! *Patterned paper:* (Daydream from June Bug collection) BasicGrey; (red polka dot from The Write Stuff collection) Stampin' Up! *Rubber stamp:* (mother's day from Teeny Tiny Wishes set) Stampin' Up! *Dye ink:* (Chocolate Chip) Stampin' Up! *Accents:* (patterned chipboard flower) BasicGrey; (white linen chipboard flower) Darice; (green button) Stampin' Up! *Fibers:* (red edged ribbon) BasicGrey; (tan floss) *Tool:* (border punch) Stampin' Up!

Finished size: 6½" x 3¼"

Sketch by: Kim Hughes

DESIGNER TIP

It's quick and easy to create a gift card holder from a sealed, standard-size envelope. Experiment with different colors and textures for an endless variety of gift-giving fun.

Birthday Wishes Gift Card Holder

Designer: Clouds Shadler

❶ Cut envelope 3¼" from one edge; punch half circle at top. Draw border.

❷ Cut rounded rectangle of cardstock with decorative-edge scissors; draw border and adhere with foam tape.

❸ Cut rounded rectangle of patterned paper; adhere. Adhere pearls.

❹ Stamp cloud on cardstock; cut out and adhere with foam tape.

❺ Affix bird and tree stickers.

❻ Stamp sentiment. Insert gift card.

Finished size: 4½" x 3¼"

SUPPLIES: *Cardstock:* (aqua) American Crafts; (white) Stampin' Up! *Patterned paper:* (Grey Grid on White Background) Scenic Route *Clear stamps:* (cloud from Sky's the Limit set) Hero Arts; (birthday wishes from Everyday Button Bits set) Papertrey Ink *Dye ink:* (Rich Razzleberry, Apricot Appeal) Stampin' Up! *Color medium:* (white gel pen) Sakura *Accents:* (purple pearls) *Stickers:* (chipboard bird, tree) American Crafts *Tools:* (corner rounder punch, 1¼" circle punch) Stampin' Up!; (decorative-edge scissors) Tonic Studios *Other:* (kraft envelope) XPEDX; (gift card)

Birthday Girl Gift Card Holder

Designer: Danielle Flanders

SUPPLIES: *Patterned paper:* (Bow and Arrow from Cupid collection) Pink Paislee *Color medium:* (brown chalk) Stampin' Up! *Accents:* (bracket, heart ticket die cuts; red glitter brads) Pink Paislee *Rub-on:* (birthday girl) Melissa Frances *Sticker:* (decorative border) Pink Paislee *Tool:* (1" circle punch) EK Success

Finished size: 5" x 3¼"

Compliments Gift Card Holder

Designer: Lisa Dorsey

SUPPLIES: *Cardstock:* (green) Bazzill Basics Paper *Patterned paper:* (Fabric Brocade from Greenhouse Paperie collection) Making Memories; (Let It Snow from Christmas Past collection, Dream a Little Dream from Baby 2 Bride collection) Graphic 45; (Cherry Cola from Lime Rickey collection) BasicGrey *Dye ink:* (Antique Linen) Ranger Industries; (black) Clearsnap *Accents:* (red berries) Jo-Ann Stores; (red glitter brads) Creative Imaginations; (Santa tag) Graphic 45; (white glitter dots) Mark Richards *Sticker:* (compliments) Graphic 45 *Fibers:* (natural twine, green polka dot ribbon) May Arts *Tools:* (decorative-edge scissors) Fiskars; (circle punch) EK Success

Finished size: 5½" x 4½"

Little Something Gift Card Holder

Designer: Kimberly Crawford

SUPPLIES: *Cardstock:* (kraft) Papertrey Ink *Patterned paper:* (Harmony from Lillian collection) Crate Paper *Clear stamp:* (little something from Everyday Button Bits set) Papertrey Ink *Chalk ink:* (Creamy Brown) Clearsnap *Specialty ink:* (Dark Chocolate hybrid) Papertrey Ink *Accents:* (glitter flower die cuts, decorative paper strip) Crate Paper *Fibers:* (yellow gingham ribbon) Offray *Die:* (circle) Spellbinders *Tool:* (border punch) Fiskars

Finished size: 4½" x 3"

Sketch by: Kim Kesti

⟨5 STEPS⟩ Spoonful of Sugar Card

Designer: Kim Kesti

1 Make card from cardstock; round one corner.

2 Print sentiment on cardstock, trim, round corner, and adhere.

3 Tie ribbon around spoon; adhere spoon and bowl with foam tape.

4 Cut patterned paper blocks; adhere.

Finished size: 6" x 4¾"

SUPPLIES: *Cardstock:* (Vienna, Jetstream) Bazzill Basics Paper *Patterned paper:* (Green Dot, brown zig zag, cream circles from Fresh Print Traveler collection) Little Yellow Bicycle *Accents:* (chipboard bowl, spoon) Zva Creative *Fibers:* (gold gingham ribbon) May Arts *Font:* (Estrangelo Edessa) Microsoft *Tool:* (corner rounder punch) We R Memory Keepers

Kangaroo Welcome Box

Designer: Kim Kesti

SUPPLIES: *Cardstock:* (Ginger, Haley, kraft) Bazzill Basics Paper *Patterned paper:* (Hide & Seek, Playday, Tag from Playday collection) SEI *Accents:* (red, yellow brads) BasicGrey *Font:* (Calibri) Microsoft

Finished size: 6¾" x 7¼" x 2¼"

Colorful Happy Birthday Card

Designer: Alli Miles

SUPPLIES: *Cardstock:* (white) Papertrey Ink *Patterned paper:* (Watching the Sun Rise, Enchanting Garden, A Day At the Beach from Simple Pleasures collection) Three Bugs in a Rug *Clear stamp:* (sentiment from Vintage Picnic set) Papertrey Ink *Specialty ink:* (Dark Chocolate hybrid) Papertrey Ink *Accents:* (green button) Papertrey Ink; (white acrylic flower) Maya Road

Finished size: 5½" x 4¼"

Grateful Spring Flowers Card

Designer: Maile Belles

SUPPLIES: All supplies from Papertrey Ink unless otherwise noted. *Cardstock:* (Melon Berry, Spring Moss, white) *Clear stamps:* (sentiment, flowers, stems from Spiral Bouquet set) *Specialty ink:* (Melon Berry, Ripe Avocado, Dark Chocolate hybrid) *Accents:* (green, pink buttons) *Fibers:* (green ribbon); (green floss) DMC *Tool:* (corner rounder punch) EK Success

Finished size: 5½" x 4¼"

Sketch by: Kim Kesti

5 STEPS — Here for You Card

Designer: Debbie Olson

Sand patterned paper edges.

① Make card from cardstock.

② Cut patterned paper panel; adhere patterned paper strip and zigzag-stitch seams. Mat panel with cardstock, adhere ribbon, and adhere to card.

③ Cut patterned paper square, adhere curved patterned paper strips, stitch, and mat with cardstock. Adhere to card.

④ Die-cut and emboss tag from cardstock. Stamp sentiment, heat-emboss, and adhere with foam tape.

⑤ Tie ribbon bow; adhere. Affix tree sticker. Thread buttons and adhere.

Finished size: 5½" x 4¼"

SUPPLIES: *Cardstock:* (Aqua Mist, kraft) Papertrey Ink *Patterned paper:* (Falling Down, colored leaves, orange clouds from Nutmeg collection) Cosmo Cricket *Clear stamp:* (sentiment from Vintage Picnic Sentiments set) Papertrey Ink *Watermark ink:* Tsukineko *Embossing powder:* (white) Papertrey Ink *Accents:* (pink, aqua buttons) Papertrey Ink *Sticker:* (chipboard tree) Cosmo Cricket *Fibers:* (aqua ribbon) Papertrey Ink *Die:* (label) Spellbinders

DESIGNER TIP

If you use an accent that faces a particular direction, place it so that it is looking at the sentiment, which will lead the viewer's eyes to that point.

Life Imagined Card

Designer: Latisha Yoast

SUPPLIES: *Cardstock:* (Dark Chocolate, kraft) Papertrey Ink; (ivory) Flourishes *Patterned paper:* (Repeat, Rethink from Earth Love collection) Cosmo Cricket *Clear stamps:* (sentiment, lemon stem from Life, Love & Lemons set) Flourishes *Dye ink:* (Rich Cocoa) Tsukineko *Accent:* (pink button) Papertrey Ink *Fibers:* (cream twine) May Arts; (cream ribbon) Papertrey Ink *Die:* (square) Spellbinders

Finished size: 6" x 3¾"

Super Star Card

Designer: Kalyn Kepner

SUPPLIES: *Cardstock:* (Orange Crush, True Teal, kraft) Bazzill Basics Paper *Patterned paper:* (Dapper Dan, Silly Sam, Handsome Henry from Lil' Man collection) Cosmo Cricket *Color medium:* (white pen) *Stickers:* (chipboard baseball player, star button) Cosmo Cricket *Fibers:* (natural twine) Westrim Crafts *Dies:* (Nutmeg alphabet) QuicKutz *Tool:* (decorative-edge scissors) Fiskars

Finished size: 7" x 3½"

Bright Be Jolly Card

Designer: Teri Anderson

SUPPLIES: *Cardstock:* (white) WorldWin *Patterned paper:* (Mistletoe Kisses, Winter Wonderland, Frosty Pines from Colorful Christmas collection; Hot Wheels from Nice Ride collection) My Mind's Eye *Accents:* (girl, trees die cuts) American Crafts *Stickers:* (Delight alphabet) American Crafts; (polka dot border) My Mind's Eye

Finished size: 5½" x 3½"

Sketch by: Kim Kesti

Happy Mother's Day

⁵⁵ₛₜₑₚₛ Brilliant Flowers Card

Designer: Kim Kesti

❶ Make card from cardstock;
  cover with patterned paper.

❷ Print sentiment on cardstock.
  Mat with cardstock and adhere.

❸ Layer flowers, attach brads, and
  adhere with foam tape.

Finished size: 6¼" x 4½"

SUPPLIES: *Cardstock:* (Lily White, Malachite) Bazzill Basics Paper *Patterned paper:* (Adirondack from Poppy collection) SEI *Accents:* (silver, flower epoxy brads) BasicGrey; (flower die cuts) SEI *Font:* (Papyrus) Microsoft

DESIGNER TIP

Tie floss around card and then through the buttons to hold them in place.

thinking of you

{Thanks}

hello chick

Fall Thanks Card
Designer: Latisha Yoast

SUPPLIES: *Cardstock:* (white) Flourishes *Patterned paper:* (Maple, Falling Down from Nutmeg collection) Cosmo Cricket *Stickers:* (chipboard bear, leaves) Cosmo Cricket; (Tiny Alpha alphabet) Making Memories

Finished size: 5½" x 4"

Buttons & Bows Card
Designer: Maile Belles

SUPPLIES: *Cardstock:* (Raspberry Fizz, white) Papertrey Ink *Clear stamp:* (sentiment from Beyond Basic Borders set) Papertrey Ink *Specialty ink:* (Raspberry Fizz) Papertrey Ink *Accents:* (assorted buttons) Papertrey Ink *Fibers:* (assorted floss) DMC *Tool:* (corner rounder punch) EK Success

Finished size: 5½" x 3½"

Hello Chick Card
Designer: Teri Anderson

SUPPLIES: *Cardstock:* (white) WorldWin *Patterned paper:* (Peaceful Easy Feeling, Sunny Day from Blue Skies collection) American Crafts *Accents:* (white buttons) Buttons Galore & More *Stickers:* (orange polka dot, bird badges; Delight alphabet) American Crafts *Fibers:* (white floss) DMC *Tools:* (circle punches) EK Success

Finished size: 5½" x 3¼"

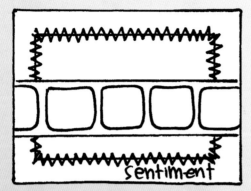

Sketch by: Kim Kesti

5 STEPS Feathered Friend Card

Designer: Julia Stainton

1. Make card from cardstock.

2. Adhere patterned paper and zigzag-stitch edges.

3. Apply rub-ons to patterned paper strip, ink edges, and adhere to card.

4. Adhere trim. Tie ribbon through button and adhere.

5. Spell "Friend" with stickers.

Finished size: 5½" x 4¼"

SUPPLIES: *Cardstock:* (Raven) Bazzill Basics Paper *Patterned paper:* (Aggie from June Bug collection) BasicGrey; (Little Nibbles from Sweet as Cherry Pie collection) Webster's Pages *Dye ink:* (Tuxedo Black) Tsukineko *Accent:* (red button) *Rub-ons:* (birds, trees) Maya Road *Stickers:* (Rockabye alphabet) American Crafts *Fibers:* (black gingham ribbon) Creative Impressions; (red pompom trim) Fancy Pants Designs

Blue Bow
Thank You Card
Designer: Heidi Van Laar

SUPPLIES: *Cardstock:* (white, kraft) American Crafts *Patterned paper:* (Cloves, Nutmeg from Kitchen Spice collection) BoBunny Press *Clear stamp:* (sentiment from All Occasion Messages) Hero Arts *Chalk ink:* (Chestnut Roan) Clearsnap *Accent:* (wood button) *Fibers:* (turquoise ribbon) Offray; (white crochet thread) Coats & Clark

Finished size: 5½" x 4¼"

Birthday
Filmstrip Card
Designer: Kim Kesti

SUPPLIES: *Cardstock:* (Beetle Black) Bazzill Basics Paper *Patterned paper:* (Confection from Sweet Marmalade collection) Sassafras Lass *Specialty paper:* (photo) *Accent:* (film negative strip die cut) Creative Imaginations *Sticker:* (sentiment) Scenic Route *Other:* (digital photos)

Finished size: 6" x 4¼"

Bird Baby Card
Designer: Tiffany Johnson

SUPPLIES: *Cardstock:* (Cream Puff, kraft) Bazzill Basics Paper *Patterned paper:* (Reuse from Earth Love collection) Cosmo Cricket *Rubber stamp:* (Sweetness) Just Johanna Rubber Stamps *Specialty ink:* (Dark Chocolate hybrid) Papertrey Ink *Stickers:* (birds, baby) Cosmo Cricket

Finished size: 8" x 3½"

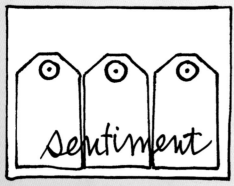

Sketch by: Kim Kesti

DESIGNER TIP

Use ordinary office supplies to incorporate new ideas into your projects.

5 STEPS Flower Tags for Mother Card

Designer: Ashley C. Newell

1. Make card from cardstock.

2. Stamp flowers on tags; adhere with foam tape.

3. Stamp sentiment on cardstock; trim and adhere with foam tape.

Finished size: 5½" x 4¼"

SUPPLIES: *Cardstock:* (Raspberry Fizz, Sweet Blush) Papertrey Ink *Clear stamps:* (sentiment from Women of Life set, flowers from Life set) Papertrey Ink *Specialty ink:* (Ripe Avocado, Raspberry Fizz hybrid) Papertrey Ink *Other:* (small tags) Nice Package

DESIGNER TIP

Use an alcohol-based marker to change the color of your embellishment to match. This works for brads, ribbons, twine, and buttons.

Father Card

Designer: Kimberly Crawford

SUPPLIES: *Cardstock:* (Rustic White, kraft) Papertrey Ink *Clear stamps:* (dad, children, star, sentiment) Stampendous! *Dye ink:* (black) Clearsnap *Watermark ink:* Tsukineko *Color medium:* (red marker) Copic *Accents:* (red heart brads) Making Memories *Fibers:* (red string) Martha Stewart Crafts *Dies:* (tags) Spellbinders

Finished size: 5½" x 4¼"

Beware Card

Designer: Ashley Harris

SUPPLIES: *Cardstock:* (white) Bazzill Basics Paper *Patterned paper:* (Undead from Halloween collection) American Crafts *Rubber stamp:* (Bat Moon) Stampendous! *Solvent ink:* (Jet Black) Tsukineko *Accent:* (yellow glitter glue) Ranger Industries *Rub-ons:* (fence, beware) American Crafts

Finished size: 5½" x 4¼"

Friend Tags Card

Designer: Kim Hughes

SUPPLIES: *Cardstock:* (Snow, Rope Swing embossed) Bazzill Basics Paper *Accents:* (pink pearls) Zva Creative *Rub-ons:* (friend) American Crafts; (flowers, dots) Crate Paper *Fibers:* (twine) Creative Impressions *Tools:* (circle punches) Marvy Uchida

Finished size: 5½" x 3¾"

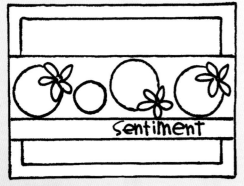

Sketch by: Besty Veldman

5 STEPS Dotty Birthday Card

Designer: Dawn McVey

① Make card from cardstock.

② Trim patterned paper and punch edge; adhere.

③ Stamp sentiment on cardstock; trim and adhere. Trim and adhere cardstock strip.

④ Punch circles and flowers from patterned paper; adhere, using foam tape as desired.

⑤ Adhere rhinestones.

Finished size: 5½" x 4¼"

SUPPLIES: All supplies from Papertrey Ink unless otherwise noted. *Cardstock:* (Dark Chocolate, Rustic Cream, Spring Moss) *Patterned paper:* (red, pink, green grid from 2008 Bitty Box Basics collection; brown, red, green polka dots from 2008 Bitty Dot Basics collection; pink, brown floral from In Bloom collection) *Clear stamps:* (sentiment from Birthday Basics set) *Specialty ink:* (Dark Chocolate hybrid) *Accents:* (green rhinestones) Kaisercraft *Tools:* (border, circle, flower punches) Stampin' Up!

DESIGNER TIP

To add volume to leaves or petals, fold them lengthwise and let edges curl up when you adhere them. This subtle technique will add both dimension and interest to your card.

Starry Dad Birthday Card

Designer: Lisa Johnson

SUPPLIES: All supplies from Papertrey Ink unless otherwise noted. *Cardstock:* (New Leaf, Enchanted Evening, white) *Clear stamps:* (happy birthday, star circle, star, star border from Let Freedom Ring set; Dad from Star Prints set) *Pigment ink:* (Fresh Snow) *Specialty ink:* (Ripe Avocado, Enchanted Evening hybrid) *Fibers:* (blue twill) *Tools:* (1⅜", 1" circle punches, star punch) Marvy Uchida

Finished size: 5½" x 4¼"

Fabric Floral Thoughts Card

Designer: Kim Kesti

SUPPLIES: *Cardstock:* (Ladybug, Lemon, Lily White) Bazzill Basics Paper *Accents:* (assorted buttons) BasicGrey *Rub-on:* (sentiment) Deja Views *Fibers:* (assorted floss) DMC *Other:* (red, yellow, multi fabric strips) Anna Griffin

Finished size: 6½" x 4"

Arigato Card

Designer: Kim Hughes

SUPPLIES: *Cardstock:* (Double Truffle) Core'dinations; (Cream Puff, Kiwi Crush, white) Bazzill Basics Paper; (dark green embossed) *Patterned paper:* (Starry Night from Eskimo Kisses collection) BasicGrey; (Cutie Pie from Sweet Cakes Collection) Pink Paislee; (Green Leaves from Wild Raspberry collection) K&Company *Stickers:* (Tiny Alpha alphabet) Making Memories

Finished size: 5½" x 4¼"

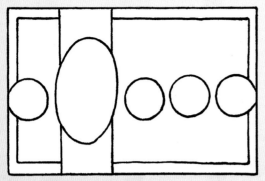

Sketch by: Betsy Veldman

Houndstooth Silhouette Card

Designer: Tiffany Johnson

1. Make card from cardstock.

2. Trim patterned paper piece and strip; adhere.

3. Print and color digital element; adhere with foam tape.

4. Die-cut circles from cardstock; adhere.

5. Thread twine through buttons; adhere.

Finished size: 5½" x 4¼"

SUPPLIES: *Cardstock:* (Lemon Tart, white) Papertrey Ink *Patterned paper:* (Norm's News from Hometown collection) October Afternoon *Color medium:* (yellow marker) Copic *Accents:* (clear, tan buttons) BasicGrey *Digital element:* (silhouette tag) vol25.typepad.com *Fibers:* (natural twine) *Die:* (circle) Provo Craft

Thumpity Thump Thump Card

Designer: Angie Tieman

SUPPLIES: *Cardstock:* (kraft) Stampin' Up! *Patterned paper:* (Sweater Weather from Jolly by Golly collection) Cosmo Cricket *Accents:* (aqua button brads) Making Memories *Stickers:* (sentiment label, decorative squares) Cosmo Cricket *Fibers:* (rainbow striped ribbon) Cosmo Cricket; (natural twine) Stampin' Up!

Finished size: 3¼" x 6½"

No Peeking Card

Designer: Rebecca Oehlers

SUPPLIES: All supplies from Papertrey Ink unless otherwise noted. *Cardstock:* (Scarlet Jewel, white, kraft) *Patterned paper:* (red polka dots from Holiday Cheer collection) *Clear stamps:* (sentiment, Santa from Holiday Button Bits set) *Specialty ink:* (Scarlet Jewel hybrid); (Noir hybrid) Stewart Superior Corp. *Color medium:* (tan, red markers) Copic *Accents:* (burgundy buttons) *Tools:* (circle, oval, scalloped oval punches) Marvy Uchida; (border punch) Fiskars

Finished size: 7" x 5"

Sock Monkey Card

Designer: Julie Campbell

SUPPLIES: *Cardstock:* (Suede Brown Dark) Prism; (Rustic Cream, kraft) Papertrey Ink *Patterned paper:* (Farmers Market from Early Bird collection) Cosmo Cricket *Rubber stamps:* (sentiment, sock monkey from …Wherever You Go set) Unity Stamp Co. *Dye ink:* (Antique Linen) Ranger Industries *Chalk ink:* (Dark Brown, Warm Red) Clearsnap *Color medium:* (red marker) Copic *Accents:* (brown buttons) *Fibers:* (brown floss, cream twine) *Dies:* (oval, scalloped oval) Spellbinders

Finished size: 6½" x 4¼"

Sentiment

Sketch by: Jessica Witty

DESIGNER TIP

Use those scraps! The thin strip of patterned paper on this card was a scrap sitting on Rae's craft table.

5 STEPS Floral Miss You Card

Designer: Rae Barthel

❶ Make card from cardstock; cover with patterned paper.

❷ Cut patterned paper block. Punch edges of patterned paper strips; adhere to block.

❸ Adhere patterned paper strip and adhere block to card.

❹ Trim patterned paper strip with decorative-edge scissors; adhere. Adhere rhinestones and spell "Miss you" with stickers.

❺ Adhere rhinestone to flower; adhere to card.

Finished size: 6" x 4½"

SUPPLIES: *Cardstock:* (kraft) DMD, Inc. *Patterned paper:* (Chocolate Mousse, Tea Cakes from Nook & Pantry collection) BasicGrey *Accents:* (pink rhinestones) Queen & Co.; (brown rhinestone, pink flower) Prima *Stickers:* (Nook & Pantry alphabet) BasicGrey *Tools:* (border punch) Martha Stewart Crafts; (decorative-edge scissors) Fiskars

Autumn Hello Card

Designer: Maren Benedict

SUPPLIES: *Cardstock:* (Dark Chocolate) Papertrey Ink *Patterned paper:* (Acorn, multi stripe, rust argyle from Nutmeg pad) Cosmo Cricket *Stickers:* (chipboard leaves, Nutmeg alphabet) Cosmo Cricket *Fibers:* (brown ribbon) Papertrey Ink

Finished size: 5½" x 4¼"

Elegant Thank You Card

Designer: Dawn McVey

SUPPLIES: *Cardstock:* (Dark Chocolate, Hibiscus Burst, white) Papertrey Ink *Clear stamps:* (damask, sentiment from Giga Guide Lines set) Papertrey Ink *Watermark ink:* Tsukineko *Specialty ink:* (Dark Chocolate hybrid) Papertrey Ink *Accent:* (pink button) Papertrey Ink *Fibers:* (brown ribbon) Papertrey Ink; (hemp twine) Wal-Mart

Finished size: 5½" x 4¼"

Get Well Wishes Card

Designer: Maile Belles

SUPPLIES: *Cardstock:* (Spring Moss, Ripe Avocado, Raspberry Fizz, Scarlet Jewel, white) Papertrey Ink *Clear stamps:* (flower, leaves from In Bloom set; tiny polka dots from Polka Dot Basics II set; stripes from Background Basics: Retro set; sentiment from Floral Frenzy set) Papertrey Ink *Watermark ink:* Tsukineko *Specialty ink:* (Ripe Avocado, Scarlet Jewel hybrid) Papertrey Ink *Embossing powder:* (white) Jo-Ann Stores *Fibers:* (olive ribbon) Papertrey Ink *Tool:* (oval punch) Stampin' Up!

Finished size: 5½" x 4¼"

Sketch by: Jessica Witty

5 STEPS Best Friend Card

Designer: Rae Barthel

❶ Make card from cardstock.

❷ Cut patterned paper piece and mat with patterned paper.

❸ Tie ribbon around piece; adhere to card. Adhere chipboard flower.

❹ Fussy-cut sentiment from patterned paper; adhere with foam tape.

Finished size: 6½" x 4½"

SUPPLIES: *Cardstock:* (Avalanche) Bazzill Basics Paper *Patterned paper:* (Friends, Friendship Tags from Friendship collection) Teresa Collins Designs *Accent:* (black chipboard flower) Teresa Collins Designs *Fibers:* (black gingham ribbon) Offray

Stitched Miss U Card

Designer: Jessica Witty

SUPPLIES: *Cardstock:* (Basic Gray) Stampin' Up!; (Raspberry Fizz, white) Papertrey Ink *Patterned paper:* (Buttercup Dot from Double Dot collection) BoBunny Press *Clear stamp:* (text from Background Basics: Text Style set) Papertrey Ink *Dye ink:* (Going Gray) Stampin' Up! *Accent:* (acrylic letter) Heidi Swapp *Stickers:* (Delight alphabet) American Crafts *Fibers:* (gray ribbon) American Crafts; (pink floss) DMC *Tools:* (2½" circle punch) Marvy Uchida; (border punch) Fiskars

Finished size: 5½" x 4¼"

Easter Eggs Card

Designer: Beatriz Jennings

SUPPLIES: *Cardstock:* (pink) Bazzill Basics Paper *Patterned paper:* (Delaney Die-Cut Stamp from Noteworthy collection) Making Memories; (Madras from Promenade collection) We R Memory Keepers *Accent:* (green button) *Stickers:* (Easter eggs tile) Making Memories; (blue oval) *Fibers:* (pink ribbon, natural twine)

Finished size: 4½" x 4¾"

Flower Pot Card

Designer: Kim Hughes

SUPPLIES: *Cardstock:* (Butter embossed) Bazzill Basics Paper; (Katydid) Core'dinations; (Tawny Dark) Prism; (kraft) *Patterned paper:* (Dotted Girl from Kraft Kuts collection) Fancy Pants Designs *Accents:* (brown, yellow buttons) Creative Café *Fibers:* (multi striped ribbon) Offray; (natural twine) Creative Impressions *Tool:* (border punch) Stampin' Up!

Finished size: 4½" x 6"

Sketch by: Jessica Witty

Designer: Windy Robinson

❶ Make card from cardstock.

❷ Trim patterned paper and adhere.

❸ Adhere ribbon; stamp celebrate.

❹ Adhere pendant.

Finished size: 7¼" x 3¾"

SUPPLIES: *Cardstock:* (kraft) DMD, Inc. *Patterned paper:* (Thin Zucchini from Minestrone collection) Jillibean Soup *Clear stamps:* (celebrate from Everyday Words set) Technique Tuesday *Specialty ink:* (Burnt Umber hybrid) Stewart Superior Corp. *Accent:* (flower pendant) Plaid *Fibers:* (brown ribbon) Michaels

DESIGNER TIP

Textured ribbon and letters are a great way to make a card more visually interesting and touchable!

In Remembrance Card

Designer: Latisha Yoast

SUPPLIES: *Cardstock:* (kraft) Papertrey Ink *Clear stamp:* (sentiment from Sweet Violets set) Flourishes *Dye ink:* (Tuxedo Black) Tsukineko *Accents:* (red flower) Prima; (brown pearls) Kaisercraft *Fibers:* (white lace) Melissa Frances

Finished size: 5½" x 3½"

Hi Birdcage Card

Designer: Julia Stainton

SUPPLIES: *Cardstock:* (kraft) Bazzill Basics Paper *Patterned paper:* (Make a Wish from Magical Wishes collection) Webster's Pages *Stickers:* (birdcage) Hambly Screen Prints; (Leg Warmers alphabet) American Crafts *Fibers:* (green ribbon) Making Memories

Finished size: 5½" x 4¼"

Love You Forever Card

Designer: Kimberly Crawford

SUPPLIES: *Cardstock:* (Stormy, Poinsettia) Core'dinations, (Rustic White) Papertrey Ink *Patterned paper:* (Sunday Dishes from Cherry Hill collection) October Afternoon *Clear stamps:* (text heart, sentiment from Heart Prints set) Papertrey Ink *Dye ink:* (L'Amour Red) Stewart Superior Corp. *Watermark ink:* Tsukineko *Embossing powder:* (white) Stampendous! *Tool:* (heart punch) EK Success

Finished size: 6" x 4¼"

Sketch by: Jessica Witty

Designer: Beth Opel

1. Make card from patterned paper.

2. Trim and adhere patterned paper block and cardstock strips.

3. Cut cake pieces from patterned paper; adhere with foam tape. Cut and punch cardstock to create stand; adhere with foam tape.

4. Adhere cardstock strips to make candles, draw wicks, and adhere rhinestones. Adhere epoxy dots.

5. Spell sentiment with stickers. *Note: Tie ribbon to one letter before affixing.*

Finished size: 7" x 6"

SUPPLIES: *Cardstock:* (Wildberry scalloped, light blue) Bazzill Basics Paper *Patterned paper:* (Pearl Bobbinhauser, Doris Spooler, Faye Needleworth from Craft Fair collection) American Crafts; (Confetti from Party It Up collection) GCD Studios; (coral grid) *Color medium:* (black pen) *Accents:* (black epoxy dots) Cloud 9 Design; (yellow rhinestones) K&Company *Stickers:* (Bold alphabet) Close To My Heart; (By the Yard alphabet) American Crafts *Fibers:* (blue dotted ribbon) Mrs. Grossman's *Tool:* (border punch) Fiskars

It's Your Birthday Card

Designer: Debbie Olson

SUPPLIES: *Cardstock:* (Vintage Cream, Pure Poppy) Papertrey Ink *Patterned paper:* (Sunrise, Apron Strings from Early Bird collection) Cosmo Cricket *Rubber stamps:* (cupcake scene, sentiment from Sweet Celebration set) Taylored Expressions *Dye ink:* (Tuxedo Black) Tsukineko; (Chamomile) Papertrey Ink *Color medium:* (assorted markers) Copic *Accents:* (red buttons) Papertrey Ink *Fibers:* (cream twine) *Die:* (tag) Spellbinders *Tools:* (corner rounder punches) Carl Brands, Mary Uchida

Finished size: 4¼" x 5½"

The Perfect Pair Card

Designer: Heidi Van Laar

SUPPLIES: *Cardstock:* (cream, brown) American Crafts *Patterned paper:* (Pear Tart, Fruit Salad, Lemon Meringue, Tea Cakes from Nook & Pantry collection) BasicGrey *Fibers:* (white crochet thread) Coats & Clark *Font:* (CAC Pinafore) www.dafont.com *Die:* (small heart) Ellison *Tools:* (decorative-edge scissors) Fiskars; (corner rounder punch) We R Memory Keepers *Other:* (chipboard)

Finished size: 6" x 5"

Wedding Congratulations Card

Designer: Latisha Yoast

SUPPLIES: *Cardstock:* (white) Flourishes; (Pure Poppy) Papertrey Ink *Patterned paper:* (Beaters from Nook & Pantry collection) BasicGrey *Rubber stamp:* (church from Wherever You Go set) Unity Stamp Co. *Clear stamp:* (congratulations from Simply Little Things set) Papertrey Ink *Dye ink:* (Tuxedo Black) Tsukineko *Color medium:* (red, brown markers) Copic *Fibers:* (red ribbon) Papertrey Ink

Finished size: 5½" x 4¼"

Sketch by: Jessica Witty

5 STEPS Dad Plaid Card

Designer: Kim Hughes

Ink all edges.

1. Make card from cardstock.

2. Trim patterned paper and cardstock strips; adhere.
   Adhere border die cut and zigzag-stitch seam.

3. Trim burlap and adhere. Stitch with floss.

4. Cut star from patterned paper and adhere.
   Thread buttons with twine and adhere.

5. Spell "Dad" with stickers.

Finished size: 4¾" x 4"

SUPPLIES: *Cardstock:* (Tawny Light) Prism *Patterned paper:* (Merry Dots from Colorful Christmas collection) My Mind's Eye; (Black Micro Dot from Vintage Red/Black collection) Jenni Bowlin Studio; (Can Beef Consommé from Grandma's Christmas Soup collection) Jillibean Soup *Chalk ink:* (Chestnut Roan) Clearsnap *Accents:* (brown plaid border die cut) My Mind's Eye; (brown buttons) Creative Café *Stickers:* (Delight alphabet) American Crafts *Fibers:* (natural twine) Creative Impressions; (black floss) DMC *Other:* (burlap)

DESIGNER TIP

To ensure the ribbon bow's shape, adhere with flat adhesive tape.

To You From Me Box

Designer: Ashley C. Newell

SUPPLIES: *Cardstock:* (Crushed Curry) Stampin' Up! *Patterned paper:* (green polka dot from 2008 Bitty Dot Basics collection) Papertrey Ink *Rubber stamp:* (sentiment from Best Yet set) Stampin' Up! *Specialty ink:* (Ripe Avocado hybrid) Papertrey Ink *Paint:* (Shopping Bag) Making Memories *Accents:* (olive buttons) Papertrey Ink; (orange rhinestones) Kaisercraft; (green, yellow stick pins) Jo-Ann Stores *Fibers:* (olive ribbon) Papertrey Ink *Tool:* (decorative-edge scissors) Fiskars *Other:* (box) Papertrey Ink; (orange, yellow, green felt) Heather Bailey

Finished size: 6½" x 3½" x 4½"

Beautiful Day Card

Designer: Nina Brackett

SUPPLIES: *Cardstock:* (Green Apple, Moonlit Fog, ivory) Gina K Designs *Patterned paper:* (Primrose, polka dot from Lotus Faded China pad) K&Company *Rubber stamps:* (topiary from Lord of the Season set, sentiment from Eclectic Summer Sayings set) Gina K Designs *Dye ink:* (London Fog) Tsukineko *Pigment Ink:* (ivory) *Color medium:* (assorted markers) Copic *Accents:* (olive buttons) Gina K Designs; (white pearls) Mark Richards *Fibers:* (olive ribbon, cream twine) *Die:* (tag) Spellbinders *Tool:* (border punch) Martha Stewart Crafts

Finished size: 4¼" x 5½"

Thanks a Bunch Birdie Card

Designer: Kim Kesti

SUPPLIES: *Cardstock:* (Rain, Lily White, Java) Bazzill Basics Paper *Patterned paper:* (Sunny Day, Walking on Sunshine from Blue Skies collection) American Crafts *Rub-on:* (sentiment) American Crafts *Stickers:* (bird, hearts, flower) American Crafts *Fibers:* (cream striped ribbon) May Arts

Finished size: 4¼" x 6½"

Sketch by: Betsy Veldman

⁵ Green & Blue Smile Card

Designer: Teri Anderson

❶ Make card from cardstock. Adhere patterned paper.

❷ Trim rectangles from patterned paper; adhere.

❸ Mat patterned paper rectangle with cardstock; adhere. Affix stickers to spell "Smile".

❹ Thread buttons with string; adhere. Tie string around buttons.

Finished size: 5½" x 4¼"

SUPPLIES: *Cardstock:* (white) WorldWin *Patterned paper:* (blue dots, green vines, yellow floral, blue swirls from Citronella pad) K&Company *Accents:* (yellow, blue, green buttons) Buttons Galore & More *Stickers:* (Delight alphabet) American Crafts *Fibers:* (white string) DMC

Rich Thanks Card
Designer: Maren Benedict

SUPPLIES: *Cardstock:* (kraft) Papertrey Ink *Patterned paper:* (Vegetable Broth from Lentil Soup collection) Jillibean Soup; (red paisley) *Stickers:* (Porcelain alphabet) BasicGrey *Fibers:* (brown twill) Papertrey Ink

Finished size: 3" x 5½"

Berry Best Birthday Card
Designer: Maile Belles

SUPPLIES: All supplies from Papertrey Ink unless otherwise noted. *Cardstock:* (Ripe Avocado, Berry Sorbet, white) *Clear stamps:* (strawberries, stems from Green Thumb set; sentiment from Year-Round Puns set; vines from With Sympathy set) *Specialty ink:* (Ripe Avocado, Berry Sorbet hybrid) *Accents:* (pink buttons) *Fibers:* (green ribbon); (white floss) DMC *Tool:* (circle punch) Marvy Uchida

Finished size: 5½" x 3½"

Peace on Earth Card
Designer: Betsy Veldman

SUPPLIES: *Cardstock:* (Vintage Cream) Papertrey Ink; (brown) *Patterned paper:* (Woodland, Alpine, Reindeer Games, Thin Ice from Eskimo Kisses collection) BasicGrey *Clear stamps:* (peace, on earth from Winter Swirls set) Papertrey Ink *Chalk ink:* (Creamy Brown) Clearsnap *Specialty ink:* (Dark Chocolate hybrid) Papertrey Ink *Accents:* (white pearls) Zva Creative; (pink/red fabric brad) BasicGrey; (white glitter) Doodlebug Design *Fibers:* (cream ribbon, natural twine) Papertrey Ink *Dies:* (snowflakes) Provo Craft

Finished size: 5½" x 4¼"

VERTICAL SKETCHES

Sentiment

Sketch by: Julia Stainton

Rainbows & Sunshine

Designer: Ashley Cannon Newell

1. Make card from cardstock.

2. Trim rainbow from patterned paper; adhere to cardstock.

3. Adhere patterned paper strip to panel. Border-punch cardstock; adhere.

4. Stamp sentiment on cardstock strip; adhere to panel. Adhere panel to card with foam tape.

5. Die-cut clouds from patterned paper; adhere with foam tape.

6. Thread buttons with twine; adhere.

Finished size: 4¼" x 5¼"

SUPPLIES: *Cardstock:* (Pure Poppy, Aqua Mist, Summer Sunrise, white) Papertrey Ink *Patterned paper:* (Rainbow from Candy Shoppe collection) Studio Calico *Clear stamp:* (sentiment from Up, Up & Away Sentiments set) Papertrey Ink *Dye ink:* (Chocolate Chip) Stampin' Up! *Accents:* (blue, red, orange buttons) Papertrey Ink *Fibers:* (white jute twine) Mary Arts *Dies:* (clouds) Papertrey Ink *Tool:* (border punch) Martha Stewart Crafts

Precious Little One

Designer: Melissa Phillips

Ink all paper edges. ① Make card from cardstock; adhere patterned paper rectangles. ② Adhere lace; stitch edges. ③ Die-cut button card from patterned paper. Stamp handmade card and homespun quality on panel. Mat with cardstock and adhere. ④ Adhere sentiment sticker to label sticker with foam tape. Affix to card. ⑤ Thread buttons with floss; adhere. Adhere ribbon bow and flower.

Finished size: 3¾" x 5¾"

Bouquet Thank You

Designer: Julia Stainton

① Make card from cardstock. ② Sand edges of patterned paper rectangle; adhere. ③ Accordion-fold crepe paper and adhere. Adhere ribbon and attach staples. ④ Adhere flowers and insert stick pins.

Finished size: 4¼" x 5"

Birthday Flags

Designer: Wendy Sue Anderson

① Make card from cardstock. Trim patterned paper slightly smaller than card front; adhere. ② Stitch edges of patterned paper rectangles; adhere. ③ Adhere flags with foam tape. Affix stickers. ④ Apply rub-on to cardstock strip; fold and trim edges. Adhere to card with foam tape. ⑤ Adhere dots.

Finished size: 5" x 6¼"

SUPPLIES: *Cardstock:* (Lavender Moon, Spring Moss, Sweet Blush) Papertrey Ink *Patterned paper:* (Lavender Leaves from Lilac House collection) Fancy Pants Designs; (Nursery Rhyme from Lullaby Girl collection) Creative Imaginations *Clear stamps:* (homespun quality, handmade card from Button Boutique set) Papertrey Ink *Pigment ink:* (Plum Pudding) Papertrey Ink *Specialty ink:* (Melon Berry hybrid) Papertrey Ink *Accents:* (white, cream buttons) Papertrey Ink; (purple flower) The Little Pink Studio *Stickers:* (label) K&Company; (sentiment) Creative Imaginations *Fibers:* (pink ribbon) My Craft Spot; (cream lace) Webster's Pages; (pink floss) Michaels *Die:* (button card) Papertrey Ink

SUPPLIES: *Cardstock:* (kraft) Bazzill Basics Paper *Patterned paper:* (Beach Chair from Seaside collection) October Afternoon *Accents:* (red, yellow flowers; green leaf stick pins) Maya Road; (silver staples) *Fibers:* (natural printed twill) Creative Impressions *Other:* (red crepe paper) Jenni Bowlin Studio

SUPPLIES: *Cardstock:* (white) American Crafts *Patterned paper:* (Cheery, Cloud Nine from Happy Go Lucky collection) Pebbles *Accents:* (patterned flags, blue dots) Pebbles *Rub-on:* (happy birthday) American Crafts *Stickers:* (Tiny Alpha alphabet) Making Memories

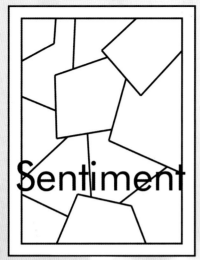

Sentiment

Sketch by: Julia Stainton

Patchwork Joy

Designer: Julia Stainton

1. Make card from cardstock.

2. Adhere patterned paper pieces together. Zigzag-stitch seams.

3. Trim edges of panel and adhere to card. Zigzag-stitch borders.

4. Paint chipboard snowflake; adhere. Affix stickers and adhere bingo number.

Finished size: 4¼" x 5¼"

SUPPLIES: *Cardstock:* (kraft) Bazzill Basics Paper *Patterned paper:* (Button Nose, Coal, Pomegranate, green snowflake, black flowers, dotted circles from Jovial collection) BasicGrey *Paint:* (Picket Fence crackle) Ranger Industries *Accents:* (chipboard snowflake, black bingo number) Maya Road *Stickers:* (By the Yard alphabet) American Crafts

Little One

Designer: Chan Vuong

① Make card from cardstock; adhere patterned paper. ② Trim patterned paper pieces; adhere. ③ Adhere label with foam tape.

Finished size: 3¾" x 4¾"

Mosaic Hello

Designer: Tenia Nelson

① Make card from cardstock. ② Trim and tear patterned paper pieces. Adhere pieces together, trim into rectangle, and round corners. ③ Mat panel with cardstock, distress edges, and adhere. ④ Affix sticker to cardstock rectangle, mat with cardstock, and adhere to card with foam tape.

Finished size: 4" x 5½"

Wouldn't Trade You

Designer: Beth Opel

① Make card from cardstock. ② Print baseball cards on cardstock, trim, and adhere to cardstock rectangle. *Note: Leave some edges curled up.* Adhere panel to card with foam tape. ③ Print sentiment on cardstock; trim. Mat with cardstock, trim, attach brads, and adhere with foam tape.

Finished size: 4¾" x 6¼"

SUPPLIES: *Cardstock:* (Rustic White) Papertrey Ink *Patterned paper:* (Skipping, Kissing Tag, Monkey Bars, Tire Swing, Passing Notes, Playground, First Dance, Skip to My Lou, Sidewalk Chalk from Hopscotch collection) BasicGrey *Accent:* (green label) Little Yellow Bicycle

SUPPLIES: *Cardstock:* (kraft, red, black) The Paper Company; (white) Georgia-Pacific *Patterned paper:* (Astaire, Chaplin, Garbo, Bette, Ginger from Circa 1934 collection) Cosmo Cricket *Sticker:* (hello) SRM Press *Tool:* (corner rounder punch) EK Success

SUPPLIES: *Cardstock:* (blue) American Crafts; (white) *Accents:* (red brads) Making Memories *Digital elements:* (baseball cards) *Fonts:* (Century Schoolbook, Cooper Black) Microsoft

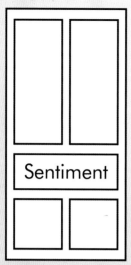

Sentiment

Sketch by: Julia Stainton

5 STEPS Welcome to the Neighborhood

Designer: Betsy Veldman

Ink all edges.

1. Make card from cardstock; paint edges.
2. Deboss cardstock, ink, trim into rectangles, and paint edges. Adhere.
3. Stamp welcome, sentiment, and medallions on cardstock strip; adhere.
4. Stamp twig wreath, leaf wreath, flowers, and dots on card.
5. Adhere twine bow.

Finished size: 3½" x 6"

SUPPLIES: All supplies from Papertrey Ink unless otherwise noted. *Cardstock:* (Rustic Cream) *Clear stamps:* (welcome, sentiment from Year-Round Puns; medallion from Borders & Corners (oval) set; twig wreath, leaf wreath, flowers, dots from Wreath for All Seasons set) *Dye ink:* (Real Red) Stampin' Up! *Chalk ink:* (Creamy Brown) Clearsnap *Specialty ink:* (Dark Chocolate, Ripe Avocado hybrid) *Paint:* (Cream) Delta *Fibers:* (natural jute twine) *Template:* (debossing woodgrain)

5 STEPS Yuletide Blessings

Designer: Dana Ford

❶ Make card from cardstock. ❷ Trim rectangles from cardstock, draw lines with marker, and ink edges. Adhere. ❸ Stamp yuletide blessings on vellum; emboss. Ink edges, adhere to cardstock, and adhere dots. Adhere to card. ❹ Wrap wired leaves in a circle; trim excess. Adhere dots and ribbon bow. Adhere to card. ❺ Attach brad.

Finished size: 4¼" x 8"

5 STEPS Monstrous Boo

Designer: Vivian Masket

❶ Make card from cardstock. ❷ Trim cardstock rectangles. ❸ Apply rub-ons and affix stickers to spell "Boo". Adhere panels to card.

Finished size: 6" x 7½"

5 STEPS Father's Day Door

Designer: Cassandra Jones

❶ Make card from cardstock. ❷ Deboss cardstock rectangles, mat with cardstock, and adhere. ❸ Stamp sentiment and flowers on card. ❹ Apply dimensional glaze to bookplate; let dry. ❺ Adhere bookplate and pearls.

Finished size: 4" x 8¼"

SUPPLIES: *Cardstock:* (Riding Hood Red, Cherry Cobbler, Whisper White) Stampin' Up! *Vellum:* (white) Stampin' Up! *Clear stamp:* (yuletide blessings from Compliments of the Season set) Waltzingmouse Stamps *Dye ink:* (Early Espresso) Stampin' Up! *Watermark ink:* Tsukineko *Embossing powder:* (gold) Stampin' Up! *Color medium:* (brown marker) Stampin' Up! *Accents:* (gold brad) Stampin' Up!; (red, gold dots) Stamping Bella; (green wired leaves) Michaels *Fibers:* (gold ribbon) Wrights

SUPPLIES: *Cardstock:* (Atlantic, Hazard, Raven) Bazzill Basics Paper *Rub-ons:* (monsters) BoBunny Press *Stickers:* (Hardcover alphabet) American Crafts

SUPPLIES: *Cardstock:* (Very Vanilla) Stampin' Up!; (Fawn, Bark) Bazzill Basics Paper *Rubber stamp:* (Happy Father's Day) Hero Arts *Clear stamp:* (flower from Mat Stack 1 Collection set) Papertrey Ink *Dye ink:* (Early Espresso) Stampin' Up! *Finish:* (clear dimensional glaze) Plaid *Accents:* (natural wood bookplate, brown pearls) Kaisercraft *Template:* (debossing woodgrain) Papertrey Ink

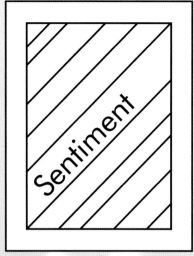

Sketch by: Julia Stainton

DESIGNER TIP

Create the same look in half the time by trimming the front cover of the 6 x 6 Stella & Rose paper pad into a rectangle and stitching lines.

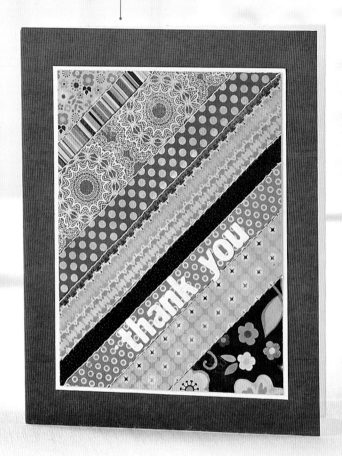

Thank You Stripes

Designer: Lucy Abrams

1. Make card from cardstock.

2. Adhere patterned paper strips together; trim into rectangle.

3. Stitch seams and mat panel with cardstock; adhere.

4. Affix stickers to spell "Thank you".

Finished size: 4¼" x 5¼"

SUPPLIES: *Cardstock:* (Punch, Snow) Hero Arts *Patterned paper:* (Delightful Sweet Stripe, Friends Forever Petals, Girly Lace, Little One Blooms, Little One Darling Dots, You & Me Ornamental, Delightful Blossom from Stella & Rose collection) My Mind's Eye *Stickers:* (Micro Mono alphabet) BasicGrey

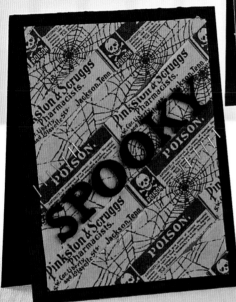

Spooky

Designer: Julia Stainton

1 Make card from cardstock. 2 Affix tape to cardstock rectangle. *Note: Curl some edges before adhering.* 3 Attach staples and adhere panel to card. 4 Affix stickers to spell "Spooky".

Finished size: 4¼" x 5½"

Happy Everything

Designer: Holly Kean

1 Make card from cardstock; die-cut scalloped square from front flap. 2 Adhere patterned paper strips together; zigzag-stitch seams. 3 Ink doily, stamp happy everything, and adhere to panel. Adhere panel behind front flap. 4 Thread button with twine; adhere.

Finished size: 4¾" square

Birthday Rules

Designer: Waleska

1 Make card from cardstock. 2 Trim patterned paper rectangle, stitch lines, and adhere. 3 Stitch lines in ribbon, trim edges, and stamp happy and birthday. Adhere. 4 Thread buttons with twine; adhere. Adhere rhinestones.

Finished size: 4¼" x 5½"

SUPPLIES: *Cardstock:* (Yam, black) Bazzill Basics Paper *Accents:* (silver staples) *Stickers:* (Emerald alphabet) American Crafts; (scull, cobweb tape) Tim Holtz

SUPPLIES: *Cardstock:* (Walnut) Core'dinations *Patterned paper:* (Coverlet, Cotton, Victoria, Ophelia, Muslin from Curio collection) BasicGrey *Rubber stamp:* (happy everything from Happy Everything Greetings set) Hero Arts *Dye ink:* (Walnut Stain) Ranger Industries *Pigment ink:* (Chestnut) Clearsnap *Accents:* (white doily) Wilton; (tan button) *Fibers:* (brown/white twine) *Die:* (scalloped square) Sizzix

SUPPLIES: *Cardstock:* (Yosemite) Bazzill Basics Paper *Patterned paper:* (Harper's Rule from Elementary collection) Studio Calico *Clear stamps:* (happy, birthday from Sentiments set) Studio Calico *Pigment ink:* (Vintage Sepia) Tsukineko *Accents:* (green buttons) Studio Calico; (blue rhinestones) My Mind's Eye *Fibers:* (natural hemp twine) May Arts; (yellow ribbon) Strano Designs

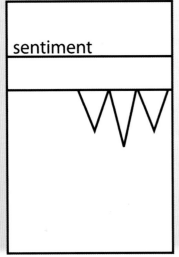

sentiment

Sketch by: Julie Campbell

5 STEPS Banner Thank You

Designer: Kimberly Crawford

1. Make card from cardstock.

2. Trim patterned paper slightly smaller than card front, distress edges, and adhere.

3. Distress edges of patterned paper strip, tie on twine, and adhere.

4. Die-cut pennants from cardstock, affix pennant stickers, and adhere to card with foam tape.

5. Affix alphabet stickers to spell "Thank you".

Finished size: 4¼" x 5½"

SUPPLIES: *Cardstock:* (True Black) Papertrey Ink *Patterned paper:* (Tablecloth from For the Record set) Echo Park Paper *Stickers:* (For the Record alphabet) Echo Park Paper; (ledger pennants) Jenni Bowlin Studio *Fibers:* (cream jute twine) May Arts *Die:* (pennant) Spellbinders

DESIGNER TIP

The mountains were cut from banner dies and turned upside down. Find unique and versatile ways to re-purpose your dies.

Creepy Boo!

Designer: Kelley Eubanks

❶ Make card from cardstock. ❷ Stamp boo! and spiders on cardstock rectangle. Round opposite corners. ❸ Adhere ribbon. Tie ribbon bow with button and twine; adhere. ❹ Adhere panel to card with foam tape.

Finished size: 4¼" x 5½"

Hit the Road Jack

Designer: Lorena Cantó Lavería

❶ Make card from cardstock; adhere cardstock rectangle. ❷ Die-cut clouds and emboss; adhere to card base. ❸ Die-cut triangles and apply ink to create snow; adhere, using foam tape on one. ❹ Stamp sentiment. ❺ Draw stitches on black cardstock with gel pen; adhere to card front with foam tape.

Finished size: 4" x 4¾"

Christmas Greetings

Designer: Colleen Dietrich

❶ Make card from cardstock. ❷ Adhere patterned paper rectangle and stamp Christmas greetings. ❸ Adhere twill and tie on twine. ❹ Stamp trees on cardstock, trim, and adhere with foam tape. ❺ Stamp star on cardstock, emboss, and trim. Adhere with foam tape.

Finished size: 4¼" x 5½"

SUPPLIES: *Cardstock:* (Orange Zest, white) Papertrey Ink *Clear stamps:* (boo!, spider from Frightful set) Hero Arts *Dye ink:* (Fountain Pen) Ranger Industries *Accent:* (orange button) Papertrey Ink *Fibers:* (orange/white twine) Divine Twine; (orange ribbon) Papertrey Ink *Tool:* (corner rounder punch) Stampin' Up!

SUPPLIES: *Cardstock:* (blue, brown, black, white) *Clear stamps:* (sentiment from Road Trip set) Inkadinkado *Pigment ink:* (Fresh Snow) Papertrey Ink; (Onyx Black) Tsukineko *Color medium:* (white gel pen) Uniball Signo *Template:* (embossing Swiss Dots) Provo Craft *Dies:* (clouds, triangles) Papertrey Ink

SUPPLIES: *Cardstock:* (kraft) Stampin' Up! *Patterned paper:* (red leaves from Calisto Christmas pad) Anna Griffin *Rubber stamps:* (star, trees from Patterned Pines set) Stampin' Up! *Clear stamp:* (Christmas greetings from Sleigh Ride set) Flourishes *Dye ink:* (Garden Green, Always Artichoke, Basic Black) Stampin' Up! *Watermark ink:* Tsukineko *Embossing powder:* (gold) Rubber Stampede *Fibers:* (cream twill) Stampin' Up!; (natural jute twine)

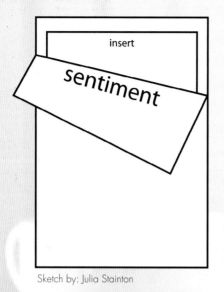

insert

sentiment

Sketch by: Julia Stainton

⁙5⁙ Shabby Pocket

Designer: Julia Stainton

Ink all patterned paper edges.

1. Trim patterned paper 4¼" x 11". Fold in half and fold down front flap. Stitch edges to create pocket.

2. Affix stickers to spell "Celebrate". Paint flowers and adhere.

3. Mat patterned paper with cardstock, stitch borders, and adhere twill. Insert panel into pocket.

4. Tie on twine bow.

Finished size: 4¼" x 5½"

SUPPLIES: *Cardstock:* (kraft) Bazzill Basics Paper *Patterned paper:* (Fresh Air, Veranda from Picket Fence collection) Lily Bee Design *Paint:* (Picket Fence crackle) Ranger Industries *Accents:* (kraft corrugated flower) Jillibean Soup; (pink flower) Prima *Stickers:* (Tiny Type alphabet) Cosmo Cricket *Fibers:* (natural jute twine) Westrim Crafts; (cream twill)

Perky Birthday
Designer: Susan R. Opel

❶ Make card from cardstock; adhere cardstock rectangle. ❷ Trim patterned paper rectangle, fold, and adhere. *Note: Adhere flap with foam tape.* ❸ Apply rub-on to cardstock strip, mat with patterned paper, and adhere to card with foam tape. ❹ Attach brad and tie on ribbon.

Finished size: 4¼" x 6"

Birdcage Hello
Designer: Anne Jo Lexander

❶ Make card from patterned paper. ❷ Trim cardstock and patterned paper rectangles. Tear and curl patterned paper and stitch to cardstock. ❸ Attach trim with staples and adhere panel to card. ❹ Trim birdcage from transparency sheet; adhere. Adhere flowers. ❺ Circle-punch cardstock; adhere. Adhere bird. ❻ Adhere rose and affix stickers to spell "Hello".

Finished size: 4" x 6"

Thanks a Million
Designer: Alicia Thelin

❶ Make card from cardstock; adhere cardstock rectangle. ❷ Fold cardstock rectangle and stitch edges to card. ❸ Stamp sentiment and insert dollar bill into pocket. ❹ Punch small star, 1" circle, and label from cardstock. Adhere together and pierce holes. Adhere to card with foam tape. ❺ Circle-punch card seam and tie on twill.

Finished size: 3¾" x 6"

SUPPLIES: *Cardstock:* (yellow, pink, white) Bazzill Basics Paper *Patterned paper:* (Pink Sparkle from Homespun Chic collection) GCD Studios *Accent:* (pink flower brad) American Crafts *Rub-on:* (sentiment) American Crafts *Fibers:* (yellow ribbon) Offray

SUPPLIES: *Cardstock:* (white, kraft corrugated) *Patterned paper:* (Bridesmaids, Honeymoon from Portrait collection) Crate Paper *Transparency sheet:* (cream cages from The Birdcages collection) Hambly Screen Prints *Specialty ink:* (Iridescent Gold shimmer spray) Tattered Angels *Accents:* (kraft bird, red rose die cuts) Crate Paper; (white flowers) Prima; (silver staples) *Stickers:* (Alpha Labels alphabet) Crate Paper *Fibers:* (cream trim) Crate Paper *Tool:* (pinked circle punch) Martha Stewart Crafts

SUPPLIES: *Cardstock:* (Wild Wasabi, Whisper White, Real Red) Stampin' Up!; (kraft) Provo Craft *Rubber stamp:* (sentiment from Thanks a Million set) Stampin' Up! *Pigment ink:* (Basic Black) Stampin' Up! *Fibers:* (black twill) Michaels *Tools:* (¾", 1" circles; small star; label punches) Stampin' Up! *Other:* (dollar bill)

Sentiment

Sketch by: Stephanie Halinski

5 STEPS Happy Happy

Designer: Jen Daloisio

1. Make card from cardstock; stamp happy repeatedly.
2. Stamp birthday.
3. Affix stickers to spell "Happy". Tie on twine.
4. Round bottom corners.

Finished size: 4¼" x 5½"

SUPPLIES: *Cardstock:* (Natural) A Muse Studio *Clear stamps:* (happy, birthday from Sentiments set) Studio Calico *Dye ink:* (Malted Milk) Ranger Industries *Chalk ink:* (Gray Whale) Clearsnap *Stickers:* (Anthology alphabet) Studio Calico *Fibers:* (gray/white twine) Divine Twine *Tool:* (corner rounder punch) We R Memory Keepers

Let's Party!

Designer: Stephanie Halinski

1 Make card from cardstock. 2 Affix stickers. *Note: Adhere let's banner with foam tape.*

Finished size: 4¼" x 5½"

Newsprint Thanks

Designer: Lindsay Amrhein

1 Make card from cardstock. Stamp Background Basics: Newsprint set on card. 2 Die-cut label from cardstock. 3 Stamp sentiment on label and adhere rhinestones. 4 Adhere label to card with foam tape.

Finished size: 4¼" x 5½"

You're Fabulous

Designer: Carina Lindholm

1 Make card from cardstock; round bottom corner. 2 Apply rub-ons and affix stickers to spell "You're fabulous". 3 Adhere rhinestones.

Finished size: 5½" x 4"

SUPPLIES: *Cardstock:* (Melon Mambo) Stampin' Up! *Stickers:* (let's banner) Me & My Big Ideas; (party) Making Memories; (Lullaby alphabet) American Crafts

SUPPLIES: All supplies from Papertrey Ink unless otherwise noted. *Cardstock:* (Soft Stone) *Clear stamps:* (sentiment from Think Big Favorites #1 set; Background Basics: Newsprint set) *Specialty ink:* (True Black, Pure Poppy hybrid) *Accents:* (clear rhinestones) Me & My Big Ideas *Die:* (label)

SUPPLIES: *Cardstock:* (white) Bazzil Basics Paper *Accents:* (clear rhinestones) Heidi Swapp *Rub-ons:* (labels) Hambly Screen Prints *Stickers:* (Micro Mono alphabet, fabulous) BasicGrey *Tool:* (corner rounder punch)

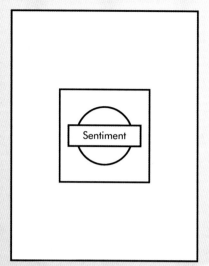

Sketch by: Stephanie Halinski

⬡5 STEPS Enjoy the Adventure

Designer: Stephanie Halinski

1. Make card from cardstock; adhere patterned paper squares.

2. Circle-punch cardstock square; adhere with foam tape.

3. Affix stickers.

Finished size: 4¼" x 5½"

SUPPLIES: *Cardstock:* (Very Vanilla, kraft) Stampin' Up! *Patterned paper:* (Great Find from The Thrift Shop collection) October Afternoon *Stickers:* (arrow) BasicGrey; (enjoy, the) Making Memories; (adventure) Martha Stewart Crafts *Tool:* (circle punch)

DESIGNER TIP

Changing the shape of card can give a whole new look to the sketch design.

5 STEPS You're a Rock Star

Designer: Kelley Eubanks

❶ Make card from cardstock; round bottom corners. ❷ Die-cut square from cardstock. Stamp striped star and sentiment. ❸ Adhere rhinestones to panel and adhere to card with foam tape.

Finished size: 4¼" x 5½"

5 STEPS Every Day is a Gift

Designer: Ellie Augustin

❶ Make card from cardstock; stamp Envelope Pattern. ❷ Stamp sentiment on cardstock square, mat with cardstock, and adhere. ❸ Circle-punch patterned paper, ink edges, and adhere. ❹ Affix sticker.

Finished size: 4" square

New Day

Designer: Agnieszka Malyszek

❶ Make card from cardstock. ❷ Trim patterned paper slightly smaller than card front, distress edges, and adhere. ❸ Circle-punch cardstock and adhere circles to cardstock square; adhere. *Note: Distress edges of cardstock square before adhering.* ❹ Accordion-fold book page, trim, and adhere into flower. Ink and adhere. ❺ Stamp sentiment on cardstock strip, trim, and adhere with foam tape. ❻ Stamp butterfly on cardstock; emboss. Trim, ink, and adhere to card. Attach brads.

Finished size: 4" x 6"

SUPPLIES: *Cardstock:* (Basic Gray) Stampin' Up!; (white) Papertrey Ink *Clear stamps:* (striped star, sentiment from Star Prints set) Papertrey Ink *Dye ink:* (Fountain Pen) Ranger Industries; (Mango) Stewart Superior Corp. *Accents:* (black rhinestones) My Mind's Eye *Die:* (square) Spellbinders *Tool:* (corner rounder punch)

SUPPLIES: *Cardstock:* (Simply Chartreuse, Fine Linen) Papertrey Ink; (white) *Patterned paper:* (True Blue Shining from Fine and Dandy collection) My Mind's Eye *Rubber stamp:* (Envelope Pattern) Hero Arts *Clear stamp:* (sentiment from Everyday Button Bits set) Papertrey Ink *Dye ink:* (Fountain Pen, Malted Milk) Ranger Industries *Watermark ink:* Tsukineko *Sticker:* (tree) KI Memories *Tool:* (circle punch) EK Success

SUPPLIES: *Cardstock:* (cream, gray) Bazzill Basics Paper *Patterned paper:* (polka dots from Black & White Basics collection) Papertrey Ink *Clear stamps:* (butterfly from Antique Engravings set) Hero Arts; (sentiment from Blooming Button Bits set) Papertrey Ink *Dye ink:* (black, green) Clearsnap *Embossing powder:* (black) Inkadinkado *Accents:* (green brads) *Tool:* (circle punch) EK Success *Other:* (book page)

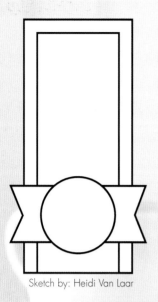

Sketch by: Heidi Van Laar

⁵⁵⁵ Sunny Days Ahead

Designer: Agnieszka Malyszek

1. Make card from cardstock.

2. Stamp Rose Background on cardstock rectangle; adhere.

3. Trim cardstock rectangle; adhere.

4. Circle-punch cardstock, stamp sentiment, and adhere. Stamp Rose Background on cardstock, trim, and adhere with foam tape.

5. Adhere pearls.

Finished size: 3" x 6"

SUPPLIES: *Cardstock:* (cream) Bazzill Basics Paper; (gold corrugated) *Rubber stamp:* (Rose Background)
Hero Arts *Clear stamps:* (sentiment from Pop Flowers set) My Cute Stamps *Pigment ink:* (pink) Studio G
Accents: (iridescent pearls) Prima *Tool:* (circle punch)

⑤ Super 8

Designer: Lori Tecler

❶ Make card from cardstock. Trim patterned paper rectangle; adhere. ❷ Trim patterned paper strip; adhere. ❸ Die-cut circle, star, and eight from cardstock. ❹ Emboss star and adhere die cuts to card. *Note: Adhere eight with foam tape.* ❺ Thread button with twine; adhere.

Finished size: 3" x 6"

SUPPLIES: *Cardstock:* (Hawaiian Shores, Orange Zest, Harvest Gold) Papertrey Ink *Patterned paper:* (True Blue Keen from Fine and Dandy collection) My Mind's Eye; (blue polka dots from Library Ledger collection) Papertrey Ink *Accent:* (orange button) Papertrey Ink *Fibers:* (blue/white twine) The Twinery *Template:* (embossing polka dots) Sizzix *Dies:* (star, eight) Papertrey Ink; (circle) Spellbinders

⑤ Say Cheese!

Designer: Jessica Fick

❶ Make card from cardstock. Trim patterned paper rectangle; adhere. ❷ Die-cut label and circle from cardstock; adhere. ❸ Attach eyelets and tie on cord. ❹ Affix camera sticker and affix alphabet stickers to spell "Say cheese!".

Finished size: 3¼" x 6½"

SUPPLIES: *Cardstock:* (Ocean, Navy) Gina K Designs; (gray) *Patterned paper:* (On the Shore from Seaside collection) October Afternoon *Accents:* (silver eyelets) *Stickers:* (Mini Market alphabet, camera) October Afternoon *Fibers:* (silver cord) *Dies:* (circle) Spellbinders; (label) My Favorite Things

⑤ Such Fabulous Friends

Designer: Heidi Van Laar

❶ Make card from cardstock; adhere patterned paper. ❷ Mat patterned paper rectangle with patterned paper; adhere. ❸ Adhere ribbon together, trim, and adhere to card. ❹ Accordion-fold patterned paper strip and adhere to create flower. Adhere to card. ❺ Adhere sticker with foam tape and insert stick pins.

Finished size: 4" x 8"

SUPPLIES: *Cardstock:* (cream) The Paper Company *Patterned paper:* (Rose Tonal Orange, Quatrefoil Pink, Quatrefoil Yellow from Carmen collection) Anna Griffin *Accents:* (pink, yellow leaf stick pins) Jo-Ann Stores *Sticker:* (fabulous friends label) Anna Griffin *Fibers:* (orange ribbon) Offray; (pink ribbon) May Arts

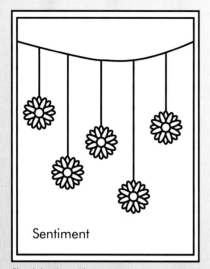

Sentiment

Sketch by: Lucy Abrams

⁵ Be Yourself

Designer: Tina Albertson

❶ Make card from cardstock. Trim patterned paper slightly smaller than card front; adhere.

❷ Stitch lines. *Note: Leave thread lengths long at top.* Cut half circle from patterned paper; adhere.

❸ Adhere butterflies and flowers. Apply rub-on.

Finished size: 4¾" x 6¾"

SUPPLIES: *Cardstock:* (white) Bazzill Basics Paper *Patterned paper:* (Botanical Gardens, Dragonflies from Butterfly Garden collection) Pink Paislee *Accents:* (beige butterflies, flowers) Pink Paislee *Rub-on:* (be yourself) American Crafts

Rhinestone Love

Designer: Jennifer Bloxsome

① Make card from cardstock. ② Stamp love and tie on twine. ③ Adhere rhinestone hearts with foam tape.

Finished size: 5¾" square

Reach for the Sky

Designer: Windy Robinson

① Make card from cardstock. ② Spritz cardstock rectangle with shimmer spray. Stamp sentiment and draw lines with marker. ③ Cut half circle from patterned paper; adhere. ④ Mat panel with cardstock; adhere. ⑤ Adhere flowers and tie on twine.

Finished size: 4¼" x 5½"

Precious Baby

Designer: Catherine Doucette

① Make card from cardstock. ② Trim cardstock slightly smaller than card front. Ink edges and stitch lines. ③ Affix sticker to panel and adhere. ④ Die-cut stars and large circle from cardstock. Trim moon shape from circle. ⑤ Apply glitter glue to die cut edges; adhere. ⑥ Apply glitter glue to stitching.

Finished size: 4¼" x 5½"

SUPPLIES: *Cardstock:* (white) Craftsworks Cards *Clear stamp:* (love from Love Tree Small set) Hot Off The Press *Pigment ink:* (Onyx Black) Tsukineko *Accents:* (red, pink rhinestone hearts) Paper Cellar *Fibers:* (blue/white twine) Divine Twine

SUPPLIES: *Cardstock:* (Classic Yellow) Bazzill Basics Paper; (kraft, white) Papertrey Ink *Patterned paper:* (Corn Kernels from Blossom Soup collection) Jillibean Soup *Clear stamp:* (sentiment from Up, Up & Away Sentiment set) Papertrey Ink *Specialty ink:* (Burnt Umber hybrid) Stewart Superior Corp.; (Blue Skies shimmer spray) Tattered Angels *Color medium:* (olive marker) Copic *Accents:* (assorted flowers) GCD Studios *Fibers:* (natural jute twine)

SUPPLIES: *Cardstock:* (Aqua Mist, Harvey Gold, kraft) Papertrey Ink; (Classic Crest) Neenah Paper *Pigment ink:* (Aqua Mist) Papertrey Ink *Accent:* (iridescent glitter glue) Ranger Industries *Sticker:* (precious baby) SRM Press *Dies:* (large circle) Spellbinders; (star) Sizzix

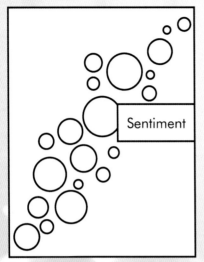

Sketch by: Emily Branch

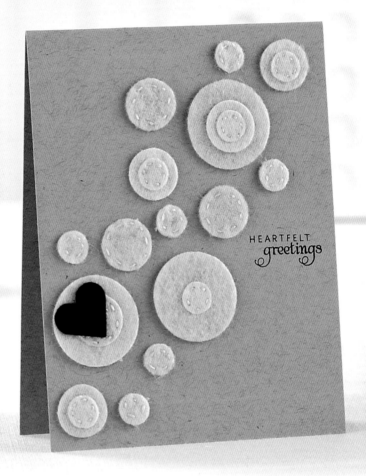

5 steps Heartfelt Greetings

Designer: Tosha Leyendekker

1. Make card from cardstock.
2. Die-cut circles and heart from felt.
   Stitch some circles with floss.
3. Adhere circles and heart to card.
4. Stamp heartfelt greetings.

Finished size: 4¼" x 5½"

SUPPLIES: *Cardstock:* (kraft) Papertrey Ink *Clear stamp:* (heartfelt greetings from Amazing Wishes set) Verve Stamps *Pigment ink:* (Onyx Black) Tsukineko *Fibers:* (cream floss) *Dies:* (circles, heart) Spellbinders *Other:* (red, cream felt)

Spooky Halloween

Designer: Ryann Salamon

❶ Make card from cardstock. ❷ Stamp images and happy Halloween.

Finished size: 4¼" x 5½"

Whale Friend

Designer: Sarah Jay

❶ Make card from cardstock; affix dots.
❷ Stamp Hello Friend on vellum rectangle, fold, and adhere with foam tape. ❸ Stamp whale on cardstock, trim, and adhere with foam tape.

Finished size: 5" x 3½"

Woodsy Birthday

Designer: Heidi Van Laar

❶ Make card from cardstock; adhere patterned paper. ❷ Stamp flowers on patterned paper and cardstock, trim, and adhere. *Note: Color some flowers with marker and adhere with foam tape.* ❸ Stamp happy birthday on cardstock rectangle. Draw and color border with markers. ❹ Round left corners of panel and adhere with foam tape. ❺ Thread buttons; adhere.

Finished size: 4¼" x 5½"

SUPPLIES: All supplies from Clear & Simple Stamps unless otherwise noted. *Cardstock:* (white) Papertrey Ink *Clear stamps:* (happy Halloween, web, spiders, skull, jack-o-lantern from Beware set) *Specialty ink:* (Perfect Little Black Dress, Creamsicle Cardigan hybrid)

SUPPLIES: *Cardstock:* (Blue Oasis) Bazzill Basics Paper *Vellum:* (white) Stampin' Up! *Rubber stamps:* (whale from Keep Swimmin' set) A Muse Studio; (Hello Friend) Rubber Soul *Dye ink:* (London Fog) Tsukineko *Pigment ink:* (Whisper White) Stampin' Up! *Stickers:* (blue dots) Michaels

SUPPLIES: *Cardstock:* (white) Georgia-Pacific *Patterned paper:* (Buddies Herringbone, Buddies Argyle, Joy Woodgrain, Little Lady Fine Flowers Love Brocade, So Sweet Herringbone from Stella & Rose collection) My Mind's Eye *Clear stamps:* (flowers from Friendly Flowers set; happy birthday from Birthday Buddies set) Paper Smooches *Pigment ink:* (Onyx Black) Tsukineko *Chalk ink:* (Bisque) Clearsnap *Color medium:* (black, white markers) Staedtler, Inc.; (yellow marker) Copic *Accents:* (orange, teal, tan buttons) Blumenthal Lansing *Tool:* (corner rounder punch) We R Memory Keepers

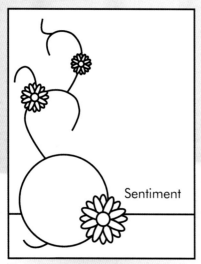

Sentiment

Sketch by: Heidi Van Laar

5 STEPS Yellow Swirl Thanks

Designer: Nicky Hsu

1. Make card from cardstock; stamp large flourish.

2. Adhere ribbon and stamp thanks.

3. Die-cut scalloped circle from cardstock and flowers from felt. Thread one flower with twine and adhere die cuts.

4. Tie button with twine; adhere. Adhere ribbon lengths.

Finished size: 4¼" x 5½"

SUPPLIES: *Cardstock:* (Rustic White, Dark Chocolate) Papertrey Ink *Clear stamps:* (large flourish from Thank You Flourishes set; thanks from So Artsy set) Hero Arts *Dye ink:* (Rich Cocoa, Dandelion) Tsukineko *Accent:* (yellow button) Papertrey Ink *Fibers:* (yellow/white twine, yellow ribbon) *Dies:* (scalloped circle, flowers) Spellbinders *Other:* (yellow, white felt)

FIND IT

Pattern on p. 284

So Fly

Designer: Tifany DeGough

❶ Make card from cardstock; score lines.
❷ Adhere patterned paper rectangles and round top corner. ❸ Affix stickers to spell sentiment. ❹ Attach twine with staples.
❺ Create airplane from patterned paper using pattern found on p. 284; adhere with foam tape.

Finished size: 4½" x 6"

Happy 4th

Designer: Heidi Van Laar

❶ Make card from cardstock. Adhere patterned paper strip and floss. ❷ Stamp "Happy th" on card; emboss. Affix sticker.
❸ Pierce flourish and stitch with floss.
❹ Die-cut circle and stars from cardstock and patterned paper. ❺ Pierce circle and stitch with floss; adhere with foam tape. ❻ Fold star die cuts and adhere with foam tape.

Finished size: 4¼" x 5½"

 Simple Joys

Designer: Kelly Schirmer

❶ Make card from cardstock; ink edges.
❷ Stamp vines on cardstock rectangle, ink edges, and adhere to card. Adhere cardstock rectangle. ❸ Die-cut circle from cardstock, stamp sentiment, and ink edges. Adhere.
❹ Stamp stems and strawberries on cardstock, trim, and adhere to card with foam tape.
❺ Adhere twine bow.

Finished size: 4¼" x 5½"

SUPPLIES: *Cardstock:* (Evening Surf) Bazzill Basics Paper *Patterned paper:* (Sailboats, In the Clouds, Rock Star from Little Boy collection) Echo Park Paper *Accents:* (silver staples) *Stickers:* (Fantastic alphabet) American Crafts; (Mini alphabet) My Little Shoebox *Fibers:* (yellow/white twine) The Twinery *Tool:* (corner rounder punch) We R Memory Keepers

SUPPLIES: *Cardstock:* (Ladybug, Admiral) Bazzill Basics Paper *Patterned paper:* (Jungle, Large Droplets, Baby Diaper Pins from Animal Crackers for Boys collection) GCD Studios *Rubber stamps:* (Times New Roman 12 pt, 24pt alphabet) JustRite *Pigment ink:* (white) Clearsnap *Embossing powder:* (white) American Crafts *Stickers:* (Heart alphabet) American Crafts *Fibers:* (white floss) *Dies:* (circle, stars) Spellbinders

SUPPLIES: *Cardstock:* (Vintage Cream, kraft) Papertrey Ink; (tan embossed) The Paper Company *Clear stamps:* (vine from Turning a New Leaf set; sentiment, stems, strawberries from Green Thumb set) Papertrey Ink *Dye ink:* (Antique Linen) Ranger Industries *Pigment ink:* (Fresh Snow) Papertrey Ink; (Strawberry) Impress Rubber Stamps *Solvent ink:* (Timber Brown) Tsukineko *Chalk ink:* (Tea Leaves) Tsukineko *Fibers:* (cream hemp twine) Darice *Die:* (circle) Spellbinders

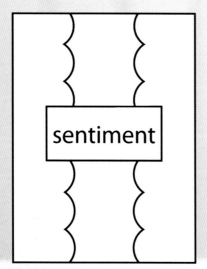

sentiment

Sketch by: Cristina Kowalczyk

Designer: Julia Stainton

1 Make card from cardstock; adhere patterned paper.

2 Trim pattered paper strips, border-punch edges, distress, and adhere. Stitch card border.

3 Die-cut clouds from felt. Mat sticker with cardstock.

4 Adhere clouds and sticker with foam tape.

Finished size: 4¼" x 5½"

SUPPLIES: *Cardstock:* (kraft) Bazzill Basics Paper *Patterned paper:* (Special Dotty Damask, Mother Ledger from Stella & Rose collection) My Mind's Eye *Sticker:* (sentiment) Glitz Design *Dies:* (clouds) Papertrey Ink *Tool:* (border punch) EK Success *Other:* (white felt) Papertrey Ink

5 Happy Happy Birthday

Designer: Lindsay Amrhein

1 Make card from cardstock. 2 Die-cut borders from patterned paper rectangles; adhere. Adhere patterned paper strips. 3 Die-cut label from cardstock. Stamp label, sentiment, and stars. Adhere to card with foam tape. 4 Thread buttons with twine; adhere.

Finished size: 4¼" x 5½"

5 Life Is Good Bear

Designer: Lorena Cantó Laveria

1 Make card from cardstock. 2 Emboss white cardstock; adhere to card base. 3 Die-cut green and blue patterned paper; adhere. 4 Stamp polar bear on patterned paper and color nose with marker; shade around edges. Trim and adhere to card base with foam tape. 5 Stamp word bubble and sentiment, fussy-cut, and adhere to card front.

Finished size: 4¾" x 4"

5 Always There

Designer: Joslyn Nielson

1 Make card from cardstock. 2 Stamp stars and stitch borders. 3 Adhere patterned paper strip. 4 Stamp sentiment on patterned paper, trim, and attach button with jump ring. 5 Adhere panel with foam tape.

Finished size: 4¼" x 5½"

SUPPLIES: *Cardstock:* (New Leaf) Papertrey Ink; (white) Georgia-Pacific *Patterned paper:* (Sailboats, Rock Star from Little Boy collection) Echo Park Paper *Clear stamps:* (frame from Fillable Frames #1 set; sentiment from Ordinary Days set) Technique Tuesday *Chalk ink:* (Yellow Cadmium) Clearsnap *Specialty ink:* (Enchanted Evening, True Black hybrid) Papertrey Ink *Accents:* (green buttons) Papertrey Ink *Fibers:* (green/white twine) Martha Stewart Crafts *Dies:* (label, medium scalloped border; label) Papertrey Ink

SUPPLIES: *Cardstock:* (white); *Patterned paper:* (Enchanted, Home from Lillian collection) Crate Paper; (Pinwheels from Sweet Summertime collection) Echo Park; (Hay Barn from Farm Fresh collection) October Afternoon *Clear stamps:* (polar bear from Critters in the Snow set) Lawn Fawn; (Life is Good sentiment from Message Bubbles set) Hero Arts *Dye ink:* (Tuxedo Black) Tsukineko *Color medium:* (pink, light grey markers) Copic *Templates:* (embossing snowflakes) Provo Craft *Die:* (scalloped border) My Favorite Things

SUPPLIES: *Cardstock:* (kraft) Papertrey Ink *Patterned paper:* (Red Wallpaper from Trendy collection) Jenni Bowlin Studio; (Spiral Orange Notebook) Creative Imaginations *Rubber stamps:* (sentiment, stars from To the Moon & Back set) Unity Stamp Co. *Specialty ink:* (L'Amour Red hybrid) Stewart Superior Corp. *Accents:* (blue button) Autumn Leaves; (silver jump ring)

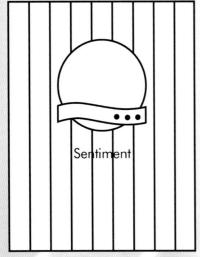

Sketch by: Lucy Abrams

5 STEPS Pucker Up!

Designer: Jocelyn Olson

1 Make card from cardstock. Adhere cardstock strips and round corners.

2 Die-cut flourished frame and circle from cardstock. Circle-punch cardstock. Adhere circles together and adhere to card with foam tape.

3 Adhere mustache with foam tape.

4 Stamp "Pucker up!" on cardstock, trim, and adhere to flourished frame; adhere.

5 Tie twill into bow tie, adhere rhinestones, and adhere to card.

Finished size: 4½" x 7"

SUPPLIES: *Cardstock:* (True Black, Hibiscus Burst, white) Papertrey Ink *Clear stamps:* (Jessie's ABCs alphabet) Lawn Fawn *Pigment ink:* (Pitch Black) Ranger Industries *Embossing powder:* (clear) Ranger Industries *Accents:* (clear rhinestones) Doodlebug Design; (mustache die cut) Imaginisce *Fibers:* (blue twill) May Arts *Dies:* (circle, flourished frame) Spellbinders *Tool:* (circle punch) Marvy Uchida; (corner rounder punch)

 Hoot

Designer: Chan Vuong

① Make card from cardstock; adhere patterned paper. ② Stamp branch on cardstock, trim, and adhere. Affix owl and adhere pearls. ③ Affix stickers to spell "Hoot".

Finished size: 3¾" x 5"

Pat on the Back

Designer: Kimberly Crawford

① Make card from cardstock; stamp Canvas Stripes. ② Die-cut scalloped circle from patterned paper. Ink edges and adhere with foam tape. ③ Adhere green flower sticker with foam tape. ④ Trim sentiment from patterned paper, curl, and adhere with foam tape. Adhere cork button and rhinestone. ⑤ Affix stickers to spell "Thanks".

Finished size: 4¼" x 5½"

Love Birds

Designer: Kim Kesti

① Make card from cardstock. ② Adhere cardstock strips to cardstock rectangle, stitch lines, and adhere. ③ Tie twill, twine, and button to tag. Adhere tag to card with foam tape.

Finished size: 4½" x 6¼"

SUPPLIES: *Cardstock:* (Vintage Cream, kraft) Papertrey Ink *Patterned paper:* (Forest Gardens from City Park collection) American Crafts *Rubber stamp:* (branch from Little Something set) Hampton Art *Chalk ink:* (Jumbo Java) Tsukineko *Accents:* (green pearls) Prima *Stickers:* (owl) My Mind's Eye; (Pink Oak alphabet) Cosmo Cricket

SUPPLIES: *Cardstock:* (kraft) Papertrey Ink *Patterned paper:* (Red Sugar from Soup Staples collection) Jillibean Soup; (Noteworthy from For the Record collection) Echo Park Paper *Rubber stamp:* (Canvas Stripes) Hero Arts *Dye ink:* (Tuxedo Black) Tsukineko; (Frayed Burlap) Ranger Industries *Accents:* (cork button) Pink Paislee; (tan rhinestone) Hero Arts *Stickers:* (green flower, For the Record alphabet) Echo Park Paper *Die:* (scalloped circle) Spellbinders

SUPPLIES: *Cardstock:* (Blossom, Berrylicious, African Daisy, Natural, kraft) Bazzill Basics Paper *Accents:* (love birds tag) We R Memory Keepers; (pink button) Pebbles *Fibers:* (cream twill, natural hemp twine)

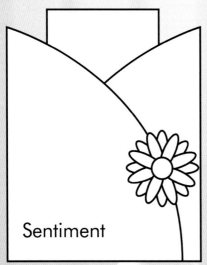

Sentiment

Sketch by: Anabelle O'Malley

DESIGNER TIP

Attach a gift card to the cardstock panel for a fun and cute way to personalize your gift!

⁵ˢᵗᵉᵖˢ Imagination Itself

Designer: Kalyn Kepner

1. Make tri-fold card from cardstock; round outside flaps.

2. Trim patterned paper to fit on flaps, stitch edges, and adhere. Adhere flaps to create pocket.

3. Stamp vine and sentiment. Affix flowers.

4. Trim cardstock rectangle to fit inside pocket; trim border with decorative-edge scissors. Adhere and stitch patterned paper rectangle.

5. Slide panel inside pocket.

Finished size: 4¼" x 5½"

SUPPLIES: *Cardstock:* (Cream Puff) Bazzill Basics Paper *Patterned paper:* (Great Find, Near Mint from The Thrift Shop collection; Strawberry Jam from Fly a Kite collection) October Afternoon *Clear stamps:* (sentiment from Grow set) Hampton Art; (vine from I Believe set) My Mind's Eye *Pigment ink:* (green, pink) Clearsnap *Accent:* (green glitter glue) Ranger Industries *Stickers:* (flowers) K&Company *Tool:* (decorative-edge scissors)

Compliments of the Season

Designer: Melissa Phillips

❶ Make card tri-fold card from cardstock.
❷ Adhere patterned paper and affix border sticker to front flaps. Round flaps and ink edges. ❸ Tie ribbon around card to create pocket. Affix sentiment and clock stickers. Adhere angel. ❹ Adhere wings and button threaded with floss to ribbon. ❺ Adhere trim. ❻ Trim patterned paper to fit inside pocket; ink edges. ❼ Trim patterned paper slightly smaller than panel, ink edges, and stamp post card and bradford stamp. Stitch to patterned paper and insert in pocket.

Finished size: 4" x 5¾"

SUPPLIES: *Cardstock:* (Cream Puff) Bazzill Basics Paper *Patterned paper:* (Geraldine, Octavia, Hattie from 5th Avenue collection) Melissa Frances; (Bo Peep from Lullaby Girl collection) Creative Imaginations *Rubber stamps:* (post card, Bradford stamp from Vintage PostCARD set) Purple Onion Designs *Specialty ink:* (Ocean Tides, Smokey Shadow hybrid) Papertrey Ink *Accents:* (cream buttons) Papertrey Ink; (white angel) The Little Pink Studio; (pink wings) MemrieMare *Stickers:* (sentiment, clock, border) Melissa Frances *Fibers:* (cream ribbon) MemriMare; (white trim) Michaels; (white floss)

⁙5⁙ Happily Ever After

Designer: Maria Gurnsey

❶ Make card from cardstock. ❷ Round cardstock panels, adhere, and stitch. ❸ Stamp church on cardstock, color with markers, trim, and adhere. ❹ Stamp conversation bubble on cardstock, trim, and adhere with foam tape. ❺ Tie twill around front flap.

Finished size: 4½" x 5½"

SUPPLIES: *Cardstock:* (Simply Chartreuse, Vintage Cream) Papertrey Ink; (white) The Paper Studio *Rubber stamps:* (sentiment from Happily Ever After set; church from Wherever You Go set) Unity Stamp Co.; (conversation bubble from Sweet Thoughts of Spring set) Ippity by Unity Stamp Co. *Dye ink:* (Tuxedo Black) Tsukineko *Color medium:* (brown, red markers) Copic *Fibers:* (green twill) Papertrey Ink

⁙5⁙ Doily Mother's Day

Designer: Julia Stainton

❶ Heart-punch cardstock rectangle. Stitch around heart, and mat with cardstock. ❷ Cut doily in half. Fold around cardstock panel and adhere flaps to create pocket. ❸ Tie twine around pocket. Adhere flower and insert stick pins. ❹ Print sentiment on cardstock, trim, and adhere.

Finished size: 3½" x 5¼"

SUPPLIES: *Cardstock:* (kraft) Bazzill Basics Paper *Accents:* (white doily) Wilton; (white flower) Prima; (white pearl, clear crystal stick pins) Maya Road *Fibers:* (natural jute twine) Westrim Crafts *Font:* (Century Schoolbook) www.myfonts.com *Tool:* (heart punch) Martha Stewart Crafts

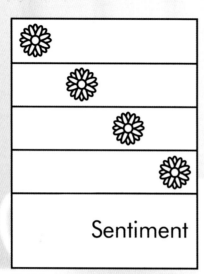

Sentiment

Sketch by: Vanessa Menhorn

{ a true friend }
{ is you friend }

⁵ You Friend

Designer: Lindsay Amrhein

1. Make card from cardstock.

2. Stamp small and medium woodgrain on cardstock strips; adhere.

3. Stamp sentiment and adhere rhinestone.

4. Thread buttons with floss; adhere.

Finished size: 4¼" x 5½"

SUPPLIES: *Cardstock:* (Sweet Blush, Berry Sorbet, Hibiscus Burst, Raspberry Fizz, white) Papertrey Ink *Clear stamps:* (small, medium woodgrain from Background Basics: Woodgrain set; sentiment from Fillable Frames #11 set) Papertrey Ink *Watermark ink:* Tsukineko *Specialty ink:* (True Black hybrid) Papertrey Ink *Embossing powder:* (clear) Hampton Art *Accents:* (pink buttons) Papertrey Ink; (clear rhinestone) Me & My Big Ideas *Fibers:* (black floss) DMC

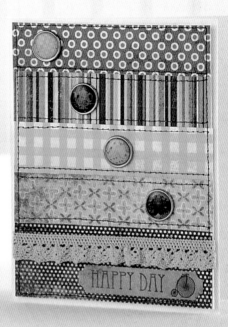

Thinking of You Roses

Designer: Sarah Jane Moerman

1 Make card from cardstock; adhere patterned paper strips. 2 Stamp sentiment. 3 Cut apart flower trim. Spritz flowers with ink, let dry, and adhere.

Finished size: 4¼" x 5½"

Birthday Ribbons

Designer: Vanessa Menhorn

1 Make card from cardstock; round bottom corners. 2 Stamp sentiment and tie on ribbon.

Finished size: 4¼" x 5½"

Happy Day

Designer: Wendy Sue Anderson

1 Make card from cardstock, adhere patterned paper strips, and stitch borders. 2 Attach brads, affix sticker, and adhere trim.

Finished size: 4½" x 5¾"

SUPPLIES: *Cardstock:* (white) Michaels *Patterned paper:* (Black Forest Strata, Eclair from Marjolaine collection; Dialect from Basics Kraft collection) BasicGrey; (Pinwheels from Togetherness collection) Cosmo Cricket *Clear stamp:* (sentiment from Find Joy set) Hero Arts *Dye ink:* (black) Memories; (Frayed Burlap, Spiced Marmalade, Broken China, Peeled Paint) Ranger Industries *Fibers:* (white flower trim) American Crafts

SUPPLIES: *Cardstock:* (kraft) Papertrey Ink *Clear stamp:* (happy birthday from Communique Curves set) Papertrey Ink *Dye ink:* (Tuxedo Black) Tsukineko *Fibers:* (pink, yellow, green, blue ribbon) Papertrey Ink *Tool:* (corner rounder punch) We R Memory Keepers

SUPPLIES: All supplies from My Mind's Eye unless otherwise noted. *Cardstock:* (white) American Crafts *Patterned paper:* (Delightful Sweet Stripe, Friends Forever Tapestry, Little One Darling Dots from Stella & Rose collection) *Accents:* (assorted epoxy brads) *Sticker:* (happy day) *Fibers:* (yellow trim)

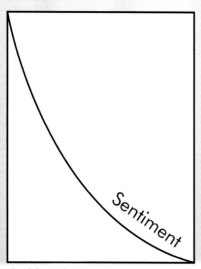

Sketch by: Kalyn Kepner

 Hello Sunshine

Designer: Kalyn Kepner

1. Make card from cardstock. Cut clouds from cardstock; adhere.

2. Trim triangles into curved edge of patterned paper; adhere. Trim patterned paper with decorative-edge scissors; adhere.

3. Trim and stitch patterned paper panel; adhere.

4. Stamp hello and sunshine.

Finished size: 4¼" x 5½"

SUPPLIES: *Cardstock:* (Light Teal) Bazzill Basics Paper; (cream) *Patterned paper:* (Dandelions from Fly a Kite collection) October Afternoon; (Colorful Umbrellas from Quite Contrary collection) My Mind's Eye *Clear stamps:* (hello from Daily Designs Sentiment set) Papertrey Ink; (Sunshine) Imaginsice *Pigment ink:* (orange) Clearsnap *Tool:* (decorative-edge scissors) Fiskars

Dino-Mite

Designer: Regina Mangum

❶ Make card from cardstock. ❷ Ink Cloudy Days Background with multiple colors; stamp on cardstock rectangle. Round right corner and adhere to card. ❸ Trim volcano, lava, and steam from cardstock. Score volcano; adhere. ❹ Ink edges of steam piece. Adhere lava and steam. ❺ Stamp dinosaur on cardstock, trim, and adhere. Stamp sentiment.

Finished size: 4¼" x 5½"

Delicate Easter Blessings

Designer: Nerina Hoffe

❶ Make card from cardstock; stamp medium damask repeatedly. ❷ Stamp large feathers repeatedly on cardstock; emboss. Trim curved edge, ink edges, and adhere. ❸ Stamp Easter blessings. ❹ Pleat and stitch ribbon; adhere. Attach brads.

Finished size: 4¼" x 5½"

Make a Wish

Designer: Lucy Abrams

❶ Make card from cardstock. ❷ Create 4" x 5¼" project in software. Stamp feather and sentiment. Print on cardstock. Stitch panel and adhere. ❸ Thread button with twine; adhere.

Finished size: 4¼" x 5½"

SUPPLIES: *Cardstock:* (white) Neenah Paper; (Real Red, Dusty Durango, Wild Wasabi, Chocolate Chip) Stampin' Up! *Rubber stamps:* (dinosaur, sentiment from Kid at Heart set; Cloudy Days Background) Taylored Expressions *Dye ink:* (Basic Black, Wild Wasabi, Basic Gray) Stampin' Up! *Pigment ink:* (Blue Brilliance, Aquatic Splash) Tsukineko *Tool:* (corner rounder punch) We R Memory Keepers

SUPPLIES: *Cardstock:* (Aqua Mist, white) Papertrey Ink *Clear stamps:* (large feather from Feathers set) Hero Arts; (Easter blessing from Tags for Spring set; medium damask from Damask Designs set) Papertrey Ink; (script from Text-It set) Waltzingmouse Stamps *Pigment ink:* (Aqua Mist, Fresh Snow) Papertrey Ink *Specialty ink:* (True Black hybrid) Papertrey Ink *Embossing powder:* (white) Stampendous! *Accents:* (pewter brads) Stampin' Up! *Fibers:* (white ribbon)

SUPPLIES: *Cardstock:* (Pool) Hero Arts; (Rustic Cream) Papertrey Ink *Accent:* (aqua button) Papertrey Ink *Digital elements:* (feather stamp from HA Bird Silhouettes collection; sentiment stamp from HA Make a Wish collection) www.twopeasinabucket.com *Fibers:* (cream hemp twine) Papertrey Ink

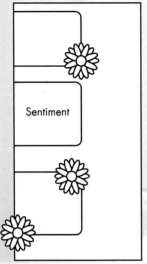

Sentiment

Sketch by: Vanessa Menhorn

5 STEPS Hello Friend

Designer: Chan Vuong

1. Make card from cardstock.
2. Round corners of patterned paper rectangles; adhere.
3. Stamp hello friend on cardstock, trim, and adhere.
4. Affix stickers.

Finished size: 3¼" x 5"

SUPPLIES: *Cardstock:* (Lemon Tart) Papertrey Ink *Patterned paper:* (Pinwheels from Togetherness collection) Cosmo Cricket *Clear stamp:* (hello friend from Hello Friend set) Lawn Fawn *Chalk ink:* (Jumbo Java) Tsukineko *Stickers:* (birds) Cosmo Cricket *Tool:* (corner rounder punch) Marvy Uchida

⟨5 STEPS⟩ Sending You Love

Designer: Angeline Yong Jeet Leen

❶ Make card from cardstock. ❷ Stamp small flowers on card to create borders. Stamp leaves and sentiment. ❸ Stamp medallions on cardstock, butterfly-punch, and adhere pearls. Adhere butterflies.

Finished size: 4" x 7"

⟨5 STEPS⟩ Happy Anniversary

Designer: Lindsay Amrhein

❶ Make card from cardstock; round bottom corner. ❷ Stamp large circled hearts on card. ❸ Stamp happy and anniversary on card and adhere rhinestone. ❹ Thread buttons with floss; adhere.

Finished size: 3½" x 5½"

⟨5 STEPS⟩ You Can Do It!

Designer: Julia Stainton

❶ Make card from cardstock; stitch rectangles. ❷ Affix stickers to spell sentiment and affix butterflies.

Finished size: 3½" x 7½"

SUPPLIES: *Cardstock:* (Raven, Snow) Bazzill Basics Paper *Clear stamps:* (leaves from Woodgrain Silhouettes Additions set; small flower, sentiment, medallion from Poinsettia Patterns set) Wplus9 Design Studio *Pigment ink:* (Graphite Black, Split Pea, Spanish Olive, Wheat) Tsukineko *Accents:* (white pearls) Kaisercraft *Tool:* (butterfly punch) Martha Stewart Crafts

SUPPLIES: *Cardstock:* (Sweet Blush) Papertrey Ink *Clear stamps:* (large circled hearts, happy, anniversary from Heart Prints set) Papertrey Ink *Pigment ink:* (Chianti) Clearsnap *Specialty ink:* (True Black hybrid) Papertrey Ink *Accents:* (black buttons) Papertrey Ink; (clear rhinestone) Me & My Big Ideas *Fibers:* (burgundy floss) DMC *Tool:* (corner rounder punch) We R Memory Keepers

SUPPLIES: *Cardstock:* (kraft) Bazzill Basics Paper *Stickers:* (butterflies) K&Company; (Tiny Type alphabet) Cosmo Cricket; (Rockabye alphabet) American Crafts

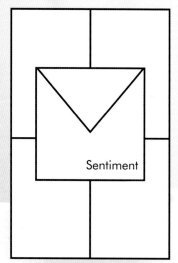

Sentiment

Sketch by: Anabelle O'Malley

⑤ Just Because Butterfly

Designer: Sarah Shewell

❶ Make card from cardstock; adhere patterned paper rectangles.

❷ Adhere envelope and stamp just because.

❸ Attach eyelet to tag, tie on ribbon, and insert into envelope.

❹ Stamp Large Highwing Butterfly on cardstock and patterned paper.

❺ Color butterfly stamped on cardstock with markers; trim and adhere. Trim wings from patterned paper and adhere.

Finished size: 4¼" x 5½"

SUPPLIES: *Cardstock:* (Very Vanilla, kraft) Stampin' Up! *Patterned paper:* (Wide Tide, Cargo, Wing-Tip, Bowling Shoes from Boxer collection) BasicGrey *Rubber stamps:* (Large Highwing Butterfly) The Rubber Cafe; (just because) A Muse Studio *Dye ink:* (Tuxedo Black) Tsukineko *Color medium:* (green, blue markers) Copic *Accents:* (white tag, kraft envelope) Melissa Frances; (brass eyelet) We R Memory Keepers *Fibers:* (green ribbon) Stampin' Up!

DESIGNER TIP

Insert a gift card inside the pocket for an added birthday bonus!

5 STEPS Made with Love

Designer: Natalie Dever

❶ Make card from cardstock. ❷ Ink edges of patterned paper rectangles; adhere. ❸ Border punch top of patterned paper rectangle. Adhere panel to cardstock and affix border sticker. ❹ Adhere button card to panel with foam tape. *Note: Ink edges before adhering.* Adhere panel to card with foam tape. ❺ Affix sentiment sticker and tie on floss.

Finished size: 4¼" x 6"

5 STEPS Birthday Banner

Designer: Julia Aston

❶ Make card from cardstock. ❷ Adhere patterned paper rectangles to cardstock rectangle; adhere to card. ❸ Stamp happy birthday on envelope, tie on twine, and adhere. ❹ Stamp pennants on cardstock, trim, and adhere with foam tape.

Finished size: 4¼" x 5½"

5 STEPS XOXO

Designer: Chan Vuong

❶ Make card from cardstock; adhere patterned paper rectangles. ❷ Adhere envelope, stamp xoxo, and adhere flowers.

Finished size: 4" x 6"

SUPPLIES: *Cardstock:* (green) Bazzill Basics Paper *Patterned paper:* (Clothespins, Canning Jar, Flour Sack, Party Line from Modern Homemaker collection) October Afternoon *Dye ink:* (Old Paper) Ranger Industries *Accents:* (cream button card with buttons) Blumenthal Lansing *Stickers:* (sentiment, border) October Afternoon *Fibers:* (red floss) *Tool:* (border punch) Fiskars

SUPPLIES: *Cardstock:* (kraft) Gina K Designs; (Orange Zest) Papertrey Ink *Patterned paper:* (Lovely Loops from Be Loved collection) My Mind's Eye *Clear stamps:* (star pennant from Bitty Banners set; happy birthday from Frame It set) Waltzingmouse Stamps *Dye ink:* (Tuxedo Black, Lady Bug, Cottage Ivy, Tangelo) Tsukineko *Accent:* (kraft envelope) Michaels *Fibers:* (orange/white, green/white twine) Martha Stewart Crafts

SUPPLIES: *Cardstock:* (kraft) Papertrey Ink *Patterned paper:* (Fancy Free, Delicate Olio, Free Composition from Mix and Mend collection) Sassafras Lass *Clear stamp:* (xoxo from Sophie's Sentiments set) Lawn Fawn *Chalk ink:* (Jumbo Java) Tsukineko *Accents:* (kraft envelope) Maya Road; (orange flowers) Prima

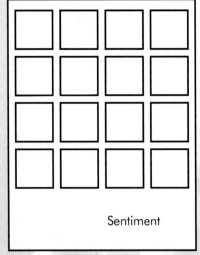

Sentiment

Sketch by: Kim Kesti

missed
you

⁵ Missed You

Designer: Chan Vuong

1. Make card from cardstock.

2. Trim patterned paper into squares;
   adhere with foam tape.

3. Stamp missed you.

Finished size: 4½" x 5¾"

SUPPLIES: *Cardstock:* (kraft) Papertrey Ink *Patterned paper:* (Shady Lane RV Park from Road Map collection) October Afternoon *Clear stamp:* (missed you from Just My Type Too set) Lawn Fawn *Pigment ink:* (Onyx Black) Tsukineko

Merry Christmas to You

Designer: Jessica Witty

1 Make card from cardstock. 2 Trim patterned paper; adhere. *Note: Adhere some panels with foam tape.* 3 Tie on twine. Trim patterned paper strip and adhere with foam tape. 4 Affix stickers to spell "To you".

Finished size: 5" x 5½"

Elegant Anniversary

Designer: Julia Stainton

1 Make card from cardstock; ink edges. 2 Trim patterned paper into squares; adhere. 3 Stamp happy anniversary. 4 Adhere twine bow and flower.

Finished size: 4¼" x 6"

Time to Give Thanks

Designer: Diana Slaughter

1 Make card from cardstock, round corners, and ink edges. 2 Stamp Foliage on cardstock, square-punch, and round corners. Adhere panels with foam tape. 3 Apply rub-on and tie on twine.

Finished size: 4¾" x 6"

SUPPLIES: *Cardstock:* (kraft) Papertrey Ink *Patterned paper:* (Refinish from Restoration collection) Crate Paper; (Flashcards from Schoolhouse collection) October Afternoon *Stickers:* (Market alphabet) The Girls' Paperie *Fibers:* (red/white twine) The Twinery

SUPPLIES: *Cardstock:* (white) Neenah Paper *Patterned paper:* (Party Looking Glass from Lost & Found collection) My Mind's Eye *Clear stamp:* (happy anniversary from All Occasion Messages set) Hero Arts *Dye ink:* (Coffee) Ranger Industries *Accents:* (white flower) Prima *Fibers:* (natural jute twine) Westrim Crafts

SUPPLIES: *Cardstock:* (Nathan, Candlelight, Papaya, Tangelo, Rain Forest) Bazzill Basics Paper *Rubber stamp:* (Foliage Cube) Stampendous! *Chalk ink:* (Hint of Pesto) Tsukineko *Watermark ink:* Tsukineko *Embossing powder:* (clear) Stampendous! *Rub-on:* (sentiment) Making Memories *Fibers:* (green twine) May Arts *Tools:* (square punch) Family Treasures; (corner rounder punch) Marvy Uchida

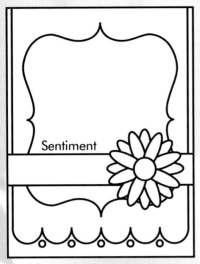

Sentiment

Sketch by: Windy Robinson

Miss You Leaf

Designer: Chris Severs

1 Make card from cardstock.

2 Die-cut medium scalloped border on patterned paper rectangle. Distress edges.

3 Stamp frame and miss you on patterned paper. Trim, ink edges, and adhere to die-cut panel.

4 Adhere ribbon and adhere panel to card.

5 Die-cut leaf from felt; adhere. Thread button with twine; adhere.

6 Adhere pearls.

Finished size: 4¼" x 5½"

SUPPLIES: *Cardstock:* (kraft) Papertrey Ink *Patterned paper:* (Refresh, Revitalize from Origins collection) BasicGrey *Rubber stamp:* (frame from Love In Return set) Ippity By Unity Stamp Co. *Clear stamp:* (miss you from Mega Mixed Messages set) Papertrey Ink *Dye ink:* (Black Soot, Antique Linen) Ranger Industries *Accents:* (black button) Papertrey Ink; (black pearls) Kaisercraft *Fibers:* (brown ribbon) Papertrey Ink; (white hemp twine) *Dies:* (leaves, medium scalloped border) Papertrey Ink *Other:* (green felt) Papertrey Ink

Summery Thanks

Designer: Windy Robinson

❶ Make card from cardstock, adhere patterned paper, and ink edges. ❷ Border-punch cardstock rectangle, ink edges, and adhere. ❸ Stamp flourish and thanks on cardstock, trim into label, ink edges, and adhere. ❹ Adhere rhinestones. ❺ Tie on ribbon. Tie on button with twine.

Finished size: 4¼" x 5½"

Wish You Were Here

Designer: Susan R. Opel

❶ Make card from cardstock; adhere cardstock. ❷ Die-cut label from patterned paper, adhere to patterned paper square, and adhere to card. ❸ Border-punch cardstock strip; adhere. ❹ Stamp sentiment on cardstock strip; adhere. Adhere rhinestones. ❺ Tie on ribbon and adhere heart.

Finished size: 4¾" x 5½"

Simply Amazing

Designer: Tosha Leyendekker

❶ Make card from cardstock. ❷ Border-punch cardstock rectangle, score lines, and adhere pearls. ❸ Die-cut large label from cardstock, stamp Cover-a-Card Quilt, and emboss. Adhere to panel. ❹ Die-cut small label from cardstock, stamp sentiment, trim, and adhere. ❺ Adhere trim and ribbon. Adhere panel to card. ❻ Loop fabric and stitch seam. Trim slits to create petals; adhere in circle shape. Attach to card with brad.

Finished size: 4¼" x 5½"

SUPPLIES: *Cardstock:* (white) Papertrey Ink; (Natural) Paper Adventures *Patterned paper:* (Fancy Free from Mix and Mend collection) Sassafras Lass *Rubber stamp:* (flourish from Floral Tattoo set) Stampers Anonymous *Clear stamp:* (thanks from Daily Designs Sentiments set) Papertrey Ink *Chalk ink:* (Chestnut Roan) Clearsnap *Accents:* (yellow rhinestones) Doodlebug Design; (white button) *Fibers:* (natural jute twine) Papertrey Ink; (white ribbon) Michaels *Tool:* (border punch)

SUPPLIES: *Cardstock:* (light blue, green, white) Bazzill Basics Paper *Patterned paper:* (Trick Pony from Fun House collection) GCD Studios; (US Map from Pack Your Bags collection) Little Yellow Bicycle *Clear stamp:* (sentiment from Wish You Were Here set) Hero Arts *Dye ink:* (Moonstruck) Close To My Heart *Accent:* (red heart) Fancy Pants Designs; (green rhinestones) Little Yellow Bicycle *Fibers:* (blue ribbon) Offray *Die:* (label) Spellbinders *Tool:* (border punch) Fiskars

SUPPLIES: *Cardstock:* (Harvest Gold, white) Papertrey Ink *Rubber stamp:* (Cover-a-Card Quilt) Impression Obsession *Clear stamp:* (sentiment from You Inspire Me set) JustRite *Pigment ink:* (Smokey Gray) Tsukineko *Watermark ink:* Tsukineko *Embossing powder:* (white) Stampin' Up! *Accents:* (pearl brad) Eyelet Outlet; (silver pearls) Michaels *Fibers:* (gray ribbon) Chatterbox; (white trim) Wild Orchid Crafts *Dies:* (large, small labels) Spellbinders *Tool:* (border punch) EK Success *Other:* (yellow organdy fabric)

Sketch by: Kim Kesti

5 STEPS Love You Letter

Designer: Angeline Yong Jeet Leen

1. Make card from cardstock.

2. Stamp September circle, postmark, bird stamp, and love on card.

3. Adhere envelope and stamp you.

4. Stamp bird stamp on cardstock, trim, and adhere bird with foam tape.

5. Thread button with twine; adhere. Attach brad.

Finished size: 4¼" x 6"

SUPPLIES: *Cardstock:* (cream) Bazzill Basics Paper *Clear stamps:* (September circle, postmark from Postmarked set; bird stamp, love, you from Spring Post set) Wplus9 Design Studio *Pigment ink:* (Sepia, brown) Kaisercraft; (Amaryllis) Martha Stewart Crafts *Accents:* (brass heart brad, brown button, kraft envelope) *Fibers:* (brown/white twine) The Twinery

⑤ One

Designer: Vivian Masket

❶ Make card from cardstock; adhere patterned paper rectangle. ❷ Trim tag from patterned paper; adhere. ❸ Adhere elephant card with foam tape; insert stick pin. ❹ Thread buttons with twine; adhere with foam tape.

Finished size: 4¼" x 5½"

⑤ Just a Note

Designer: Glenda J. Wyatt

❶ Make card from cardstock. ❷ Punch circle and scalloped circle from patterned paper; adhere. ❸ Stamp sentiment. ❹ Make envelope using template on p. 284. ❺ Tie envelope with twine and adhere.

Finished size: 5¾" x 5½"

⑤ Wish Big

Designer: Angela Hathikhanavala

Ink all patterned paper edges. ❶ Make card from cardstock. ❷ Trim patterned paper slightly smaller than card front; adhere. ❸ Die-cut circle and scalloped circles from patterned paper; adhere. ❹ Mat envelope with patterned paper; adhere. Tie on twine. ❺ Stamp wish big.

Finished size: 5" x 6"

SUPPLIES: *Cardstock:* (Maraschino) Bazzill Basics Paper *Patterned paper:* (Chalkboard from Schoolhouse collection) October Afternoon; (Step Right Up from Animal Crackers collection) Imaginisce *Accents:* (clear crystal stick pin) Maya Road; (cream elephant card) October Afternoon *Stickers:* (green, blue buttons) October Afternoon *Fibers:* (red/white twine) Martha Stewart Crafts

SUPPLIES: *Cardstock:* (Crumb Cake) Stampin' Up! *Patterned paper:* (Exploration Words from Panorama collection) Making Memories *Clear stamp:* (sentiment from Take Three Fall set) Papertrey Ink *Dye ink:* (Real Red) Stampin' Up! *Accent:* (white envelope) *Fibers:* (natural jute twine) Papertrey Ink *Tools:* (scalloped circle, circle punches) EK Success

SUPPLIES: *Cardstock:* (kraft) Papertrey Ink *Patterned paper:* (Table Cloth, Lace Stripes from For the Record collection) Echo Park Paper *Clear stamp:* (wish big from Big & Bold Wishes set) Papertrey Ink *Dye ink:* (Basic Black) Stampin' Up! *Chalk ink:* (Creamy Brown) Clearsnap *Accent:* (kraft envelope) Maya Road *Fibers:* (yellow/white twine) The Twinery *Dies:* (scalloped circles, circles) Spellbinders

Sketch by: Chan Vuong

5 STEPS Scooting By

Designer: Heidi Van Laar

1. Make card from cardstock. Adhere patterned paper and round top corners.
2. Die-cut circle from patterned paper, ink edges, and adhere.
3. Stamp scooter and flag on cardstock and patterned paper, trim, and adhere together. Adhere to card with foam tape.
4. Stamp sentiment and adhere twine bow.

Finished size: 4½" x 6"

SUPPLIES: *Cardstock:* (white) Georgia-Pacific; (gray) The Paper Company *Patterned paper:* (Head in the Clouds, Up Town, Pristine Plaid from Good Day Sunshine Girl collection) My Mind's Eye *Clear stamps:* (sentiment, scooter, flag from Spiffy Scooters set) Paper Smooches *Pigment ink:* (Sky Gray) Clearsnap *Fibers:* (green/white twine) The Twinery *Die:* (circle) Spellbinders *Tool:* (corner rounder punch) We R Memory Keepers

Outlook Good

Designer: Regina Mangum

1 Make card from specialty paper. 2 Print "Outlook good" on cardstock; adhere. 3 Die-cut circle from specialty paper; adhere. 4 Print "8" on cardstock, die-cut into circle, and adhere.

Finished size: 4¼" x 5½"

Doily Thanks

Designer: Kimberly Crawford

1 Make card from cardstock; adhere patterned paper rectangle. 2 Stamp Circle Lace on cardstock; emboss. Trim and adhere. 3 Stamp thanks on card and tie on twine. 4 Punch butterflies from patterned paper, clip together with clothespins, and adhere to card with foam tape.

Finished size: 4¼" x 5½"

You Make My Day

Designer: Jennifer Rzasa

1 Make card from cardstock; tie on floss. 2 Cut circle from cardstock rectangle, stamp sentiment, and adhere with foam tape. 3 Adhere rhinestone.

Finished size: 4¼" x 5½"

SUPPLIES: *Cardstock:* (white) Nennah Paper *Specialty paper:* (black foil) American Crafts *Font:* (Arial) Microsoft *Dies:* (circles) Spellbinders

SUPPLIES: *Cardstock:* (kraft) Papertrey Ink *Patterned paper:* (Last One, One-of-a Kind from The Thrift Shop collection) October Afternoon *Rubber stamp:* (Circle Lace) Hero Arts *Clear stamp:* (thanks from Type set) Hero Arts *Dye ink:* (Tuxedo Black) Tsukineko *Watermark ink:* Tsukineko *Embossing power:* (white) Stanpendous! *Accents:* (natural clothespins) Canvas Corp. *Fibers:* (black/white twine) Divine Twine *Tool:* (butterfly punch) Martha Stewart Crafts

SUPPLIES: *Cardstock:* (white) Michaels *Clear stamp:* (sentiment from How Delightful set) Lawn Fawn *Pigment ink:* (Still of the Night) Fiskars *Accent:* (clear rhinestone) Me & My Big Ideas *Fibers:* (assorted floss) DMC *Tool:* (circle cutter) Fiskars

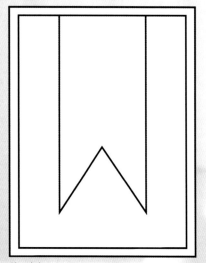

Sketch by: AJ Otto

Balloons for You

Designer: Angeline Yong Jeet Leen

1 Make card from cardstock. Adhere slightly smaller cardstock rectangle.

2 Trim cardstock rectangle; adhere.

3 Stamp balloons on cardstock and card. Adhere twine.

4 Trim stamped balloons from cardstock; adhere with foam tape.

5 Adhere rhinestones and ribbon bow.

Finished size: 3¾" x 5½"

SUPPLIES: *Cardstock:* (Glow, Sea Water, Petunia, white, kraft) Bazzill Basics Paper *Clear stamps:* (balloons from Party Time set) Verve Stamps *Pigment ink:* (brown) Kaisercraft *Accents:* (clear, purple, blue rhinestones) Kaisercraft *Fibers:* (yellow/white, blue/white, purple/white twine) The Twinery; (white ribbon)

DESIGNER TIP

Take liberties with the sketch. Flip it or invert it and let your imagination soar.

Groom

Designer: Regina Mangum

1 Make card from cardstock; adhere cardstock rectangle. 2 Trim collar in cardstock rectangle, score lines, and adhere. 3 Adhere cardstock strip and attach brads. 4 Trim bow tie from cardstock; adhere. Circle-punch cardstock, trim, and adhere with foam tape. 5 Trim lapels in cardstock panels, fold, and adhere. 6 Adhere cardstock strip and affix sticker.

Finished size: 4" x 8"

Best Friends

Designer: Wendy Sue Anderson

1 Make card from cardstock. 2 Trim patterned paper slightly smaller than card front; adhere. Trim patterned paper rectangle, stitch edges, and adhere. 3 Trim label from patterned paper; adhere. Affix sticker. 4 Thread buttons with twine; adhere.

Finished size: 4½" x 5¾"

Birthday Pennant

Designer: Rae Barthel

Ink all paper edges. 1 Make card from cardstock; adhere patterned paper rectangles. 2 Adhere die cut and tie on twine.

Finished size: 6" x 4½"

SUPPLIES: *Cardstock:* (white) Neenah Paper (Basic Black) Stampin' Up! *Accents:* (red brads) My Mind's Eye *Sticker:* (groom) K&Company *Tool:* (circle punch) EK Success

SUPPLIES: All supplies from Cosmo Cricket unless otherwise noted. *Cardstock:* (white) American Crafts *Patterned paper:* (Elements, blue vines, cream stitching from Social Club pad) *Accents:* (green, blue buttons) *Sticker:* (best friend) *Fibers:* (cream jute twine) Papertrey Ink

SUPPLIES: *Cardstock:* (Rustic White) Papertrey Ink *Patterned paper:* (Happy Birthday Dictionary, Happy Birthday Tapestry from Lost & Found collection) My Mind's Eye *Chalk ink:* (Creamy Brown) Clearsnap *Accent:* (cream happy birthday die cut) My Mind's Eye *Fibers:* (natural jute twine) Papertrey Ink

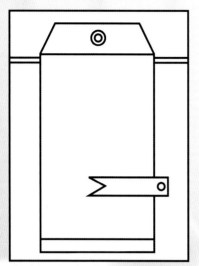

Sketch by: Windy Robinson

Hello Spring

Designer: Cristina Kowalczyk

1. Make card from cardstock.

2. Adhere patterned paper rectangle and stamp double lines.

3. Trim tag shape from cardstock.

4. Stamp branch and leaves on cardstock, adhere to tag, and adhere to card with foam tape.

5. Die-cut double ended banner from cardstock, stamp hello, and trim; adhere.

6. Thread button with twine and adhere.

Finished size: 4¼" x 5½"

SUPPLIES: *Cardstock:* (kraft, white) Papertrey Ink *Patterned paper:* (Meatballs from Pasta Fagioli collection) Jillibean Soup *Clear stamps:* (double lines from Faux Ribbon set; hello from Mat Stack 3 Collection set; branch, leaves from Falling Leaves set) Papertrey Ink *Dye ink:* (Rich Cocoa) Tsukineko *Pigment ink:* (Moss Green) Clearsnap *Accent:* (brown button) The Paper Studio *Fibers:* (natural jute twine) Papertrey Ink *Die:* (double ended banner) Papertrey Ink

Be Merry

Designer: Teri Anderson

❶ Make card from cardstock; adhere patterned paper rectangles. ❷ Die-cut button card from coaster board. Stamp border, sentiment, and dotted grid. Tie die cut onto card with twine. ❸ Die-cut buttons from coaster board and stamp buttons. ❹ Adhere patterned paper strip and affix stickers to spell "Be merry". ❺ Adhere buttons. *Note: Thread one button with floss before adhering.* ❻ Insert stick pins.

Finished size: 4¼" x 5½"

Just for You Pocket

Designer: Daniela Dobson

❶ Make card from cardstock. Spritz Cover-a-Card Corduroy with shimmer spray; stamp. ❷ Ink edges and affix border. ❸ Stamp Silhouette 16 on envelope; adhere doily. ❹ Tie ribbon around envelope. Tie on button with raffia. Adhere envelope to card. ❺ Paint edges of tag; insert in envelope. ❻ Stamp sentiment on cardstock, trim, ink edges, and adhere with foam tape. Adhere button.

Finished size: 4¼" x 5½"

Peas, Love, & Happiness

Designer: Valerie Stangle

❶ Make card from cardstock; round top corner. ❷ Distress edges of patterned paper rectangle; adhere. ❸ Punch top corners of cardstock rectangles with tag corner punch. ❹ Attach eyelet, adhere cardstock strip, and border-punch one tag. Tie on ribbon and adhere tags to card with foam tape. ❺ Stamp peas, eggplant, and carrot on cardstock. Trim and adhere. *Note: Adhere some with foam tape.* ❻ Stamp sentiment on cardstock strip, trim, attach brad, and adhere to card with foam tape.

Finished size: 3¾" x 5½"

SUPPLIES: *Cardstock:* (white) Georgia-Pacific; (Vintage Cream) Papertrey Ink *Patterned paper:* (Picnic Table, Happy Camper, Ponderosa from The Great Outdoors collection) GCD Studios *Clear stamps:* (buttons, border, sentiment, dotted grid from Button Boutique set) Papertrey Ink *Dye ink:* (Old Olive, Real Red) Stampin' Up! *Accents:* (white pearl stick pins) Jenni Bowlin Studio *Stickers:* (Tiny Type alphabet) Cosmo Cricket *Fibers:* (red/white twine) The Twinery; (white floss) DMC *Dies:* (buttons, button card) Papertrey Ink *Other:* (cream coaster board) Papertrey Ink

SUPPLIES: *Cardstock:* (white) Papertrey Ink *Rubber stamps:* (Cover-a-Card Corduroy, Silhouette 16) Impression Obsession *Clear stamp:* (sentiment from Anytime Sentiments set) Impression Obsession *Dye ink:* (Latte) Ranger Industries *Pigment ink:* (Moss Green) Clearsnap *Specialty ink:* (Peacock shimmer spray) Tattered Angels *Paint:* (Malted Milk) Ranger Industries *Accents:* (green buttons) Papertrey Ink; (white doily) Wilton; (cream tag) Avery; (kraft envelope) DMD, Inc. *Sticker:* (border) Sassafras Lass *Fibers:* (tan raffia) Karen Foster Design; (white ribbon)

SUPPLIES: *Cardstock:* (Lovely Lavender, white) Gina K Designs; (Old Olive, Certainly Celery, Rich Razzleberry, Pumpkin Pie) Stampin' Up! *Patterned paper:* (Violet Dot from Double Dot collection) BoBunny Press *Clear stamps:* (eggplant, peas, carrot, sentiment from Vegtastic set) Paper Smooches *Pigment ink:* (Onyx Black) Tsukineko *Embossing powder:* (clear) *Accents:* (orange eyelet) Oriental Trading Company; (orange brad) *Fibers:* (black gingham ribbon) Gina K Designs *Tools:* (border punch) We R Memory Keepers; (corner rounder, tag corner punches) Stampin' Up!

Sentiment

Sketch by: Jessica Witty

5 STEPS Lovely Hello

Designer: Teri Anderson

1. Make card from cardstock; adhere patterned paper rectangles.
2. Affix medallion sticker; trim.
3. Adhere ribbon and pearls.
4. Affix alphabet stickers to spell "Hello".

Finished size: 4¼" x 5½"

SUPPLIES: *Cardstock:* (white) Georgia-Pacific *Patterned paper:* (Succulent, Inviting, Lemon Zest from Hello Luscious collection) BasicGrey *Accents:* (cream pearls) Kaisercraft *Stickers:* (Berry alphabet) American Crafts; (medallion) BasicGrey *Fibers:* (cream ribbon) May Arts

⁵⁵ Be Your Own Beautiful

Designer: Glenda J. Wyatt

① Make card from cardstock. ② Stamp sentiment on cardstock; pierce line. ③ Mat stamped panel with cardstock and adhere to card. Adhere patterned paper. ④ Border-punch cardstock strip; adhere. ⑤ Adhere buttons.

Finished size: 4¼" x 5½"

⁵⁵ Snazzy Best Wishes

Designer: Susan R. Opel

① Make card from cardstock. ② Adhere cardstock and patterned paper strips to card. Adhere ribbon. ③ Stamp best wishes. Tie ribbon bow and adhere.

Finished size: 5½" x 4¼"

⁵⁵ Dapper Dude

Designer: Beth Opel

① Make card from patterned paper. ② Adhere patterned paper rectangles and borders. ③ Print sentiment on cardstock strip, round bottom corners, and adhere. Adhere patterned paper strip. ④ Affix sticker.

Finished size: 4¼" x 6"

SUPPLIES: *Cardstock:* (Very Vanilla, Crumb Cake, and Tangerine Tango) Stampin' Up! *Patterned paper:* (Best Thing Red Chevron Paper from So Sophie collection) My Mind's Eye *Rubber stamp:* (sentiment from Be Your Own Cosmo Itty Bitty) Unity Stamp Co. *Dye ink:* (Real Red) Stampin' Up! *Accents:* (green, red buttons) BasicGrey (orange buttons) Stampin' Up! *Tool:* (border punch) EK Success

SUPPLIES: *Cardstock:* (Intense Yellow, Aqua) Bazzill Basics Paper; (Bumblebee glittered) Doodlebug Design *Patterned paper:* (Dorian Gray from The Classics collection) American Crafts *Clear stamp:* (best wishes from Fancy Phrases set) Waltzingmouse Stamps *Dye ink:* (black) Hero Arts *Fibers:* (teal ribbon) Offray

SUPPLIES: *Cardstock:* (white) *Patterned paper:* (Deep Sea Dot from Double Dot collection) BoBunny Press; (Tango from Socialite collection) Bella Blvd; (Peek-a-Boo from Ducks in a Row collection) October Afternoon *Accents:* (black rickrack borders) Doodlebug Design *Sticker:* (man) Cosmo Cricket *Font:* (Busso Extended) www.fontyukle.com *Tool:* (corner rounder punch) EK Success

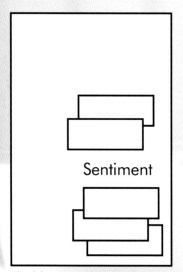

Sentiment

Sketch by: Jessica Witty

life
IS GOOD

Life is Good

Designer: Teri Anderson

1. Make card from cardstock; stamp sentiment.
2. Adhere twine around cardstock strips; adhere.
3. Attach brads.

Finished size: 4¼" x 5½"

SUPPLIES: *Cardstock:* (white) Georgia-Pacific *Clear stamp:* (sentiment from Kids Are Cool set) Technique Tuesday *Dye ink:* (Tuxedo Black) Tsukineko *Accents:* (orange, green brads) Making Memories; (yellow brad) Creative Imaginations *Fibers:* (assorted twine) The Twinery

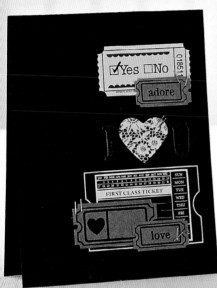

⁵ I Heart You

Designer: Julia Stainton

1. Make card from cardstock; apply rub-on.
2. Adhere tickets. Punch heart from patterned paper; adhere. Attach staples. 3. Affix stickers.

Finished size: 4¼" x 5½"

⁵ Good Luck

Designer: Anabelle O'Malley

1. Make card from cardstock; round right corners. 2. Stamp good luck and pierce line. 3. Border-punch cardstock strips; adhere. Trim patterned paper with decorative-edge scissors; adhere. 4. Adhere trim. Trim patterned paper with decorative-edge scissors, zigzag-stitch, and adhere. 5. Adhere twine bow and butterfly with foam tape.

Finished size: 4¼" x 5½"

⁵ Beautiful Best Friends

Designer: Lisa Dorsey

1. Make card from cardstock. 2. Trim patterned paper rectangles. Stitch and ink edges; adhere to card. 3. Adhere trim and pearls. 4. Adhere label and affix butterfly.

Finished size: 5½" x 7½"

SUPPLIES: *Cardstock:* (Pomegranate) Bazzill Basics Paper *Patterned paper:* (Picnic Lunch from Play Date collection) Jenni Bowlin Studio *Accents:* (kraft tickets) Maya Road; (white ticket) Jenni Bowlin Studio; (silver staples) Maya Road *Rub-on:* (ticket) Maya Road *Stickers:* (Rockabye alphabet) American Crafts *Tool:* (heart punch) Martha Stewart Crafts

SUPPLIES: *Cardstock:* (kraft) Papertrey Ink *Patterned paper:* (Doilies from Restoration collection) Crate Paper; (Sunshine from A Walk in the Park collection) Echo Park Paper *Clear stamp:* (good luck from Fancy Phrases set) Waltzingmouse Stamps *Specialty ink:* (True Black hybrid) Papertrey Ink *Accent:* (white butterfly with pearls) Jenni Bowlin Studio *Fibers:* (natural jute twine) Papertrey Ink; (cream trim) Wrights *Tools:* (corner rounder punch) EK Success; (decorative-edge scissors) Provo Craft; (border punch) Martha Stewart Crafts

SUPPLIES: *Cardstock:* (brown) Bazzill Basics Paper *Patterned paper:* (Little Lady Fine Flowers, Play Damask, Play Silly Stripe, Love Letters from Stella & Rose collection) My Mind's Eye; (Cherry Blossom from Lush collection) Kaisercraft *Chalk ink:* (Chestnut) Clearsnap *Accents:* (white pearls) Creative Charms; (bronze best friends label) Making Memories *Sticker:* (butterfly) K&Company *Fibers:* (cream trim) Webster's Pages

Sketch by: Kim Hughes

⬢5⬢ All Star

Designer: Lori Tecler

1. Make card from cardstock. Trim patterned paper slightly smaller than card front; adhere.
2. Die-cut ticket borders from cardstock. Stamp star tickets and sentiment. Ink edges, trim, and adhere.
3. Adhere ribbon loop.
4. Die-cut stars from felt; adhere.
5. Tie button with twine; adhere.

Finished size: 5½" x 4¼"

SUPPLIES: *Cardstock:* (Dark Chocolate, kraft) Papertrey Ink *Patterned paper:* (True Blue Fabulous from Fine and Dandy collection) My Mind's Eye *Clear stamps:* (star ticket, sentiment from Just the Ticket set) Papertrey Ink *Dye ink:* (Rich Cocoa) Tsukineko *Accent:* (yellow button) Papertrey Ink *Fibers:* (tan/white twine) The Twinery; (brown ribbon) Papertrey Ink *Dies:* (stars, ticket border) Papertrey Ink *Other:* (yellow, blue felt) Papertrey Ink

DESIGNER TIP

Create extra dimension by trimming a camera lens from your patterned paper and adhering it to your punched patterned paper circle with foam tape.

 A Life She Loves

Designer: Carisa Zglobicki

❶ Make card from cardstock. ❷ Trim patterned paper slightly smaller than card front, distress edges, and adhere. ❸ Stamp sentiment. ❹ Adhere patterned paper behind filmstrip strips; adhere. Adhere gear. ❺ Trim circles from patterned paper. Roll into flowers; adhere. Adhere pearls.

Finished size: 4¼" x 5½"

Picture Perfect

Designer: Tiffany Heilman

❶ Make card from cardstock; adhere patterned paper strips. ❷ Die-cut scalloped circle from cardstock. Circle-punch patterned paper. Adhere pieces together and adhere to card with foam tape. ❸ Thread button with twine; adhere. ❹ Stamp picture perfect.

Finished size: 4¼" x 5½"

Get Well Soon

Designer: Sarah Jay

❶ Make card from patterned paper. ❷ Stamp Envelope Pattern on cardstock strips, score, and fold. Adhere with foam tape. ❸ Heart-punch cardstock, apply glitter glue, and adhere with foam tape. ❹ Stamp sentiment.

Finished size: 4¼" x 5½"

SUPPLIES: *Cardstock:* (kraft) The Paper Company *Patterned paper:* (Mechanical Mind, Steampunk Debutante from Steampunk Debutante collection) Graphic 45 *Rubber stamp:* (sentiment from She Said set) Unity Stamp Co. *Dye ink:* (Tuxedo Black) Tsukineko *Accents:* (white, pink pearls) Kaisercraft; (clear filmstrip strips) Tim Holtz; (brass gear) 7gypsies

SUPPLIES: *Cardstock:* (Riding Hood Red, kraft) Stampin' Up! *Patterned paper:* (Italian Seasoning, Blended Beans from Pasta Fagioli collection) Jillibean Soup *Rubber stamp:* (picture perfect from Picture Perfect set) My Favorite Things *Accent:* (blue button) Autumn Leaves *Fibers:* (yellow/white twine) The Twinery *Die:* (scalloped circle) Papertrey Ink *Tool:* (circle punch) Stampin' Up!

SUPPLIES: *Cardstock:* (kraft) Papertrey Ink; (red) *Patterned paper:* (Frost Dot from Double Dot collection) BoBunny Press *Rubber stamp:* (Envelope Pattern) Hero Arts *Clear stamp:* (sentiment from Everyday Sayings set) Hero Arts *Dye ink:* (Rich Cocoa) Tsukineko *Watermark ink:* Tsukineko *Accent:* (red glitter glue) Ranger Industries *Tool:* (heart punch) Stampin' Up!

Sketch by: Kim Hughes

Wishes Your Heart Makes

Designer: Latisha Yoast

1. Make card from cardstock. Border-punch patterned paper strip; adhere.

2. Adhere patterned paper rectangle.

3. Die-cut labels from patterned paper. Stamp dreams and sentiment on small label. Adhere labels to card with foam tape.

4. Affix sticker.

Finished size: 4¼" x 5½"

SUPPLIES: *Cardstock:* (white) Papertrey Ink *Patterned paper:* (Wedding Day, Tulle from Mr. & Mrs. Collection) Pebbles *Clear stamps:* (dreams, sentiment from Spiral Bouquet set) Papertrey Ink *Dye ink:* (Tuxedo Black) Tsukineko *Sticker:* (white flower) Pebbles *Dies:* (labels) Spellbinders *Tool:* (border punch) Stampin' Up!

5 STEPS Best Teacher

Designer: Teri Anderson

1 Make card from cardstock. Adhere patterned paper strips, affix sticker, and adhere twine. 2 Trim label from patterned paper, mat with cardstock, and stamp the, best, and teacher. Attach paperclip and adhere to card. 3 Trim apples from patterned paper; adhere. Adhere pearls.

Finished size: 4¼" x 5½"

5 STEPS Simply Amazing

Designer: Tosha Leyendekker

1 Make card from cardstock. Mat patterned paper rectangle with cardstock; adhere. 2 Mat patterned paper strip with cardstock, adhere trim, and adhere to card. 3 Die-cut doily, circle, star, and tag from cardstock and patterned paper. Trim doily and circle; adhere. 4 Score star and adhere. 5 Stamp simply amazing on tag; adhere. Thread button with twine and adhere.

Finished size: 4¼" x 5½"

5 STEPS Deepest Sympathy

Designer: Melissa Phillips

1 Make card from cardstock; paint edges. 2 Adhere patterned paper panels together. Adhere trim and ink edges. Stitch to card. 3 Adhere patterned paper strip and label. 4 Die-cut doily from patterned paper; adhere. Ink ribbon; tie on card. 5 Adhere flower and button. Stamp sentiment.

Finished size: 3¾" x 5¼"

SUPPLIES: *Cardstock:* (white) Georgia-Pacific *Patterned paper:* (Show Your Work, Nibbles, Library from Elementary collection) Studio Calico *Clear stamps:* (the, best, teacher from School Basics set) I {heart} papers *Dye ink:* (Tuxedo Black) Tsukineko *Accents:* (white pearls) Kaisercraft; (silver paperclip) Target *Sticker:* (alphabet border) Studio Calico *Fibers:* (white hemp twine) Hemptique

SUPPLIES: *Cardstock:* (Vintage Cream, Fine Linen, True Black) Papertrey Ink *Patterned paper:* (Pantomime, Applause from Curtain Call) Graphic 45 *Clear stamp:* (simply amazing from Bountiful Backgrounds set) Verve Stamps *Pigment ink:* (Onyx Black) Tsukineko *Chalk ink:* (Brick Red) Tsukineko *Accent:* (black button) Papertrey Ink *Fibers:* (cream trim, jute twine) May Arts *Dies:* (doily) My Favorite Things; (star, circle, tag) Spellbinders

SUPPLIES: *Cardstock:* (Aqua Mist) Papertrey Ink *Patterned paper:* (blue stripe from 5th Avenue collection; Lauren from Kitschy Kitchen collection) Melissa Frances; (Glossary from Basics Manila collection) BasicGrey; (Love Mail) Crafty Secrets *Clear stamp:* (sentiment from Card Sentiments set) Crafty Secrets *Specialty ink:* (Dark Chocolate hybrid) Papertrey Ink *Paint:* (cream) *Accents:* (pink flower) Prima; (pink label) Melissa Frances; (cream button) *Fibers:* (cream trim) Maya Road; (cream ribbon) MemrieMare *Die:* (doily) Papertrey Ink

Sketch by: Maile Belles

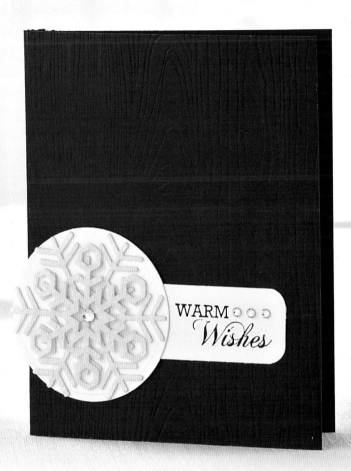

⁙5⁙ Warm Wishes
STEPS

Designer: Cristina Kowalczyk

1. Make card from cardstock; deboss.

2. Stamp Warm Wishes on cardstock rectangle, round right corners, and adhere.

3. Die-cut circle from cardstock; adhere snowflake. Adhere to card.

4. Adhere rhinestones.

Finished size: 4¼" x 5½"

SUPPLIES: *Cardstock:* (Pure Poppy, Vintage Cream) Papertrey Ink *Rubber stamp:* (Warm Wishes) Savvy Stamps *Pigment ink:* (Onyx Black) Tsukineko *Accents:* (clear rhinestones) Stampin' Up!; (cream snowflake) Little Yellow Bicycle *Template:* (debossing woodgrain) Papertrey Ink *Die:* (circle) Spellbinders *Tool:* (corner rounder punch) We R Memory Keepers

Simply with Sympathy

Designer: Angeline Yong Jeet Leen

❶ Make card from cardstock. ❷ Stamp with sympathy on cardstock strip, trim with decorative-edge scissors, and adhere. ❸ Stamp large flower outline on vellum, trim, and adhere. ❹ Thread button with twine; adhere.

Finished size: 3¾" x 5¾"

Tie the Knot

Designer: Cate Shaw

❶ Make card from cardstock; stamp La Lettre. ❷ Ink doily; adhere. ❸ Trim image from patterned paper; adhere. ❹ Tie on ribbon. ❺ Stamp sentiment on cardstock, trim, and adhere to card with foam tape. Insert stick pins.

Finished size: 4¼" x 5½"

Hello Butterfly

Designer: Teri Anderson

❶ Make card from cardstock; adhere patterned paper. ❷ Trim tag from patterned paper, adhere patterned paper strip, and tie on twine. Adhere to card. ❸ Adhere butterfly. ❹ Affix stickers to spell "Hello". *Note: Adhere patterned paper behind letter openings.*

Finished size: 4¼" x 5½"

SUPPLIES: *Cardstock:* (kraft) Bazzill Basics Paper *Vellum:* (white polka dots) Cristina Re *Rubber stamp:* (with sympathy from Regal Greetings set) Ippity by Unity Stamp Co. *Clear stamp:* (large flower outline from Great Friend set) Verve Stamps *Pigment ink:* (brown) Kaisercraft *Accent:* (brown button) Kaisercraft *Fibers:* (brown/white twine) The Twinery *Tool:* (decorative-edge scissors) Smiggle

SUPPLIES: *Cardstock:* (kraft) The Paper Studio *Patterned paper:* (Nouveau Artistry from Steampunk Debutante) Graphic 45 *Rubber stamp:* (La Lettre) Hero Arts *Clear stamp:* (sentiment from Bouquet set) American Cards *Dye ink:* (Old Paper) Ranger Industries; (black) Stewart Superior Corp. *Accents:* (white flower stick pins) Little Yellow Bicycle; (white doily) Little Yellow Bicycle *Fibers:* (aqua ribbon) American Crafts

SUPPLIES: *Cardstock:* (white) Georgia-Pacific *Patterned paper:* (Wholegrain Mustard from Dutch Mustard Soup collection; Dark Brown Sugar from Soup Staples collection; Lime Wedges from Blossom Soup collection) Jillibean Soup *Accent:* (kraft corrugated butterfly) Jillibean Soup *Stickers:* (Blue Line alphabet) Cosmo Cricket *Fibers:* (natural hemp twine)

Sketch by: Betsy Veldman

BONUS IDEA

Change the color of cardstock and ribbon to personalize for the type of cancer.

Cancer is so limited...

It cannot cripple *LOVE*
It cannot shatter *HOPE*
It cannot corrode *FAITH*
It cannot destroy *PEACE*
It cannot kill *FRIENDSHIPS*
It cannot suppress *MEMORIES*
It cannot silence *COURAGE*
It cannot invade the *SOUL*
It cannot steal eternal *LIFE*
It cannot conquer the *SPIRIT*
~ Anonymous

5 STEPS Cancer Cannot

Designer: Virginia Brennan

1. Make card from cardstock.
2. Print poem on cardstock, trim, and adhere ribbon.
3. Adhere panel to card.

Finished size: 5" x 7"

SUPPLIES: *Cardstock:* (Blush) American Crafts; (white) Neenah Paper *Fibers:* (pink ribbon) *Fonts:* (Georgia, Lucida Handwriting) Microsoft

5 STEPS Seriously

Designer: Daniela Dobson

❶ Make card from cardstock. ❷ Ink and stitch edges of patterned paper rectangle; adhere. ❸ Stamp This Life on cardstock, trim, and, adhere. Zigzag-stitch sides and stitch line. ❹ Stamp label and sentiment on cardstock, color with marker, trim, and adhere with foam tape. ❺ Tie on twine and attach brad.

Finished size: 4¼" x 5½"

5 STEPS Sew Stylish

Designer: Julie Lacey

❶ Make card from cardstock. ❷ Adhere patterned paper rectangles to patterned paper. ❸ Stamp girl with cape and sew stylish on panel. Tie on ribbon. ❹ Zigzag-stitch seams and adhere panel to card. ❺ Thread button with twine; adhere.

Finished size: 4¼" x 5½"

5 STEPS Love is Patient

Designer: Nina Brackett

❶ Make card from cardstock. ❷ Stamp scripture on vellum rectangle; emboss. Mat with cardstock. ❸ Adhere trim to panel and tie on ribbon; adhere to card. ❹ Adhere pearls and flower.

Finished size: 4¼" x 6¼"

SUPPLIES: *Cardstock:* (white) Papertrey Ink *Patterned paper:* (Snowfall from Tinsel & Twig collection) The Girls' Paperie *Clear stamps:* (label, sentiment from Sweet Somethings set; This Life) Technique Tuesday *Dye ink:* (black) Ranger Industries *Color medium:* (pink marker) Sakura *Paint:* (Stick Candy) Ranger Industries *Accent:* (pink brad) American Crafts *Fibers:* (natural hemp twine) Wal-Mart

SUPPLIES: *Cardstock:* (Vintage Cream) Papertrey Ink *Patterned paper:* (Cocktail, Peacock, Jazz from Social Club collection) Cosmo Cricket *Clear stamps:* (girl with cape, sew stylish from Sew Stylish set) Hero Arts *Specialty ink:* (Noir hybrid) Stewart Superior Corp. *Accent:* (black button) My Mind's Eye *Fibers:* (red ribbon) Stampin' Up!; (natural jute twine) Papertrey Ink

SUPPLIES: *Cardstock:* (Innocent Pink) Gina K Designs *Patterned paper:* (Breezeway from Country Estate collection) Webster's Pages *Vellum:* (white) 3M *Rubber stamp:* (scripture from The Love Chapter set) Layers of Color Art Stamps *Watermark ink:* Tsukineko *Embossing powder:* (white) Stampin' Up! *Accents:* (white flower) Wild Orchid Crafts; (white pearls) Mark Richards Enterprises *Fibers:* (cream trim, pink ribbon)

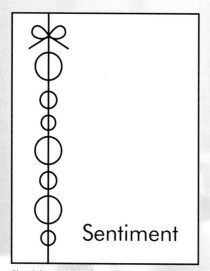

Sentiment

Sketch by: Kim Hughes

YOU MAKE ME *smile*

Make Me Smile

Designer: Kalyn Kepner

1. Make card from cardstock.

2. Stamp sentiment.

3. Border-punch patterned paper strip; adhere. Adhere twill. Ink and stitch edges.

4. Thread buttons with floss. Adhere and attach accents; affix sticker.

5. Adhere twill bow.

Finished size: 4¼" x 5½"

SUPPLIES: *Cardstock:* (kraft) Bazzill Basics Paper *Patterned paper:* (In Love Splendid Surroundings from So Sophie collection) My Mind's Eye *Clear stamp:* (sentiment from Simple Messages set) Hero Arts *Pigment ink:* (white) Tsukineko *Chalk ink:* (Chestnut) Clearsnap *Accents:* (pink, green buttons) Papertrey Ink; (pink flower, burgundy medallion brads) K&Company; (aqua brad) American Crafts *Sticker:* (green badge) American Crafts *Fibers:* (white twill) Papertrey Ink; (white floss) DMC *Tool:* (decorative-edge scissors)

Always with You

Designer: Betsy Veldman

Ink all edges. ❶ Make card from cardstock.
❷ Trim patterned paper slightly smaller than
card front, trim bottom with decorative-edge
scissors, and stitch edges. Adhere to card.
❸ Die-cut large heart from patterned paper.
Trim and adhere. ❹ Stamp sentiment and small
heart on card. ❺ Die-cut tags from cardstock.
Stamp circled heart, heart on circle text, small
heart, and medium heart. Tie on twine to some
tags and adhere. ❻ Stitch tags. Thread buttons
with twine; adhere. Insert stick pin.

Finished size: 4¼" x 5½

⑤ Birthday Numbers

Designer: Terri Trotter Earley

❶ Make card from cardstock; round bottom
corners. ❷ Die-cut numbers from patterned
paper; adhere. ❸ Stitch numbers to card and
stamp sentiment.

Finished size: 5½" x 4¼"

⑤ Belated Birthday

Designer: Anabelle O'Malley

❶ Make card from cardstock; adhere
cardstock rectangle. ❷ Stamp sentiment on
patterned paper rectangle. Border-punch
patterned paper, adhere to panel, and stitch
edges. ❸ Adhere trim to panel and adhere
to card. ❹ Adhere buttons and flowers.
❺ Die-cut flower from cardstock, ink edges,
and adhere twine bow. Trim flower from trim
and adhere to die cut. Adhere piece to card
with foam tape.

Finished size: 4" x 5¾"

SUPPLIES: *Cardstock:* (Vintage Cream) Papertrey
Ink *Patterned paper:* (Chiffon Dot from Double Dot
collection) BoBunny Press; (Sparkling from Hello Luscious
collection) BasicGrey *Rubber stamp:* (circled heart from
Itty Bitty Bits set) Stampin' Up! *Clear stamps:* (sentiment,
heart on circle text, small heart, medium heart from
Love Lives Here set) Papertrey Ink *Dye ink:* (Real Red)
Stampin' Up! *Chalk ink:* (Creamy Brown) Clearsnap
Specialty ink: (True Black, Scarlet Jewel, Ocean Tides
hybrid) Papertrey Ink *Accents:* (cream buttons) Papertrey
Ink; (red heart stick pin) Maya Road *Fibers:* (white jute
twine) Papertrey Ink *Dies:* (tiny tags, large heart) Provo
Craft *Tool:* (decorative-edge scissors)

SUPPLIES: All supplies from Papertrey Ink unless
otherwise noted. *Cardstock:* (kraft) *Patterned paper:*
(aqua, green, orange polka dots from Dotty Biscotti
collection) *Clear stamp:* (sentiment from Birthday Bash
Sentiments set) *Dye ink:* (Crumb Cake) Stampin' Up!
Dies: (numbers) *Tool:* (corner rounder punch) We R
Memory Keepers

SUPPLIES: *Cardstock:* (Vintage Cream, kraft) Papertrey
Ink *Patterned paper:* (Time of My Life from Ladies
& Gents collection) Webster's Pages *Clear stamp:*
(sentiment from Fancy Phrases set) Waltzingmouse
Stamps *Dye ink:* (Creamy Caramel) Stampin' Up!;
(Chai) Papertrey Ink *Accents:* (tan, white, green
flowers) Webster's Pages; (cream buttons) Papertrey
Ink *Fibers:* (yellow flower, cream trim) Webster's
Pages; (natural hemp twine) Papertrey Ink *Die:*
(flower) Papertrey Ink *Tool:* (border punch) Martha
Stewart Crafts

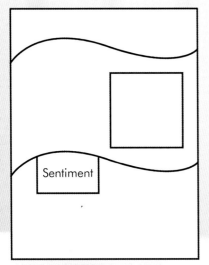

Sentiment

Sketch by: Kim Hughes

happy
birthday
to moo

⁵STEPS Moo to You

Designer: Kim Kelley

❶ Make card from cardstock.

❷ Print sentiment on cardstock, trim, and adhere.
Trim patterned paper and adhere.

❸ Stamp cow on cardstock rectangle, color with
marker, and adhere.

❹ Stamp party hat on cardstock, color with markers, trim,
and adhere glitter. Adhere to card with foam tape.

Finished size: 4¼" x 5½"

SUPPLIES: *Cardstock:* (white, blue) *Patterned paper:* (green polka dots) Making Memories *Rubber stamp:* (cow) Vap! Scrap *Clear stamp:* (party hat from Let's Party Hat and Cake set) Studio G *Dye ink:* (black) Making Memories *Color medium:* (pink, blue, yellow markers) Marvy Uchida *Accent:* (silver glitter) Mark Richards Enterprises *Font:* (CK Toggle) Creating Keepsakes *Tool:* (corner rounder punch) Fiskars

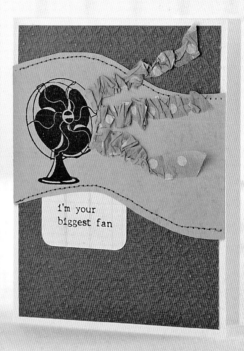

5 steps More than Words

Designer: Beth Opel

1 Make card from cardstock; adhere patterned paper. 2 Print sentiment on cardstock, trim, round corners, and adhere. 3 Trim specialty paper and adhere. 4 Affix sticker and adhere pearls.

Finished size: 4¼" x 5½"

Forever

Designer: Anne Harada

1 Make card from cardstock. 2 Adhere patterned paper rectangle. 3 Trim patterned paper, adhere trim, and adhere piece to card. 4 Affix stickers to spell "Forever". 5 Stitch trim to create flower; adhere. 6 Die-cut flowers from patterned paper. Stitch flowers and button together with twine; adhere.

Finished size: 4¼" x 5½"

5 steps Biggest Fan

Designer: Kim Kesti

1 Make card from cardstock. Trim cardstock slightly smaller than card front; adhere. 2 Print sentiment on patterned paper, trim, round corners, and adhere. 3 Trim cardstock, stitch edges, and stamp fan; adhere. 4 Wrinkle crepe paper and adhere.

Finished size: 4¾" x 6¼"

SUPPLIES: *Cardstock:* (white) American Crafts *Patterned paper:* (Pucker Up from Material Girl collection) GCD Studios *Specialty paper:* (gray embossed) FiberMark *Accents:* (white pearls) Zva Creative *Sticker:* (typewriter) American Crafts *Font:* (Rockwell) Microsoft *Tool:* (corner rounder punch) EK Success

SUPPLIES: *Cardstock:* (Very Vanilla) Stampin' Up! *Patterned paper:* (Light the Way, Pure Grace from Lullaby Lane collection) Webster's Pages *Accent:* (cream button) Stampin' Up! *Stickers:* (Lullaby alphabet) Webster's Pages *Fibers:* (cream trim) The Paper Studio; (cream hemp twine) *Dies:* (flowers) Stampin' Up!

SUPPLIES: *Cardstock:* (Wildberry embossed, Natural, Strawberry Splash) Bazzill Basics Paper *Patterned paper:* (ledger) *Rubber stamp:* (fan from Vintage set) Hero Arts *Dye ink:* (Tuxedo Black) Tsukineko *Font:* (Chunk Type) www.simplythebest.net *Tool:* (corner rounder punch) We R Memory Keepers *Other:* (teal crepe paper) Jenni Bowlin Studio

Sketch by: Chan Vuong

5 STEPS

Heart All a Flutter

Designer: Jenny Chesnick

1. Make card from patterned paper.

2. Paint frame; let dry. Adhere patterned paper and affix sentiment sticker behind frame.

3. Tie on twine and affix flower sticker. Adhere to card with foam tape.

4. Adhere pearls.

Finished size: 3½" x 5"

SUPPLIES: *Patterned paper:* (All You Need, Can't Help Falling from Love Line collection) American Crafts *Paint:* (Pearl Metallic) Ranger Industries *Accents:* (blue pearls) BasicGrey; (chipboard frame) Maya Road *Stickers:* (flower, sentiment) American Crafts *Fibers:* (teal/white twine) The Twinery

Across the Miles

Designer: Chan Vuong

1 Make card from cardstock. 2 Stamp Postage Stamp and sentiment on cardstock. 3 Color stamped image with markers, tie on wine, and adhere to card with foam tape. 4 Stamp smiley face on cardstock square; adhere with foam tape. Adhere pearls.

Finished size: 3¼" x 4¼"

Eclectic Congratulations

Designer: Waleska

1 Make card from cardstock. 2 Stamp Hot Air Balloon on cardstock rectangle, emboss, and trim. 3 Adhere fabric behind stamped frame and stamp congratulations. 4 Trim patterned paper; adhere. Tie on floss and adhere panel to card. 5 Apply rub-on to butterfly. Adhere pearls and adhere to card with foam tape.

Finished size: 4¼" x 5½"

Strawberry Get Well

Designer: Julia Stainton

1 Make card from cardstock, adhere patterned paper, and ink edges. 2 Trim patterned paper rectangle with decorative-edge scissors; ink edges. 3 Stamp sentiment on cardstock, trim, tear, and attach to panel with staples. 4 Tie twine around panel and adhere to card.

Finished size: 3½" x 6"

SUPPLIES: *Cardstock:* (Real Red) Stampin' Up!; (white) Papertrey Ink; (Aqua) We R Memory Keepers *Clear stamps:* (Postage Stamp) Studio Calico; (sentiment from Hello Friend set; smiley face from Say Cheese set) Lawn Fawn *Dye ink:* (Tuxedo Black) Tsukineko *Pigment ink:* (Onyx Black) Tsukineko *Color medium:* (aqua marker) Copic *Accents:* (red pearls) Prima *Fibers:* (red/white/blue twine) Divine Twine

SUPPLIES: *Cardstock:* (kraft) Bazzill Basics Paper *Patterned paper:* (Best in Show from State Fair collection) Studio Calico *Clear stamps:* (congratulations from Everyday Sayings set) Hero Arts; (Hot Air Balloon) Studio Calico *Dye ink:* (Brown Sugar) Ranger Industries *Watermark ink:* Hero Arts *Embossing powder:* (Aqua) American Crafts *Accents:* (wood butterfly) Studio Calico; (white pearls) BasicGrey *Rub-on:* (butterfly) Studio Calico *Fibers:* (yellow floss) DMC *Other:* (pink fabric) Studio Calico

SUPPLIES: *Cardstock:* (kraft) Bazzill Basics Paper *Patterned paper:* (Frozen Strawberries, Cup Sour Cream from Chilled Strawberry Soup collection) Jillibean Soup *Rubber stamp:* (sentiment from Heartfelt Sentiments set) Unity Stamp Co. *Dye ink:* (Jet Black) Ranger Industries *Pigment ink:* (Frost White) Clearsnap *Accents:* (silver staples) *Fibers:* (red/white twine) Jillibean Soup *Tool:* (decorative-edge scissors)

Sketch by: Teri Anderson

Floral Mother Card

Designer: Latisha Yoast

1 Make card from cardstock.

2 Die-cut and emboss cardstock; adhere.

3 Stamp mother on card. Adhere flowers and pearls.

Finished size: 2½" x 5¼"

SUPPLIES: *Cardstock:* (kraft) Papertrey Ink; (cream) Flourishes *Clear stamp:* (mother from Mixed Message set) Papertrey Ink *Dye ink:* (Tuxedo Black) Tsukineko *Accents:* (purple, white flowers) Prima; (purple pearls) Kaisercraft *Template:* (Floral & Stone embossing) Spellbinders *Die:* (rectangle) Spellbinders

Two Trees Hi Card

Designer: Teri Anderson

SUPPLIES: *Cardstock:* (white) WorldWin *Patterned paper:* (Hot Wheels from Nice Ride collection; Scenery from Round & Round collection) My Mind's Eye *Accents:* (copper brads) American Label & Tag; (green tree die cuts) My Mind's Eye *Stickers:* (Delight alphabet) American Crafts

Finished size: 3¼" x 5½"

The Best Dreams Card

Designer: Danielle Flanders

SUPPLIES: *Cardstock:* (kraft) WorldWin *Patterned paper:* (Mary's Journal from Secret Garden collection) Dream Street Papers *Accents:* (white glitter chipboard stars, white pearls) Melissa Frances *Rub-on:* (sentiment) Dream Street Papers

Finished size: 4¾" x 5"

10th Birthday Card

Designer: Betsy Veldman

SUPPLIES: *Cardstock:* (Pure Poppy) Papertrey Ink; (white) *Patterned paper:* (blue denim from Citrus collection) Die Cuts With a View; (Edith Fitzbolt from Craft Fair collection) American Crafts; (Cookie Jar from Cherry Hill collection) October Afternoon; (Peace from About a Boy collection) Fancy Pants Designs *Clear stamp:* (sentiment from Birthday Basics set) Papertrey Ink *Pigment ink:* (Fresh Snow) Papertrey Ink *Chalk ink:* (Creamy Brown) Clearsnap *Accents:* (green glitter brads) Doodlebug Design; (white scalloped journaling tags) Jillibean Soup *Tools:* (star punches, border punch) Fiskars

Finished size: 3½" x 6½"

Sketch by: Teri Anderson

⁙5⁙ Snowflake Joy Card

Designer: Heidi Van Laar

① Make card from cardstock; adhere cardstock panel.

② Die-cut snowflakes and circles from cardstock. Punch snowflakes and circles from cardstock.

③ Stitch large circles with crochet thread and adhere.

④ Adhere remaining circles and snowflakes.

⑤ Paint stickers, let dry, and affix to spell "Joy".

Finished size: 5" x 7"

SUPPLIES: *Cardstock:* (red, white) American Crafts; (Dragonfly) Bazzill Basics *Paper Paint:* (red) Liquitex *Stickers:* (Hat Box alphabet) American Crafts *Fibers:* (white crochet thread) Coats & Clark *Dies:* (small, large circles) Spellbinders; (snowflake) Ellison *Tools:* (½" circle punch) EK Success; (snowflake punches) Martha Stewart Crafts

Circle & Flower Hi Card

Designer: Teri Anderson

SUPPLIES: *Cardstock:* (Rustic Cream) Papertrey Ink; (white) Bazzill Basics Paper; (red) WorldWin *Patterned paper:* (Red Wallpaper from Trendy collection) Jenni Bowlin Studio *Dye ink:* (Old Paper) Ranger Industries *Accents:* (clear buttons) Buttons Galore & More; (cream ledger chipboard buttons) Jenni Bowlin Studio; (red, tan newsprint flowers) Prima; (white pearls) Zva Creative *Stickers:* (MoMA alphabet) American Crafts *Fibers:* (white floss) DMC; (jute twine) DCC *Tool:* (corner rounder punch) Zutter

Finished size: 3½" x 6"

Poinsettia Card

Designer: Kim Hughes

SUPPLIES: *Cardstock:* (Tawny Light) Prism *Rubber stamps:* (sentiment circle, flowers from Merry Little Christmas Borders & Centers Round set) Justrite *Dye ink:* (Espresso) Ranger Industries *Color medium:* (red, green, yellow pencils) Prismacolor *Accents:* (green, yellow glitter brads) We R Memory Keepers; (red poinsettias) Imaginisce

Finished size: 4" x 6"

Look Who's 10 Card

Designer: Maren Benedict

SUPPLIES: *Cardstock:* (Ripe Avocado) Papertrey Ink; (Whisper White) Stampin' Up! *Rubber stamp:* (sentiment from U R A Hoot set) Cornish Heritage Farms *Dye ink:* (Black Soot) Ranger Industries *Stickers:* (circles, numbers, arrow, rainbow) BasicGrey

Finished size: 4" x 6½"

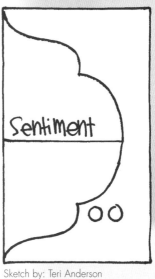

Sentiment

Sketch by: Teri Anderson

we aRe so **PROUD** of you

5 STEPS So Proud Card

Designer: Teri Anderson

1 Make card from cardstock; adhere patterned paper.

2 Attach brads to cardstock piece; adhere.

3 Trim die cut; tie on ribbon and adhere.

4 Apply rub-on.

Finished size: 3" x 4"

SUPPLIES: *Cardstock:* (white) WorldWin *Patterned paper:* (Yellow Tablecloth from Citronella collection) K&Company *Accents:* (yellow brads) Making Memories; (blue journaling die cut) Anna Griffin *Rub-on:* (sentiment) Melissa Frances *Fibers:* (yellow gingham ribbon) Offray

Kwanzaa Card

Designer: Kim Kesti

SUPPLIES: *Cardstock:* (Lily White, Beetle Black, Grenadine, Patch, kraft) Bazzill Basics Paper *Accent:* gold glitter glue) Ranger Industries *Stickers:* (Delight alphabet) American Crafts

Finished size: 6½" x 5¼"

Dotty Thanks Card

Designer: Lisa Johnson

SUPPLIES: All supplies from Papertrey Ink unless otherwise noted. *Cardstock:* (Raspberry Fizz, Aqua Mist, white) *Clear stamps:* (polka dots from Polka Dot Basics set; thank you from On My Couch set; label from Vintage Labels set) *Specialty ink:* (Raspberry Fizz, Orange Zest hybrid) *Accents:* (orange, aqua, pink buttons) *Fibers:* (natural twine) *Tool:* (2½" circle punch) Marvy Uchida

Finished size: 3¾" x 5½"

Mom Bracket Card

Designer: Rae Barthel

SUPPLIES: *Cardstock:* (Burgundy) Core'dinations *Patterned paper:* (Cabbage Rose, Sunshine, Strawberry Patch from Lemonade collection) BasicGrey; (bracketed from Noteworthy collection notebook) Making Memories *Chalk ink:* (Maroon) Clearsnap *Accents:* (pink rhinestones) Michaels *Stickers:* (pink journaling tag) October Afternoon; (Indian Summer alphabet) BasicGrey *Fibers:* (pink ribbon) Offray

Finished size: 4" x 6½"

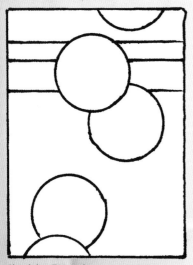

Sketch by: Teri Anderson

5 STEPS Thanks a Bunch Card

Designer: Angie Hagist

1. Make card from cardstock; round two corners.
2. Adhere cardstock strips. Affix stickers.
3. Punch circles from patterned paper; adhere.
   Note: Adhere one with foam tape.
4. Apply rub-on to cardstock; trim and adhere with foam tape.
5. Draw borders.

Finished size: 3¾" x 6¾"

SUPPLIES: *Cardstock:* (kraft) The Paper Company; (Aqua Mist, Ripe Avocado) Papertrey Ink; (Sunflowers Light) Prism *Patterned paper:* (Forever Rings from Sisters collection, Round 7 Round from Scenery collection) My Mind's Eye *Color medium:* (black marker) Sanford *Rub-on:* (sentiment) American Crafts *Stickers:* (squares) American Crafts *Tools:* (2" circle punch) Fiskars; (corner rounder punch)

Tumbling Skulls Card

Designer: Heidi Van Laar

SUPPLIES: *Cardstock:* (black) Bazzill Basics Paper; (orange) Die Cuts With a View *Patterned paper:* (Horror, Scream from Halloween collection) American Craft *Fibers:* (white crochet thread) Coats & Clark *Font:* (Attic Antique) www.fonts.com

Finished size: 4¼" x 5½"

Delightful Little Things Card

Designer: Teri Anderson

SUPPLIES: *Cardstock:* (white, black) WorldWin; (kraft) Neenah Paper *Patterned paper:* (Typography from Communique collection) Graphic 45 *Clear stamps:* (memories, sentiment from Favorite Memories set) Technique Tuesday *Dye ink:* (Tuxedo Black) Tsukineko *Fibers:* (jute cord) DCC *Tool:* (1¾" circle punch) Fiskars

Finished size: 4¼" x 5½"

Flourish Thanks Card

Designer: Sarah Martina Parker

SUPPLIES: *Cardstock:* (Lemon Tart, New Leaf, white) Papertrey Ink; (blue) Bazzill Basics Paper *Patterned paper:* (Borders from Invisibles collection) Heidi Swapp *Clear stamp:* (thank you from Damask Designs set) Papertrey Ink *Pigment ink:* (Wasabi, Stem Green, Leaf Bud, Ocean, Dusk Blue) Martha Stewart Crafts *Tool:* (1½" circle punch) EK Success

Finished size: 4¼" x 5½"

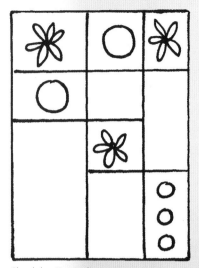

Sketch by: Teri Anderson

Patchwork Hello Card

Designer: Heidi Van Laar

1 Make card from cardstock.

2 Cut squares and rectangles from patterned paper. Cut rectangles from cardstock and emboss two.

3 Adhere cardstock and patterned paper pieces; zigzag-stitch seams.

4 Thread buttons and adhere.

5 Trim butterfly, apple, and flower from patterned paper; adhere with foam tape.

6 Stamp sentiment.

Finished size: 3½" x 5¼"

SUPPLIES: *Cardstock:* (white) Georgia-Pacific; (kraft) The Paper Company *Patterned paper:* (green grid, orange wheels, bold stripes, brown wheat, red flowers from Greenhouse pad) K&Company *Clear stamp:* (hello from All Occasion Messages set) Hero Arts *Pigment ink:* (white) *Accents:* (brown wood buttons) *Fibers:* (cream crochet thread) Coats & Clark *Die:* (Herringbone embossing) Provo Craft

Special Mom Card
Designer: Jessica Witty

SUPPLIES: *Cardstock:* (kraft) Papertrey Ink *Patterned paper:* (Wildflower from Jackson Lodge collection) Collage Press; (Leah) Melissa Frances; (Nutmeg from Kitchen Spice collection) BoBunny Press; (Cubicle from Office Lingo collection) Pink Paislee; (Double Take Detail from Curious collection) My Mind's Eye *Clear stamps:* (damask from Baroque set) Melissa Frances; (Elegant Memoir alphabet) Scrappy Cat; (special from Faux Ribbon set) Papertrey Ink *Dye ink:* (Chocolate Chip) Stampin' Up!; (Antique Linen) Ranger Industries *Pigment ink:* (Vintage Cream) Papertrey Ink *Accents:* (blue, green buttons) Papertrey Ink *Fibers:* (white twine) Papertrey Ink

Finished size: 5½" x 4¼"

Trio of Hugs Card
Designer: Teri Anderson

SUPPLIES: *Cardstock:* (white) WorldWin *Patterned paper:* (Reuse, Relive, Repeat from Earth Love collection) Cosmo Cricket *Clear stamp:* (hugs & kisses from All You Need is Love set) Technique Tuesday *Dye ink:* (Tuxedo Black) Tsukineko *Accents:* (white buttons) Buttons Galore & More; (aqua, yellow, orange chipboard hearts) Cosmo Cricket *Fibers:* (white floss) DMC

Finished size: 4¼" x 5½"

Birds for Baby Card
Designer: Kim Hughes

SUPPLIES: *Cardstock:* (Sunset Glow) SEI *Patterned paper:* (Repeat, Relive from Earth Love collection) Cosmo Cricket; (Finch from Wisteria collection) BasicGrey *Stickers:* (Earth Love alphabet) Cosmo Cricket; (blue cloud, tree badges) American Crafts *Tool:* (corner rounder punch)

Finished size: 5¾" x 3¼"

Sketch by: Kim Hughes

Groovy Love Card

Designer: Latisha Yoast

1. Make card from cardstock.

2. Cut strip of patterned paper; trim to form curve and adhere.

3. Cut strip of patterned paper; punch border and adhere.

4. Die-cut hearts from patterned paper; adhere.

5. Stamp sentiment on cardstock; trim and adhere with foam tape.

6. Thread button with twine; attach stick pin and tie bow. Adhere button.

Finished size: 4¼" x 5¾"

SUPPLIES: *Cardstock:* (white) Flourishes *Patterned paper:* (Birdy Gossip from Animal Bash collection) Prima *Clear stamp:* (groovy love sentiment from Feeling Groovy set) Verve Stamps *Dye ink:* (Tuxedo Black) Tsukineko *Accents:* (red heart stick pin) Making Memories; (yellow button) Autumn Leaves *Fibers:* (white twine) May Arts *Die:* (heart) Spellbinders *Tool:* (border punch) Martha Stewart Crafts

DESIGNER TIP

Keep black, white, and cream patterned paper on hand to create classic wedding and anniversary cards.

DESIGNER TIP

Use strong adhesive to attach the scalloped edge to the base—it will have to bear the weight of the card.

Best Wishes Card
Designer: Rae Barthel

SUPPLIES: *Cardstock:* (black) Hobby Lobby *Patterned paper:* (Tan Floral with Black Flocking, tan textured, small squares, tiny polka dots from La Crème pad) Die Cuts With a View *Chalk ink:* (Blackbird) Clearsnap *Accents:* (chipboard hearts) Making Memories; (white felt flower) Zva Creative; (black rhinestone) Kaisercraft *Font:* (Garton) www.fontstock.net *Tool:* (½" circle punch) EK Success

Finished size: 4¼" x 6¼"

Joy Hearts Card
Designer: Beatriz Jennings

SUPPLIES: *Cardstock:* (kraft) DMD, Inc. *Patterned paper:* (Thankful from Thankful collection) Melissa Frances *Dye ink:* (Vintage Photo) Ranger Industries *Specialty ink:* (gold shimmer spray) Tattered Angels *Accents:* (cream chipboard wings) Tattered Angels; (date tag, flower die cut) K&Company; (white glitter chipboard hearts, white button, green-rimmed button, white pearls) *Rub-on:* (joy) Melissa Frances *Fibers:* (aqua ribbon, white lace trim, twine)

Finished size: 3½" x 6"

Two Hearts
Miss You Card
Designer: Maile Belles

SUPPLIES: *Cardstock:* (Melon Berry, Vintage Cream, Dark Chocolate, kraft) Papertrey Ink *Clear stamps:* (miss you from Beyond Basic Borders set) Papertrey Ink; (Houndstooth Block) Studio Calico *Specialty ink:* (Aqua Mist, Dark Chocolate hybrid) Papertrey Ink *Accents:* (brown buttons) Papertrey Ink *Fibers:* (pink floss) DMC *Dies:* (heart, heart frame) Provo Craft *Tools:* (border punch) Stampin' Up!; (circle cutter)

Finished size: 3½" x 7¼"

Sketch by: Kim Hughes

BONUS IDEA

Use this unique card to wish someone good luck on a new job, or to celebrate an upcoming trip. For an added treat, insert a gift card to the recipient's favorite Chinese restaurant!

FIND IT

Pattern on p. 282

Good Fortune Card

Designer: Kim Hughes

1. Make card from cardstock.

2. Cut pocket, following pattern on p. 282. Stitch edges.

3. Punch circles from cardstock; attach to pocket body and flap with brads. Tie twine around circle on flap and wrap around both circles to close.

4. Cut branch from cardstock; adhere. Attach flowers with brads.

5. Print sentiment on cardstock; trim and adhere.

6. Cut circle of cardstock; fold in half and bend into fortune cookie shape; adhere. Insert chopsticks and close pocket.

Finished size: 4" x 8½"

SUPPLIES: *Cardstock:* (Tawny Light) Prism; (Beach, Vanilla Cream, French Roast, Café Sombre) Core'dinations; (white) Bazzill Basics Paper *Accents:* (brown glitter brads) We R Memory Keepers; (pink glitter brads) Doodlebug Design; (white flowers) Making Memories *Fibers:* (twine) Creative Impressions *Font:* (AL Landscape) Autumn Leaves *Tool:* (½" circle punch) EK Success *Other:* (wood chopsticks)

BONUS IDEA

Give a child a fun back-to-school greeting by decorating this card with classroom-themed embellishments like apples, chalkboards, notebooks, and school buses. The pencils will come in handy!

DESIGNER TIP

Make this project easy by creating your bookmark and pocket first and then designing your card around it.

Cheery Bookmark Card

Designer: Heidi Van Laar

SUPPLIES: *Cardstock:* (white) Georgia-Pacific; (yellow) Bazzill Basics Paper *Patterned paper:* (Jana from Little Ladies collection) My Little Shoebox *Accents:* (white flower) Prima; (yellow buttons) *Fibers:* (white string) Coats & Clark; (red polka dot ribbon) American Crafts *Font:* (Hobby Horse) www.1001fonts.com *Template:* (polka dots embossing) QuicKutz *Tools:* (decorative-edge scissors) Fiskars; (1½" circle punch) EK Success

Finished size: 4½" x 7"

All I Want For Christmas Card

Designer: Beth Opel

SUPPLIES: *Cardstock:* (red, green, white) Bazzill Basics Paper *Patterned paper:* (Kissing Santa Claus from Christmas 2008 collection) American Crafts *Specialty paper:* (photo) *Accents:* (red chipboard arrow) American Crafts; (white pearls) Zva Creative *Fibers:* (green polka dot ribbon) Making Memories *Fonts:* (Caslon Open Face, Century Gothic) www.fonts.com; (CK Squiggly) Creating Keepsakes *Software:* (photo editing) *Other:* (digital photo)

Finished size: 4¾" x 8"

Halloween Pencils Card

Designer: Kim Hughes

SUPPLIES: *Cardstock:* (black) Core'dinations *Patterned paper:* (Bewitching Webs from BOO! to You collection) My Mind's Eye *Accents:* (Frankenstein die cut, paper word strip) My Mind's Eye; (purple brads) BasicGrey *Other:* (pencils)

Finished size: 4¼" x 8"

Sketch by: Kim Kesti

DESIGNER TIP

Overlap alphabet stickers to allow for longer words in small spaces. Patterned paper on this card was a scrap sitting on Rae's craft table.

5 STEPS Congrats Gift Card Holder

Designer: Maren Benedict

1. Make card from cardstock.

2. Adhere cardstock panel. Adhere envelope.

3. Spell "Congrats" with stickers and adhere badge with foam tape.

4. Cut strip of patterned paper, adhere rhinestones, and adhere with foam tape.

Finished size: 4¼" x 5½"

SUPPLIES: *Cardstock:* (Dark Chocolate) Papertrey Ink *Patterned paper:* (Skip To My Lou from Blue skies collection) American Crafts *Accents:* (orange rhinestones) Me & My Big Ideas *Stickers:* (Delight alphabet; cherry badge) American Crafts *Other:* (kraft envelope) Maya Road

Just for You Gift Card Holder

Designer: Julia Stainton

SUPPLIES: *Cardstock:* (kraft) Bazzill Basics Paper *Patterned paper:* (La Boutique de Jardin from Postcards from Paris collection) Webster's Pages *Rubber stamp:* (sentiment from Classic Essential Expressions set) Cornish Heritage Farms *Dye ink:* (Rich Cocoa) Tsukineko *Pigment ink:* (Frost White) Clearsnap *Accents:* (pink flower stick pins) Maya Road; (newsprint flowers) Prima; (pewter buttons) Melissa Frances *Fibers:* (white ribbon) Michaels; (natural twine) *Other:* (kraft envelope) Maya Road

Finished size: 4¼" x 5½"

Rudolph Gift Card Holder

Designer: Maren Benedict

SUPPLIES: *Cardstock:* (Scarlet Jewel, Spring Rain) Papertrey Ink; (white) Stampin' Up! *Patterned paper:* (Snow Globe from Eskimo Kisses collection) BasicGrey *Rubber stamp:* (sentiment from Deck the Halls set) Lizzie Anne Designs *Dye ink:* (Black Soot) Ranger Industries *Accents:* (blue button) BasicGrey; (red rhinestones) Me & My Big Ideas *Sticker:* (felt deer) BasicGrey

Finished size: 4¼" x 5½"

Head of the Class Gift Card Holder

Designer: Beth Opel

SUPPLIES: *Cardstock:* (orange, red) Prism Papers; (Vanilla) American Crafts *Patterned paper:* (Midnight Blooms from Duck Pond collection) Black River Designs *Accents:* (bingo card) Jenni Bowlin Studio; (black, red brads) American Crafts *Fibers:* (red stitched ribbon) Li'l Davis Designs; (red floss) Bazzill Basics Paper *Font:* (Team MT) www.dafont.com

Finished size: 4" x 5½"

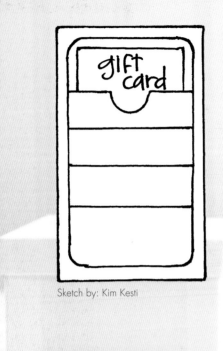

Sketch by: Kim Kesti

DESIGNER TIP

Using a gradient color scheme is a great way to incorporate lots of color without being overwhelming.

⋮5⋮ For You Gift Card Holder

Designer: Maile Belles

❶ Make card from cardstock.

❷ Cut pocket front and back from cardstock; round back piece corners.

❸ Cut cardstock strips; stamp polka dots and emboss. Adhere to pocket front.

❹ Punch half circle from top of pocket front and round bottom corners. Tie on twine and adhere three sides to pocket back. Adhere to card with foam tape.

❺ Stamp sentiment on cardstock; adhere. Adhere buttons.

Finished size: 3½" x 5½"

SUPPLIES: *Cardstock:* (Berry Sorbet, Melon Berry, Summer Sunrise, white) Papertrey Ink; (yellow) Core'dinations *Clear stamps:* (assorted polka dots from Polka Dot Basics II set; sentiment from Men of Life) Papertrey Ink *Watermark ink:* Tsukineko *Specialty ink:* (Berry Sorbet hybrid) Papertrey Ink *Embossing powder:* (clear) Jo-Ann Stores *Accents:* (pink buttons) Papertrey Ink *Fibers:* (white twine) Michaels *Tools:* (corner rounder punch) EK Success; (circle punch) Marvy Uchida

DESIGNER TIP

Tie ribbon around the gift card for a unique way to pull it out.

Enjoy Gift Card Holder

Designer: Kim Hughes

SUPPLIES: *Cardstock:* (Tawny Light, Intense Kiwi) Prism; (white embossed) Bazzill Basics Paper *Patterned paper:* (Falling Flakes, Merry Dots from Colorful Christmas collection) My Mind's Eye; (One Fine Day from Blue Skies collection) American Crafts *Sticker:* (enjoy) American Crafts *Fibers:* (tree ribbon) American Crafts *Tool:* (circle punch) Marvy Uchida *Other:* (gift card)

Finished size: 2¾" x 5½"

Fabric Gift Card Holder

Designer: Ashley C. Newell

SUPPLIES: *Cardstock:* (Vintage Cream) Papertrey Ink; (Kiwi Kiss, Soft Suede) Stampin' Up! *Fibers:* (orange ribbon) Papertrey Ink *Tool:* (corner rounder punch) We R Memory Keepers *Other:* (orange, brown, cream fabric) Moda Fabrics; (brown felt, gift card)

Finished size: 4¼" x 5½"

Fall Leaves Gift Card Holder

Designer: Maren Benedict

SUPPLIES: *Cardstock:* (Dark Chocolate) Papertrey Ink *Patterned paper:* (Plum Wine, Brandied Melon, Aspen, Maize, Woodrose from Indian Summer collection) BasicGrey *Accent:* (brown button) BasicGrey *Sticker:* (felt flower) BasicGrey *Fibers:* (pink ribbon) May Arts; (brown rope) Canvas Corp. *Tools:* (corner rounder punch) Creative Memories; (circle punch) Stampin' Up! *Other:* (gift card)

Finished size: 4¼" x 5½"

Sketch by: Betsy Veldman

DESIGNER TIP

Get more mileage from your stamps and papers by creating multiples of the same card design. Substitute papers and sentiments for a bounty of fresh looks.

5 STEPS So Sweet of You Card

Designer: Debbie Olson

1. Make card from cardstock.

2. Trim patterned paper square, sand edges, and stitch to larger patterned paper piece; sand edges.

3. Die-cut and emboss label from cardstock; cut in half diagonally and ink edges.

4. Mat top edge with patterned paper. Stamp sentiment and adhere.

5. Tie twill around block; adhere to card. Thread button and adhere.

Finished size: 4¼" x 5½"

SUPPLIES: All supplies from Papertrey Ink unless otherwise noted. *Cardstock:* (Vintage Cream) *Patterned paper:* (Cherry Pie, Farmers Market from Early Bird collection) Cosmo Cricket *Clear stamps:* (sentiment from Signature Greetings set) *Dye ink:* (Chamomile) *Specialty ink:* (Pure Poppy hybrid) *Accent:* (red button) *Fibers:* (cream twill) *Die:* (label) Spellbinders

Sniffles Get Well Card

Designer: Latisha Yoast

SUPPLIES: *Cardstock:* (white) Flourishes; (coral) Bazzill Basics Paper *Rubber stamp:* (Tissue Box) Lockhart Stamp *Clear stamp:* (polka dots from Polka Dot Basics set) Papertrey Ink *Dye ink:* (Tuxedo Black) Tsukineko *Specialty ink:* (Landscape hybrid) Stewart Superior Corp. *Color media:* (green, orange, peach markers) Copic; (white glaze pen) Sakura *Accent:* (white button) Papertrey Ink *Stickers:* (My Neighborhood Mini alphabet) My Little Shoebox *Fibers:* (green ribbon) Stampin' Up!

Finished size: 4¼" x 5½"

Cheery Home Congrats Card

Designer: Jessica Witty

SUPPLIES: *Cardstock:* (white) Papertrey Ink *Patterned paper:* (Bewitching from Fascinating collection) Pink Paislee; (Nutmeg from Kitchen Spice collection) BoBunny Press; (Pocketful of Sunshine, Sunny Day from Blue Skies collection) American Crafts *Rubber stamp:* (sentiment from Congrats set) Stampin' Up! *Dye ink:* (Chocolate Chip) Stampin' Up! *Accents:* (felt sun, cloud) American Crafts *Stickers:* (trees) American Crafts

Finished size: 4¼" x 7"

O Holy Night Card

Designer: Beth Opel

SUPPLIES: *Cardstock:* (kraft) Bazzill Basics Paper *Patterned paper:* (Denim Dot, Decaf Dot from Double Dot collection) BoBunny Press *Accent:* (gold chipboard star) American Crafts *Stickers:* (Center of Attention alphabet) Heidi Swapp *Fibers:* (cream twill)

Finished size: 4½" x 7"

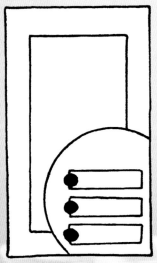

Sketch by: Betsy Veldman

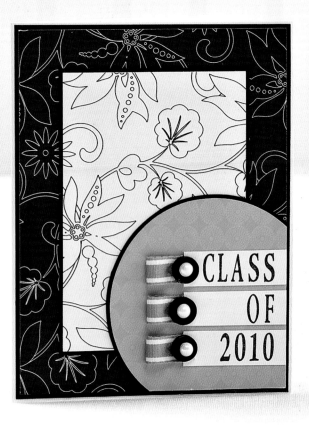

⟨5 STEPS⟩ Class of 2010 Card

Designer: Debbie Olson

1 Make card from cardstock.

2 Mat patterned paper rectangles with cardstock; adhere.

3 Cut circles from patterned paper and cardstock. Trim edges and adhere.

4 Stamp sentiment on cardstock strips; adhere.

5 Adhere ribbon behind buttons. Adhere pearls and adhere to card.

Finished size: 4¼" x 5½"

SUPPLIES: *Cardstock:* (True Black, white) Papertrey Ink *Patterned paper:* (Ocean Brise, Milou Mist, Dorada Vista from Black Orchid collection) SEI *Rubber stamps:* (Times New Roman Uppercase set) JustRite *Specialty ink:* (True Black hybrid) Papertrey Ink *Accents:* (black buttons) Papertrey Ink; (white pearls) Kaisercraft *Fibers:* (teal/white ribbon) SEI *Tool:* (circle cutter) Martha Stewart Crafts

Bulleted
Thank You Card

Designer: Latisha Yoast

SUPPLIES: *Cardstock:* (Not Quite Navy) Stampin' Up!; (white) *Patterned paper:* (Ads from Vintage Findings collection) Making Memories *Clear stamps:* (sentiment from Seaside Life set) Flourishes *Specialty ink:* (Enchanted Evening hybrid) Papertrey Ink *Accents:* (brass brads) Making Memories *Tool:* (circle cutter) *Other:* (adhesive-backed cork sheet) QuicKutz

Finished size: 2¾" x 5½"

Get Well
Crossword Card

Designer: Jessica Witty

SUPPLIES: *Cardstock:* (Berry Sorbet) Papertrey Ink *Patterned paper:* (Terrassa from Barcelona collection) 7gypsies; (Sugar Pie from Sweet Cakes collection) Pink Paislee; (Vacationer Motel from Road Map collection) October Afternoon *Color medium:* (black marker) Stampin' Up! *Accents:* (black brads) Making Memories *Die:* (bracket label) Spellbinders

Finished size: 4¼" x 5½"

Note To Self Notebook

Designer: Betsy Veldman

SUPPLIES: *Cardstock:* (Vintage Cream, Melon Berry) Papertrey Ink *Patterned paper:* (Repeat, Rethink, Elements from Earth Love collection) Cosmo Cricket *Clear stamps:* (note to self, pencil, circle frame from Take Note set; polka dots from Polka Dot Basics II set) Papertrey Ink *Chalk ink:* (Creamy Brown) Clearsnap *Specialty ink:* (Dark Chocolate, Melon Berry hybrid) Papertrey Ink *Accents:* (orange button) Papertrey Ink; (white pearls) Zva Creative *Fibers:* (striped ribbon) Cosmo Cricket; (cream twine) Papertrey Ink *Tools:* (decorative-edge scissors) Provo Craft; (binding machine) Zutter; (butterfly punch) EK Success *Other:* (white spiral binding) Zutter; (chipboard)

Finished size: 6" x 3½"

Sketch by: Jessica Witty

Love Blooms Card

Designer: Betsy Veldman

1 Make card from cardstock.

2 Stamp medallion repeatedly, stitch, and ink edges.

3 Die-cut bracketed label from cardstock; stamp frame, ink edges, and adhere. Affix tag sticker, stamp sentiment, and adhere pearls.

4 Stamp leaves on cardstock; trim and adhere.

5 Trim flower from patterned paper, ink edges, and adhere.

6 Die-cut flowers from patterned paper; ink edges, attach brad, and adhere.

Finished size: 4¼" x 5½"

SUPPLIES: *Cardstock:* (Vintage Cream, Sweet Blush) Papertrey Ink *Patterned paper:* (Hope from Calypso collection) BoBunny Press; (Tea Towel from Cherry Hill collection) October Afternoon *Clear stamps:* (sentiment from Favor It Weddings set, leaves from Beautiful Blooms set, medallion from Giga Guide Lines set, frame from Vintage Labels set) Papertrey Ink *Chalk ink:* (Creamy Brown) Clearsnap *Specialty ink:* (Dark Chocolate, Ripe Avocado hybrid) Papertrey Ink *Accents:* (pink polka dot fabric brad) BasicGrey; (white pearls) Zva Creative *Sticker:* (remember tag) October Afternoon *Dies:* (flowers) Provo Craft; (bracketed label) Spellbinders

Sassy Hello Card

Designer: Roree Rumph

SUPPLIES: *Patterned paper:* (Tudor Rose from Renaissance Faire collection) Graphic 45; (Catalonia from Barcelona collection) 7gypsies *Accents:* (definitions die cut) October Afternoon; (ivory flower) Prima *Stickers:* (label) October Afternoon; (Glitter alphabet) Pink Paislee *Fibers:* (green ribbon) Michaels

Finished size: 4¼" x 5½"

Autumn Thinking of You Card

Designer: Latisha Yoast

SUPPLIES: *Cardstock:* (kraft) Papertrey Ink *Clear stamps:* (sentiment from Vintage Picnic Sentiments set) Papertrey Ink *Dye ink:* (Tuxedo Black) Tsukineko *Color medium:* (orange glaze pen) Sakura *Stickers:* (felt tree, autumn chipboard) BasicGrey *Tool:* (corner rounder punch) Stampin' Up!

Finished size: 4¼" x 5½"

Dictionary Congrats Card

Designer: Kim Kesti

SUPPLIES: *Cardstock:* (Vanilla) Bazzill Basics Paper *Patterned paper:* (Tea Towel from Cherry Hill collection) October Afternoon *Transparency sheet:* (brown scroll) *Accents:* (brown/yellow flower) Bella Blvd; (gold filigree square, white pearl brad) *Rub-on:* (congrats) American Crafts *Tool:* (corner rounder punch) We R Memory Keepers

Finished size: 4½" x 6"

Sketch by: Jessica Witty

Birthday Hat Card

Designer: Jessica Witty

1. Make card from cardstock. Stamp polka dots; emboss.

2. Stamp sentiment on cardstock strip; adhere.

3. Cut triangle from patterned paper; adhere and stitch edges.

4. Gather ribbon, adhere, and stitch.

5. Wrap floss repeatedly around 1" cardstock scrap. Slide floss off cardstock, tie around center of floss loops, and cut loops to create pompom. Adhere to card.

Finished size: 4¼" x 5½"

SUPPLIES: *Cardstock:* (kraft, white) Papertrey Ink *Patterned paper:* (Wasabi Dot from Double Dot collection) BoBunny Press *Clear stamps:* (sentiment from Mega Mixed Messages set, polka dots from Polka Dot Basics set) Papertrey Ink *Dye ink:* (Summer Sun) Stampin' Up! *Watermark ink:* Tsukineko *Embossing powder:* (white) Stampin' Up! *Fibers:* (yellow polka dot ribbon) BoBunny Press; (yellow floss) DMC

DESIGNER TIP

Don't be afraid to mix fun patterns and colors. It's like getting to make your own clothes—only they're on a card and require no sewing!

Happy Holidays Tree Card

Designer: Angie Tieman

SUPPLIES: *Cardstock:* (kraft) Stampin' Up! *Patterned paper:* (Sweater Weather from Jolly by Golly collection) Cosmo Cricket; (brown polka dot from Chocolate Chip Patterns collection) Stampin' Up! *Accent:* (brown corduroy button) Stampin' Up! *Sticker:* (happy holidays) Cosmo Cricket *Fibers:* (red pompom trim) The Scarlet Lime; (natural linen thread) Stampin' Up! *Tool:* (oval punch) Stampin' Up!

Finished size: 4¼" x 5½"

Birthday Dress Card

Designer: Tina Fussell

SUPPLIES: *Cardstock:* (white) Papertrey Ink *Patterned paper:* (Picnic from Hello Sunshine collection, Playtime from Jack's World collection, Something Old from Everafter collection) Cosmo Cricket; (Ladybug from Urban Prairie collection) BasicGrey; (Red Circle Flower from Front Porch collection) Jenni Bowlin Studio; (brown polka dot from 2008 Bitty Dot Basics collection) Papertrey Ink *Clear stamp:* (birthday from Borders & Corners Monogram Mini set) Papertrey Ink *Dye ink:* (Chocolate Chip) Stampin' Up! *Accents:* (clear rhinestone) Hero Arts; (brown flower rhinestone) *Stickers:* (Polka Dot alphabet) Webster's Pages *Fibers:* (white ribbon) Stampin' Up! *Tool:* (scallop trimmer) Fiskars

Finished size: 4¼" x 5½"

Joy Tree Tag

Designer: Heidi Van Laar

SUPPLIES: *Cardstock:* (cream, kraft) The Paper Company *Patterned paper:* (Argyle from Mistletoe collection) Making Memories *Accents:* (red star stick pin, chipboard tree) Making Memories *Stickers:* (Metro alphabet) Making Memories *Fibers:* (hemp twine)

Finished size: 2½" x 4¼"

Sketch by: Jessica Witty

With Sympathy Bird Card

Designer: Rae Barthel

1 Make card from patterned paper.

2 Mat patterned paper piece with patterned paper; adhere to card.

3 Tie on ribbon.

4 Print sentiment on label; mat with patterned paper and adhere with foam tape.

5 Fussy-cut bird trio from patterned paper; adhere.

Finished size: 4½" x 6"

SUPPLIES: *Patterned paper:* (tiny red floral, blue grid, black filigree from Mi Casa pad) Die Cuts With a View *Accent:* (label die cut) Making Memories *Fibers:* (gold ribbon) Offray *Font:* (Fling) www.fonts.com

I Love You Flower Card

Designer: Windy Robinson

SUPPLIES: *Cardstock:* (kraft) DMD, Inc. *Patterned paper:* (Saloon from Town Square collection) Jenni Bowlin Studio; (Tweet Hearts from Whoo Loves You? collection) My Little Shoebox *Clear stamp:* (sentiment from Call Me set) Renaissance By Design *Chalk ink:* (Chestnut Roan) Clearsnap *Specialty ink:* (Burnt Umber hybrid) Stewart Superior Corp. *Accents:* (white flower) Prima; (green felt leaves) Jillibean Soup

Finished size: 5½" x 4¼"

Alphabet Thanks Card

Designer: Tiffany Johnson

SUPPLIES: *Cardstock:* (white) Papertrey Ink *Patterned paper:* (Ledger from Character collection) American Crafts *Clear stamps:* (thanks from Thank You set) Close To My Heart *Dye ink:* (Outdoor Denim) Close To My Heart *Accent:* (silver staple) *Fibers:* (white ribbon) Papertrey Ink

Finished size: 4¼" x 5½"

Airplane Boy Card

Designer: Kalyn Kepner

SUPPLIES: *Cardstock:* (kraft) Bazzill Basics Paper *Patterned paper:* (Mischievous Max from Lil' Man collection) Cosmo Cricket *Chalk ink:* (Creamy Brown, Chestnut Roan) Clearsnap *Stickers:* (chipboard airplane, button) Cosmo Cricket; (Rockabye alphabet) American Crafts *Fibers:* (natural twine) Westrim Crafts; (orange twill, striped ribbon) Cosmo Cricket *Tool:* (decorative-edge scissors) *Other:* (brown felt)

Finished size: 3¾" x 6¾"

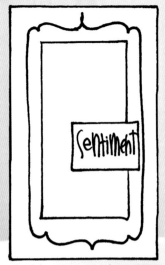

Sketch by: Maren Benedict

5 STEPS You Rock, Dad Card

Designer: Rae Barthel

1. Make card from cardstock; adhere patterned paper and ink edges.

2. Cut patterned paper and ink edges. Affix brackets; adhere.

3. Trim guitar from patterned paper and cover with glitter. Adhere with foam tape.

4. Stamp frame on patterned paper and trim. Affix letters; adhere with foam tape.

5. Affix letters to spell "Dad".

Finished size: 4" x 6"

SUPPLIES: *Cardstock:* (black) *Patterned paper:* (Sabadell, Catalonia from Barcelona collection) 7gypsies; (Revolution from Rock Star collection) Creative Imaginations *Clear stamp:* (frame from Round and Round set) Autumn Leaves *Pigment ink:* (Onyx Black) Tsukineko *Chalk ink:* (Blackbird) Clearsnap *Accent:* (black glitter) Making Memories *Stickers:* (Mini Shimmer, Tiny Alpha alphabets) Making Memories; (chipboard brackets) American Crafts

Houndstooth Hi Card

Designer: Tiffany Johnson

SUPPLIES: *Cardstock:* (Melon Berry) Papertrey Ink; (white) *Patterned paper:* (Retro from Moda Bella collection) American Crafts *Vellum:* Papertrey Ink *Clear stamps:* (Friendship Alphabet set) Close To My Heart *Pigment ink:* (Turquoise) Tsukineko *Accent:* (clear rhinestone) Close To My Heart *Die:* (label) Stampin' Up!

Finished size: 4¼" x 5½"

Boo-ed Card

Designer: Kim Kesti

SUPPLIES: *Cardstock:* (Festive, white, black) Bazzill Basics Paper *Patterned paper:* (Tricky Sticks, Web Page from Eerie Allie collection) SEI *Embossing powder:* (Orange Glitter) American Crafts *Accents:* (black buttons) BasicGrey *Fibers:* (black polka dot ribbon) May Arts *Font:* (Delicious Small Caps) www.josbuivenga.demon.nl *Dies:* (Haunted Mini Alphabet, frame) QuicKutz *Tool:* (corner rounder punch) We R Memory Keepers

Finished size: 4" x 7½"

Holiday Planner

Designer: Debbie Olson

SUPPLIES: *Cardstock:* (Rustic White) Papertrey Ink *Patterned paper:* (peppermints, red sheet music from Jolly By Golly pad) Cosmo Cricket *Clear stamps:* (stocking from Stocking Prints set, sentiment from Take Note set) Papertrey Ink *Dye ink:* (Chamomile) Papertrey Ink; (Tuxedo Black) Tsukineko *Specialty ink:* (Pure Poppy hybrid) Papertrey Ink *Color medium:* (pink, red, dark red, gray markers) Copic *Accents:* (red rhinestone) A Muse Artstamps; (ivory textured sprinkles) Flower Soft *Fibers:* (natural twill) Twilltape.com; (red ribbon) Papertrey Ink *Die:* (label) Spellbinders *Other:* (mini composition book)

Finished size: 3½" x 4¼"

Thoughts of You Tag

Designer: Kim Hughes

SUPPLIES: *Cardstock:* (French Garden White embossed) Bazzill Basics Paper; (white) *Patterned paper:* (Whirlybird from Shine collection, Two-Wheeler from Road Trip collection) My Mind's Eye; (Bermudas from Plastino collection) Bella Blvd *Accents:* (ivory button) Creative Impressions; (ivory flowers) *Fibers:* (white twill, twine) Creative Impressions *Font:* (your choice) *Die:* (frame) Ellison *Tool:* (½" circle punch) Marvy Uchida

Finished size: 4" x 6"

Nurture Today Card

Designer: Maren Benedict

SUPPLIES: *Cardstock:* (kraft) Papertrey Ink *Rubber stamps:* (tree, sentiment from The Artist in You set) Unity Stamp Co. *Dye ink:* (Vintage Photo) Ranger Industries

Finished size: 4¼" x 6"

Wildflower Thanks Card

Designer: Julie Cameron

SUPPLIES: *Cardstock:* (kraft) Papertrey Ink; (Herbal Garden Light, black) Prism; (white) *Clear stamps:* (flowers from Life set, sentiment from Tags for Spring set) Papertrey Ink; (leaf background from Texture Tile set) Stampendous! *Dye ink:* (Antique Linen) Ranger Industries *Specialty ink:* (Noir, Water Lily Green hybrid) Stewart Superior Corp. *Color medium:* (gold glitter pen) Sakura *Dies:* (label) QuicKutz; (curved rectangle) Spellbinders *Tools:* (flower punch) Fiskars; (butterfly punch) Martha Stewart Crafts

Finished size: 3½" x 5"

Sketch by: Kim Kesti

✦5✦ Christmas Tree Buttons Card
STEPS

Designer: Wendy Sue Anderson

1 Make card from cardstock, cover with cardstock, and round top corners.

2 Round top corners of patterned paper piece; adhere. Adhere patterned paper panel.

3 Adhere ribbon to seam. Tie ribbon bow and adhere.

4 Apply rub-on and affix tree sticker.

Finished size: 3¾" x 6½"

SUPPLIES: *Cardstock:* (white, black) American Crafts *Patterned paper:* (Argyle and Big Green Dot from Mistletoe collection) Making Memories *Rub-on:* (sentiment) Making Memories *Sticker:* (felt tree) Making Memories *Fibers:* (black/cream striped ribbon) *Tool:* (corner rounder punch) EK Success

Thanks Box

Designer: Lisa Dorsey

SUPPLIES: *Cardstock:* (Blackberry Swirl, Sea Breeze, Pear Crush, Cherry Splash) Bazzill Basics Paper *Patterned paper:* (Dots from Jack Frost collection) BoBunny Press; (Distress Notebook from Spirit collection) Creative Café; (blue/green polka dots) *Pigment ink:* (black) Clearsnap *Color medium:* (black marker) *Accent:* (green button) Creative Imaginations *Fibers:* (black ribbon) Papertrey Ink; (natural twine) May Arts *Font:* (Edwardian Script) www.fonts.com *Template:* (paisley, flowers embossing) Ellison *Die:* (tag) Ellison *Other:* (kraft gift box) Emma's Paperie

Finished size: 3¾" x 5¾" x 1¼"

Boo Bling Card

Designer: Rae Barthel

SUPPLIES: *Cardstock:* (Avalanche) Bazzill Basics Paper *Patterned paper:* (Argyle from Spellbound collection) Making Memories *Chalk ink:* (Blackbird) Clearsnap *Accents:* (clear rhinestones) Kaisercraft; (clear rhinestone brad) Michaels *Stickers:* (Shin-Dig alphabet) Doodlebug Design *Fibers:* (black/white stripe ribbon) Hobby Lobby

Finished size: 4" x 6"

Thinking of You Quilt Card

Designer: Nina Brackett

SUPPLIES: *Cardstock:* (Rocket Red, Sweet Corn, Black Onyx) Gina K Designs *Patterned paper:* (red leaf from Christmas pad) Die Cuts With a View; (Black Toile) The Paper Studio *Rubber stamp:* (sentiment from Elegant Post set) Gina K Designs *Clear stamp:* (script from Background Basics: Text Style set) Papertrey Ink *Dye ink:* (Tuxedo Black) Tsukineko *Accents:* (silver pearls) Mark Richards; (red button) Gina K Designs *Fibers:* (yellow ribbon) Stampin' Up!; (white string)

Finished size: 4½" x 5¾"

DESIGNER TIP

Use a gridline acrylic block to align and evenly space your line stamps.

Feel Better Soon Gift Bag

Designer: Kim Hughes

SUPPLIES: *Cardstock:* (pale green) Bazzill Basics Paper *Clear stamp:* (sentiment from Large Sentiments set) American Crafts *Dye ink:* (Desert Sand) Close To My Heart *Accents:* (pink flower) Making Memories; (white/red epoxy brad) BasicGrey *Fibers:* (pink, tan floss) DMC; (cream ribbon) *Tool:* (decorative-edge scissors) Fiskars *Other:* (brown bag)

Finished size: 3¼" x 6¼"

Fatherhood Gift Bag

Designer: Betsy Veldman

SUPPLIES: *Cardstock:* (Vintage Cream) Papertrey Ink *Patterned paper:* (Bleu Striped, FulFilled, Sophie from BellaBella collection) My Mind's Eye *Clear stamp:* (father from Mega Mixed Messages set) Papertrey Ink *Pigment ink:* (Vintage Cream) Papertrey Ink *Chalk ink:* (Creamy Brown) Clearsnap *Accents:* (green buttons) Papertrey Ink; (black glitter brads) We R Memory Keepers; (copper eyelet) Provo Craft *Fibers:* (blue twill) Papertrey Ink *Font:* (Baskerville Old) Microsoft *Dies:* (tie, argyle, gift box) Provo Craft

Finished size: 4" x 6¼" x 1¼"

Rhinestones & Argyle Card

Designer: Lisa Johnson

SUPPLIES: All supplies from Papertrey Ink unless otherwise noted. *Cardstock:* (Pure Poppy, Spring Moss, Sweet Blush, white) *Clear stamps:* (dotted lines, five stripes from Background Basics: Retro set; dual stripes from Faux Ribbon set; sentiment from 2009 Holiday Tag Collection set) *Pigment ink:* (Fresh Snow) *Specialty ink:* (Pure Poppy, Spring Moss, Sweet Blush hybrid) *Accents:* (clear rhinestones) Zva Creative

Finished size: 3½" x 5"

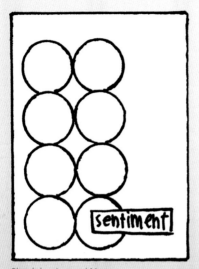

Sketch by: Jessica Witty

5 STEPS Circles of Thanks Card

Designer: Tina Fussell

1. Make card from cardstock.

2. Punch circles from patterned paper; adhere.

3. Stamp sentiment on cardstock; trim and adhere.

Finished size: 4¼" x 5½"

SUPPLIES: *Cardstock:* (white) Papertrey Ink *Patterned paper:* (Chronicle from Character collection) American Crafts; (Frolic from Little Sprout collection) Crate Paper; (Harvest from Urban Prairie collection) BasicGrey; (gold loops from Urban Oasis collection) Stampin' Up! *Clear stamp:* (sentiment from Thank You Messages set) Hero Arts *Dye ink:* (Basic Gray) Stampin' Up! *Tool:* (⅞" circle punch) Creative Memories

Thanksgiving Gift Bag

Designer: Lisa Johnson

SUPPLIES: All supplies from Papertrey Ink unless otherwise noted. *Cardstock:* (Dark Chocolate) *Patterned paper:* (large, small leaves; stripes, polka dots from Autumn Abundance collection) *Clear stamps:* text from Background Basics: Text Style II set, sentiment from 2009 Autumn Tags set, dotted circle from Borders & Corners {circle} set) *Pigment ink:* (Fresh White) *Specialty ink:* (Dark Chocolate hybrid) *Tools:* (1⅜" circle punch) Marvy Uchida; (decorative-edge scissors) Fiskars *Other:* (kraft bag)

Finished size: 4¼" x 10¼"

8 Button Birthday Card

Designer: Betsy Veldman

SUPPLIES: *Cardstock:* (Vintage Cream, kraft) Papertrey Ink *Clear stamps:* (polka dots from Polka Dot Basics II set, sentiment from Mega Mixed Messages set) Papertrey Ink *Chalk ink:* (Creamy Brown) Clearsnap *Specialty ink:* (Pure Poppy, Dark Chocolate hybrid) Papertrey Ink *Accents:* (assorted buttons) Papertrey Ink; (journaling card) My Mind's Eye; (orange glitter brads) Doodlebug Design; (green check fabric brad) BasicGrey *Fibers:* (multi striped ribbon) Cosmo Cricket; (pink, yellow twine) The Beadery; (white twine) Papertrey Ink *Die:* (tag) Provo Craft

Finished size: 4¼" x 5½"

Miss You Flowers Card

Designer: Lisa Johnson

SUPPLIES: All supplies from Papertrey Ink unless otherwise noted. *Cardstock:* (Spring Moss, Dark Chocolate, kraft) *Patterned paper:* (yellow, green, pink, brown polka dots from 2008 Bitty Dot Basics collection) *Clear stamps:* (vine, sentiment from Beyond Basic Borders set) *Pigment ink:* (Fresh White) *Specialty ink:* (Dark Chocolate hybrid) *Accents:* (yellow buttons) *Fibers:* (natural twine) *Tools:* (flower, corner rounder punches) Marvy Uchida

Finished size: 4¼" x 5½"

Season's Button Greetings Card

Designer: Ryann Salamon

SUPPLIES: *Cardstock:* (Vintage Cream, kraft) Papertrey Ink *Accents:* (assorted chipboard buttons) Making Memories; (red button) Creative Café *Rub-on:* (sentiment) Making Memories

Finished size: 4¼" x 5½"

Ruff Day? Card

Designer: Kim Hughes

SUPPLIES: *Cardstock:* (Tawny Light, white) Prism; (Seven Seas) SEI *Patterned paper:* (Aggie from June Bug collection) BasicGrey; (Choo Choo! From Let's Roll collection) Imaginisce; (Tailored from French Couture collection) Lily Bee Design; (Peppermint Stripes from The Merry Days of Christmas collection, Scattered Flowers from Best Friends collection, Pumpkin Patch from The Spider's Web collection) My Mind's Eye *Color medium:* (black pen) Sakura *Accent:* (red button) Creative Café *Fibers:* (white twine) Creative Impressions *Tools:* (1¼" circle punch) Marvy Uchida; (paw punch) EK Success

Finished size: 4¼" x 5¾"

Missing You Dots Card

Designer: Teri Anderson

SUPPLIES: *Cardstock:* (red, yellow, orange, green, light blue, blue, purple, gray) Core'dinations; (white) WorldWin; (Vintage Cream) Papertrey Ink *Accent:* (silver brad) Making Memories *Rub-ons:* (Alex alphabet) American Crafts *Stickers:* (MoMa alphabet) American Crafts *Tools:* (1" circle punch) Martha Stewart Crafts; (corner rounder punch) Zutter

Finished size: 4¼" x 5½"

Sketch by: Teri Anderson

Birthday Flower Silhouette Card

5 STEPS

Designer: Natasha Trupp

❶ Make card from cardstock.

❷ Round top corners of patterned paper; mat with cardstock and adhere.

❸ Stamp flowers on cardstock. Fussy-cut and adhere with foam tape.

❹ Stamp happy birthday on cardstock; mat with cardstock. Attach brad and adhere.

Finished size: 4¼" x 5¼"

SUPPLIES: *Cardstock:* (Vintage Cream, Dark Chocolate) Papertrey Ink *Patterned paper:* (blue grid from Bashful Blue collection) Stampin' Up! *Rubber stamp:* (flowers from Feel the Joy set) Unity Stamp Co.
Clear stamp: (happy birthday from Vintage Picnic set) Papertrey Ink *Dye ink:* (Rich Cocoa) Tsukineko
Accent: (blue brad) Making Memories *Tool:* (corner rounder punch) EK Success

To You Card

Designer: Gretchen Clark

SUPPLIES: *Cardstock:* (Ocean Tides) Papertrey Ink; (Whisper White, Chocolate Chip, kraft) Stampin' Up! *Clear stamps:* (flower petals, stem, center, leaf from Floral Frenzy set; sentiment from Everyday Button Bits set) Papertrey Ink *Dye ink:* (Chocolate Chip) Stampin' Up! *Specialty ink:* (Ocean Tides, Ripe Avocado hybrid) Papertrey Ink *Fibers:* (brown ribbon) Stampin' Up! *Dies:* (tag, ribbon slide) Spellbinders *Tools:* (corner rounder, border, ½" circle punches) Stampin' Up!

Finished size: 4¼" x 5½"

'Tis the Season Card

Designer: Maile Belles

SUPPLIES: All supplies from Papertrey Ink unless otherwise noted. *Cardstock:* (Ripe Avocado, Ocean Tides, Aqua Mist, white) *Clear stamps:* (tree, star from Tree Trimming Trio set; sentiment from Signature Christmas set) *Specialty ink:* (Ripe Avocado, Dark Chocolate, Summer Sunrise hybrid) *Accents:* (blue buttons) *Fibers:* (white floss) DMC *Tool:* (corner rounder punch) EK Success

Finished size: 4¼" x 5½"

Get Well Soon Card

Designer: Latisha Yoast

SUPPLIES: *Cardstock:* (Classic Ivory) Flourishes *Patterned paper:* (Remember from Earth Love collection) Cosmo Cricket *Dye ink:* (Walnut Stain) Ranger Industries *Stickers:* (blue chipboard flower, chipboard flower trio) Cosmo Cricket; (Tiny Alpha alphabet) Making Memories *Fibers:* (yellow ribbon) Papertrey Ink *Tool:* (ticket corner punch) Stampin' Up!

Finished size: 4¼" x 5½"

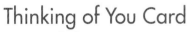

Thinking of You Card
Designer: Charlene Austin

SUPPLIES: *Cardstock:* (Rustic Cream, Scarlet Jewel) Papertrey Ink *Patterned paper:* (Girl Vine Dot from Just Chillin collection) Making Memories *Rubber stamp:* (sentiment from Simply Sentiments set) Lizzie Anne Designs *Dye ink:* (Walnut Stain) Ranger Industries *Accent:* (pink paper flower) Prima *Fibers:* (green leaf trim) Papertrey Ink

Finished size: 5½" square

Happy Easter Card
Designer: Rae Barthel

SUPPLIES: *Cardstock:* (Dandelion) Core'dinations *Patterned paper:* (New Apron, Recipe Box from Cherry Hill collection) October Afternoon *Accents:* (pink flower, happy yellow scallop die cuts) October Afternoon *Stickers:* (Nutmeg alphabet) American Crafts *Fibers:* (pink polka dot ribbon) American Crafts *Tool:* (corner rounder punch) EK Success

Finished size: 4½" x 6"

Flower Patch Thank You Card
Designer: Davinie Fiero

SUPPLIES: *Cardstock:* (Vanilla) American Crafts *Patterned paper:* (Apron Strings from Early Bird collection) Cosmo Cricket; (Sleep Tight from Ducks in a Row collection) October Afternoon; (Bow & Arrow from Cupid collection) Pink Paislee *Dye ink:* (brown) *Accents:* (blue buttons) Tessa Ann Designs; (orange tag die cut) Collage Press *Rub-on:* (bluebird) Lily Bee Design *Stickers:* (Whimsies alphabet) Pink Paislee *Fibers:* (green ribbon) Cosmo Cricket; (white waxed floss) Karen Foster Design *Tools:* (corner rounder punch; 1", 1½" circle punches) Fiskars

Finished size: 4½" x 6"

Sketch by: Kim Hughes

DESIGNER TIP

This box was initially used as food packaging. You can also look to nature to embellish your projects, including twigs, leaves, petals, and more.

Where the Heart Lives Gift Box

Designer: Julie Campbell

1. Cut strip of patterned paper; stitch border and adhere.

2. Cut cardstock to fit behind frame; adhere. Adhere frame and feather.

3. Apply rub-on to cardstock; color with markers, cut out, and adhere with foam tape.

4. Adhere beaded swirl.

5. Cut strip of cardstock; punch/emboss border and adhere.

6. Adhere twig; tie ribbon bow and adhere.

Finished size: 3¾" x 7½" x 3¾"

SUPPLIES: *Cardstock:* (Suede Brown Dark, Simply Smooth Natural, kraft) Prism *Patterned paper:* (Saloon from Town Square collection) Jenni Bowlin Studio *Color medium:* (assorted markers) Copic *Accents:* (brown beaded swirl) Zva Creative; (red chipboard frame) Sassafras Lass; (black feather) *Rub-on:* (home definition) Jenni Bowlin Studio *Fibers:* (brown ribbon) Martha Stewart Crafts *Tool:* (embossing border punch) EK Success *Other:* (corrugated cardboard box, twig)

BONUS IDEA

Stamp a background pattern onto the bag instead of using die cut cardstock or patterned paper strips.

THERE'S NOTHING BETTER THAN A TRUE *friend*

SWEET

You Can Do It Card
Designer: Alicia Thelin

SUPPLIES: *Cardstock:* (white, green, teal, brown) Stampin' Up!; (yellow) Hobby Lobby *Rubber stamp:* (good luck block from In Good Form set) Stampin' Up! *Dye ink:* (Chocolate Chip) Stampin' Up! *Accents:* (yellow buttons) Oriental Trading Co. *Fibers:* (white floss) *Tools:* (border, rounded rectangle, circle punches) Stampin' Up!

Finished size: 3½" x 5½"

True Friend Gift Bag
Designer: Sarah Martina Parker

SUPPLIES: *Cardstock:* (Hibiscus Burst, white) Papertrey Ink; (white) Bazzill Basics Paper *Patterned paper:* (Tea Party from June Bug collection) BasicGrey *Specialty paper:* (yellow die cut) Creative Imaginations *Clear stamp:* (friend sentiment from In Bloom set) Papertrey Ink *Specialty ink:* (Hibiscus Burst hybrid) Papertrey Ink *Accents:* (pink rhinestones) Kaisercraft *Fibers:* (pink ribbon) Papertrey Ink *Tool:* (embossing border punch) EK Success *Other:* (white gift bag)

Finished size: 5¼" x 8½"

Oh So Sweet Card
Designer: Betsy Veldman

SUPPLIES: *Cardstock:* (Vintage Cream, Melon Berry) Papertrey Ink *Patterned paper:* (Remember from Earth Love collection; Apron Strings from Early Bird collection) Cosmo Cricket; (Straw from Urban Prairie collection) BasicGrey *Clear stamps:* (special delivery from Favor it Baby set; polka dot background from Polka Dot Basics II set) Papertrey Ink *Chalk ink:* (Creamy Brown) Clearsnap *Specialty ink:* (Summer Sunrise, Ocean Tides hybrid) Papertrey Ink *Accents:* (orange, green, blue buttons) Papertrey Ink *Sticker:* (oh so sweet) Cosmo Cricket *Fibers:* (jute twine) Papertrey Ink *Dies:* (clouds, tiny tag) Provo Craft

Finished size: 4¼" x 5½"

DESIGNER TIP

If you want your bow to
lie perfectly, try tying it
separately and attaching it
to the main length of ribbon
with a mini glue dot.

DESIGNER TIP

Get more versatility from your stamps
by using a flourish as a background,
and to emphasize your sentiment.
This also helps coordinate the
sentiment label with the card base.

Sustaining Hope Card

Designer: Debbie Olson

SUPPLIES: *Cardstock:* (Vintage Cream, Sweet Blush)
Papertrey Ink *Patterned paper:* (La Boutique de Jardin,
Tres Magique from Postcards from Paris collection)
Webster's Pages *Clear stamps:* (butterfly, hope
sentiment from With Sympathy set) Papertrey Ink *Dye
ink:* (Chamomile) Papertrey Ink *Specialty ink:* (Dark
Chocolate, Sweet Blush, Berry Sorbet, Spring Moss,
Ripe Avocado hybrid) Papertrey Ink *Color medium:*
(green, aqua markers) Copic *Accents:* (white button)
Papertrey Ink; (pink rhinestones) Hero Arts *Fibers:*
(aqua ribbon) Papertrey Ink; (cream floss) *Die:* (label)
Spellbinders *Tools:* (embossing border punch) EK
Success; (butterfly punch) Martha Stewart Crafts

Finished size: 4¼" x 5½"

Celebrate Card

Designer: Maile Belles

SUPPLIES: *Cardstock:* (Ripe Avocado, Spring Moss,
Vintage Cream, kraft) Papertrey Ink *Clear stamps:*
(label, flourishes from Vintage Labels set; celebrate
from Damask Designs set) Papertrey Ink *Specialty ink:*
(Ripe Avocado, Spring Moss, Dark Chocolate hybrid)
Papertrey Ink *Accents:* (white pearls) Kaisercraft *Fibers:*
(brown ribbon) Papertrey Ink *Tools:* (corner rounder
punch) EK Success; (border punch) Fiskars

Finished size: 4¼" x 5½"

Starry Noel Card

Designer: Beatriz Jennings

SUPPLIES: *Cardstock:* (Rustic Cream) Papertrey
Ink *Patterned paper:* (Noel from Wassail collection)
BasicGrey; (Reindeer Games, Cassy) Melissa Frances;
(vintage sheet music) *Clear stamps:* (noel from Glitzmas
set) SEI; (frame from Framework set) Melissa Frances
Dye ink: (Vintage Photo) Ranger Industries *Pigment ink:*
(black, red) Clearsnap *Accents:* (white glitter chipboard
star) Melissa Frances; (white flower, white pearls, brown
button) *Fibers:* (white lace trim, natural cord)

Finished size: 4¼" x 5½"

Card Sketches | bonus sketches
FOR PAPER CRAFTERS

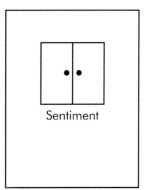

Sketch by: Lucy Abrams

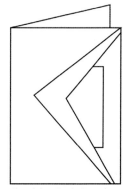

Sketch by: Emily Branch

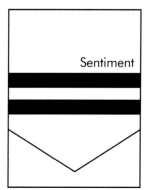

Sketch by: Emily Branch

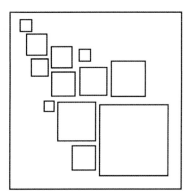

Sketch by: Heidi Van Laar

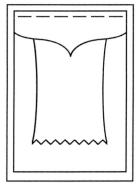

Sketch by: Betsy Veldman

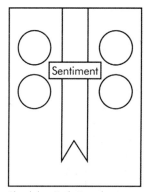

Sketch by: Emily Branch

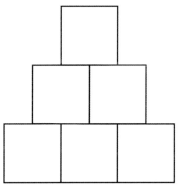

Sketch by: Heidi Van Laar

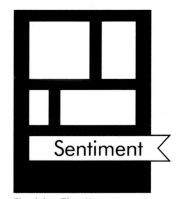

Sketch by: Chan Vuong

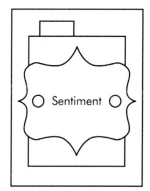

Sketch by: Betsy Veldman

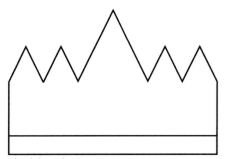

Sketch by: Julia Stainton

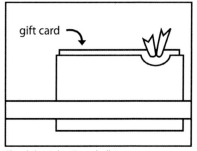

Sketch by: Julie Campbell

Sketch by: Chan Vuong

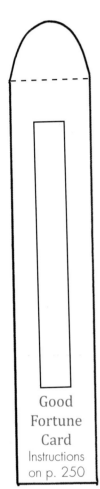

Good Fortune Card
Instructions on p. 250

Pocket pattern
Cut from Café Sombre cardstock

Easter Basket Card
Instructions on p.36

Basket & handle pattern
Cut from white cardstock

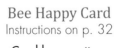

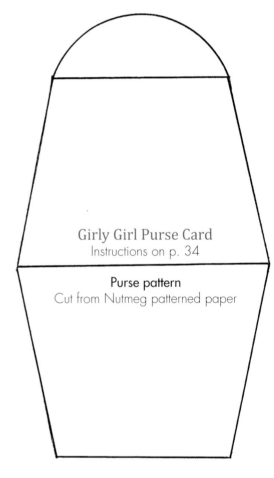

Girly Girl Purse Card
Instructions on p. 34

Purse pattern
Cut from Nutmeg patterned paper

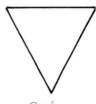

Bee Happy Card
Instructions on p. 32

Card base pattern
Cut from gray cardstock

Happy Hanukkah Card
Instructions on p. 25

Dreidel pattern

Cut from white cardstock

Cut from lemon yellow cardstock

Cut from dark blue cardstock

*Enlarge all patterns by 200%

Mr. Gnome Card
Instructions on p. 23

Hat pattern
Cut from felt

Mr. Gnome Card
Instructions on p. 23

Gnome base pattern
Cut from cardstock

Have a Blast Card
Instructions on p. 14

Star pattern
Cut from
silver cardstock

Wassup Gnomey?
Instructions on p. 7

Gnome pattern
Cut from white cardstock

You're a Star Card
Instructions on p. 15

Inside star pattern
Cut from patterned paper

You're a Star Card
Instructions on p. 15

Outside star pattern
Cut from cardstock

Cheese & Thank You Card
Instructions on p. 23

Cheese base pattern
Cut 2, one from cardstock &
one from patterned paper

Cheese & Thank You Card
Instructions on p. 23

Cheese top pattern
Cut from patterned paper

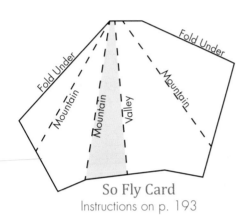

So Fly Card
Instructions on p. 193

Airplane pattern
Cut & fold from patterned paper

Mermaid Wish Card
Instructions on p. 107

Hair pattern
Cut from cardstock

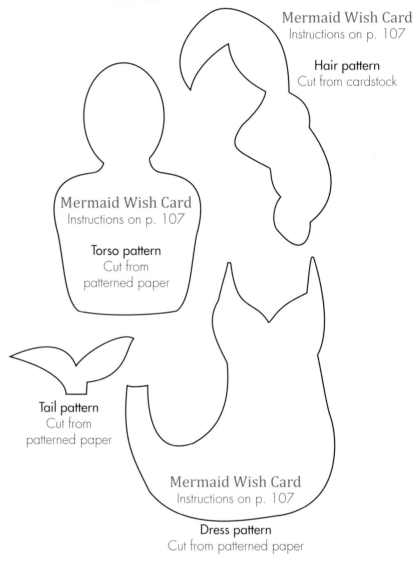

Mermaid Wish Card
Instructions on p. 107

Torso pattern
Cut from patterned paper

Tail pattern
Cut from patterned paper

Mermaid Wish Card
Instructions on p. 107

Dress pattern
Cut from patterned paper

Sailboat Birthday Card
Instructions on p. 21

Sail pattern
Cut from patterned paper

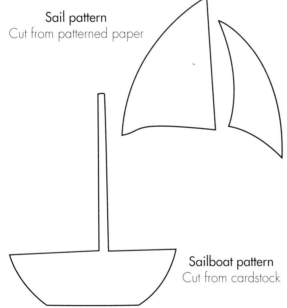

Sailboat pattern
Cut from cardstock

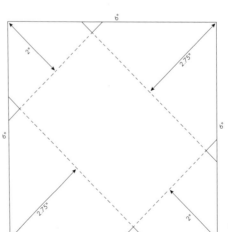

Just a Note Card
Instructions on p. 213

Envelope template
Cut & fold from cardstock

Card Sketches

FOR PAPER CRAFTERS | index